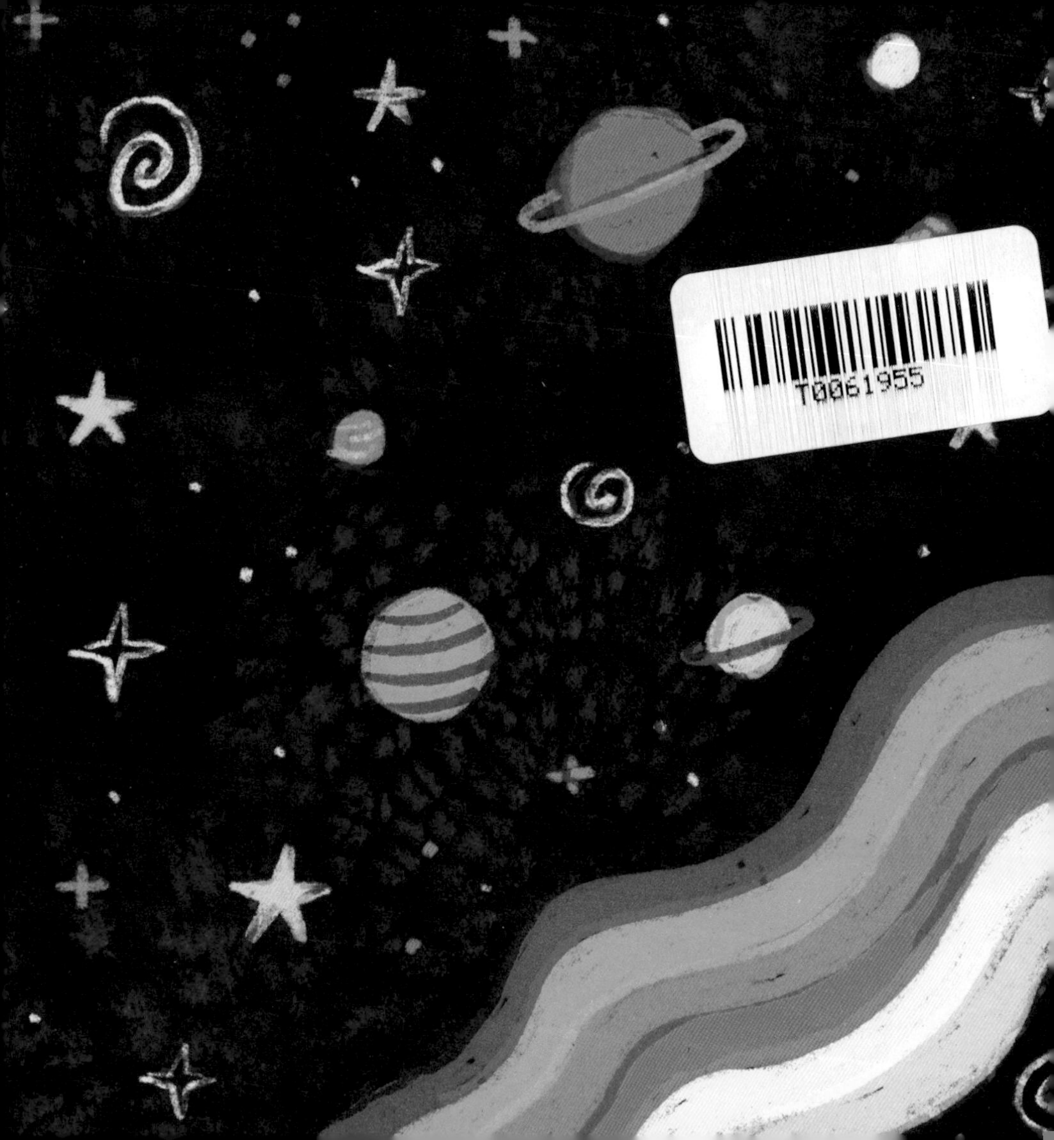

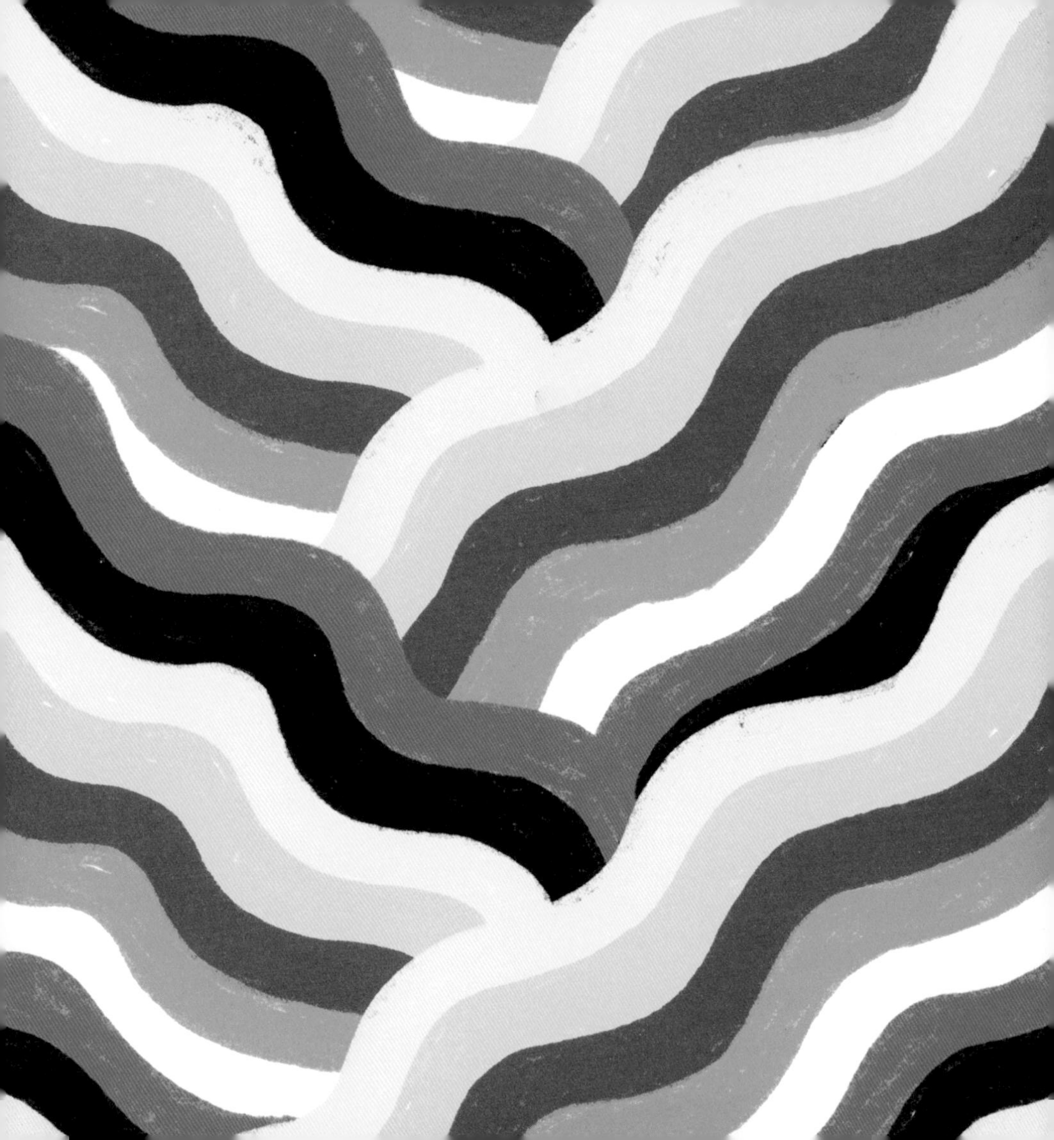

SAVE ME!

(FROM MYSELF)

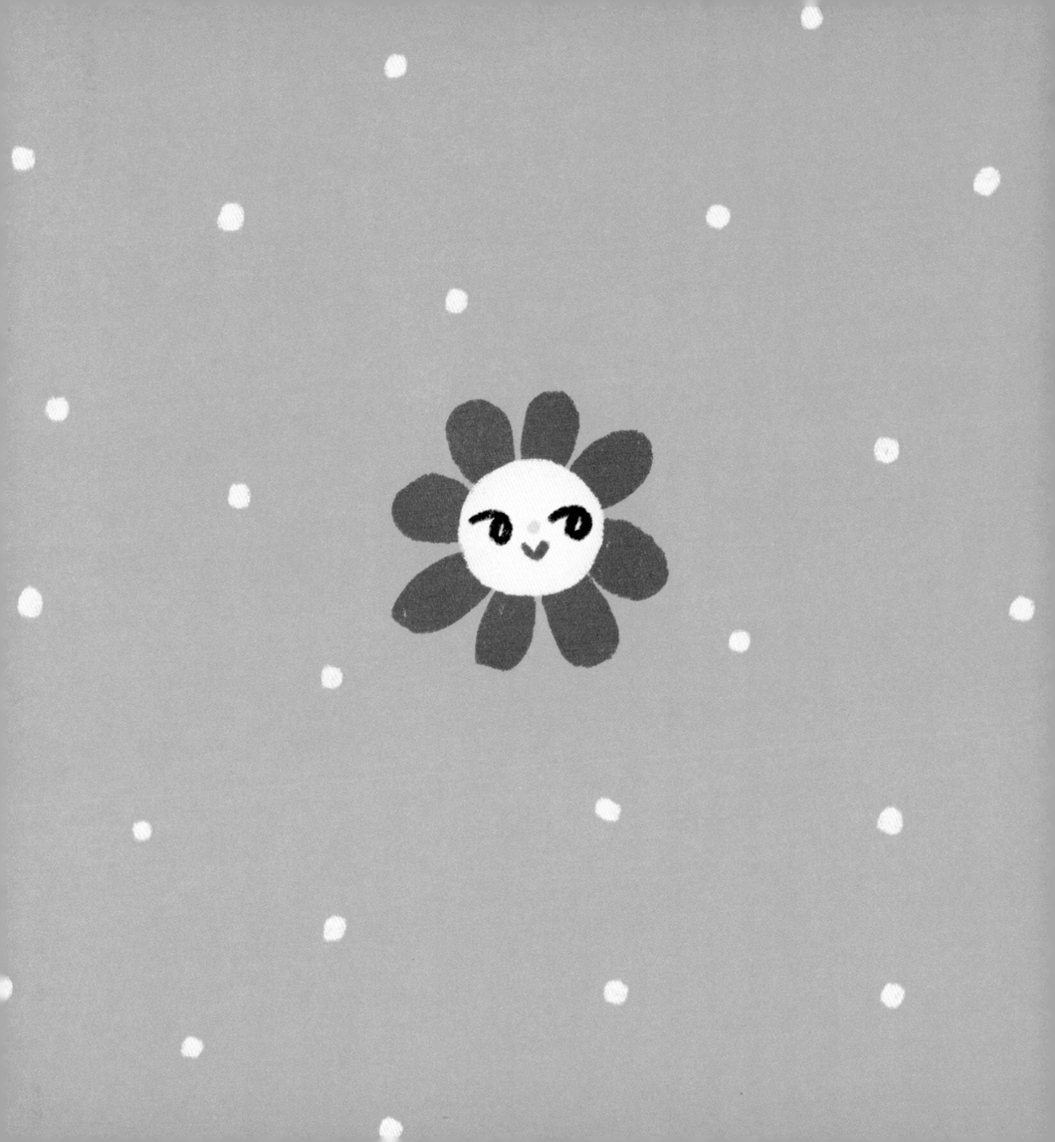

SAVE ME!

(FROM MYSELF)

the Existential CRISES of a CREATIVE INtRoVERt

♥

SO LAZO

CHRONICLE BOOKS

SAN FRANCISCO

Library of Congress Cataloging-in-Publication Data available.

ISBN 978-1-7972-0341-6

Manufactured in China.

MIX
Paper from responsible sources
FSC™ C008047
FSC www.fsc.org

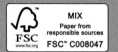

10 9 8 7 6 5 4 3 2

Chronicle books and gifts are available at special quantity discounts to corporations, professional associations, literacy programs, and other organizations. For details and discount information, please contact our premiums department at corporatesales@chroniclebooks.com or at 1-800-759-0190.

Chronicle Books LLC
680 Second Street
San Francisco, California 94107
www.chroniclebooks.com

To Those who feel too much
And don't like to talk about it.

Hello! So you've picked up this book. That means you're intrigued by the title, right? (Maybe just a little bit?) Well, I'm just going to give you a brief introduction to what you'll find inside these pages. You see, this book is filled with SO many feelings, and emotions and thoughts and FEARS and anxiety and just LOTS of existential crises.

This book is EXTREMELY personal; it's my diary, it's hope, it's heartbreak, it's revenge, it's life, it's RAW.

But even though it does seem like a lot of "me, me, me," this book is also about (you) and about your friends, maybe, or your family, or anyone close to you. Because let's be honest here, I'm not tHAT special, and that's a really good thing. I'm not the only person in the world who feels these feelings and fears these fears, even though sometimes it might feel that way. And maybe if you can relate to some of the things you'll find here, you'll feel a bit better, because in the end there's so many of us searching for answers to the same questions. So let me just share this with you, and at least for now, we won't be alone.

♥ SØ

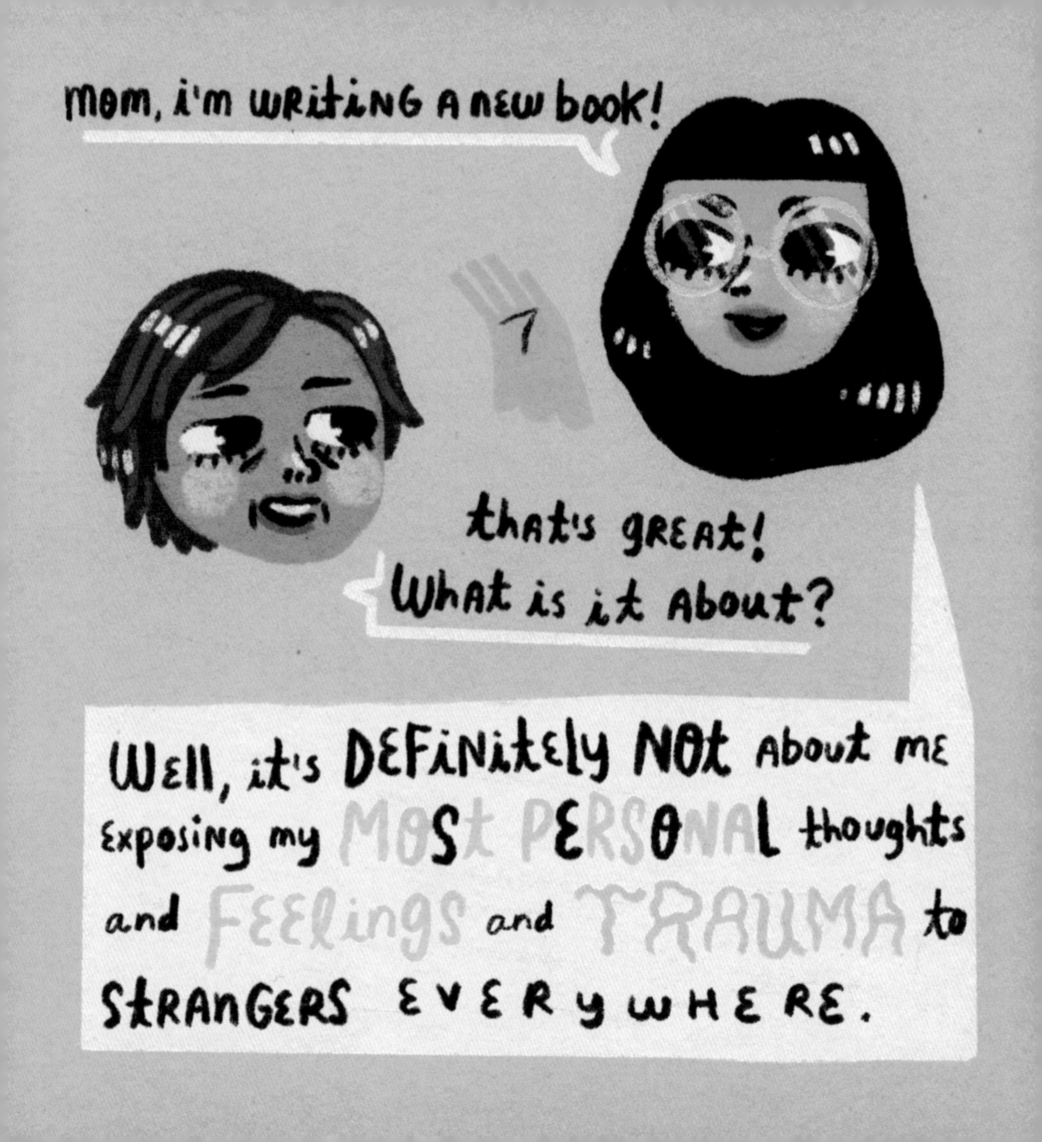
mom, i'm writing a new book!
that's great! What is it about?
Well, it's DEFINITELY NOT about me exposing my MOST PERSONAL thoughts and FEELINGS and TRAUMA to STRANGERS EVERYWHERE.

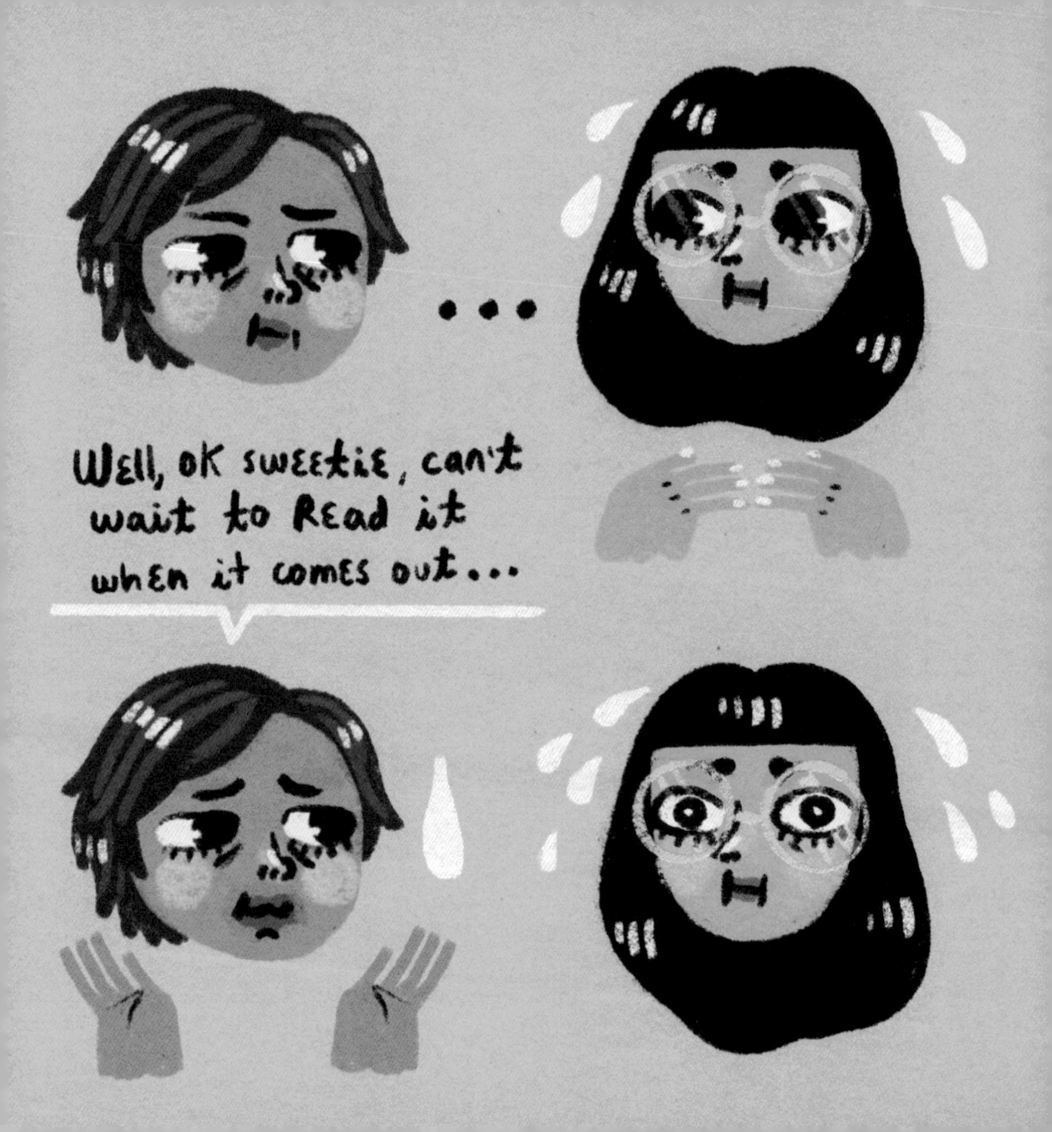
...
Well, ok sweetie, can't wait to read it when it comes out...

Reminder

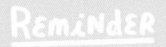

WE ALL MAKE

MISTAKES

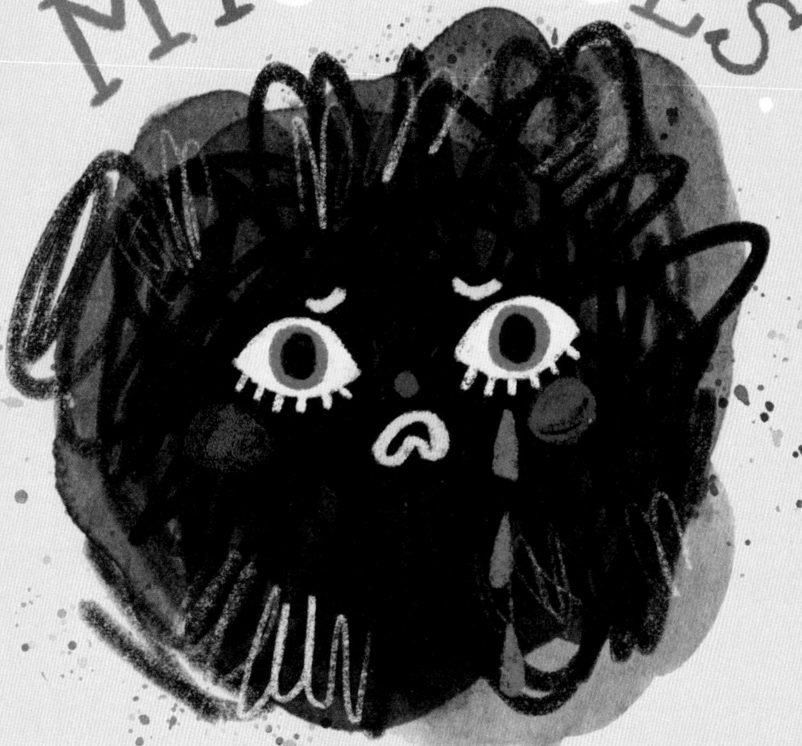

AND it's OK.

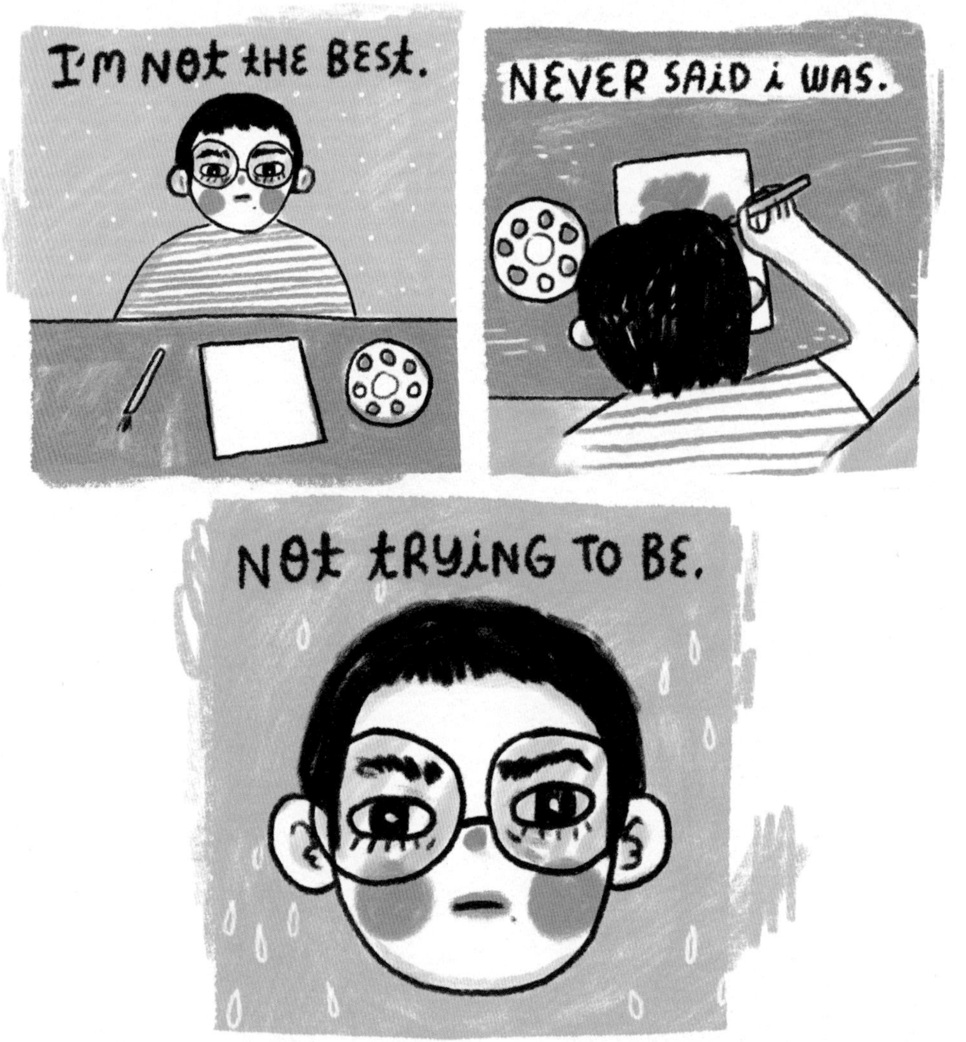
I'M NOT THE BEST.
NEVER SAID I WAS.
NOT TRYING TO BE.

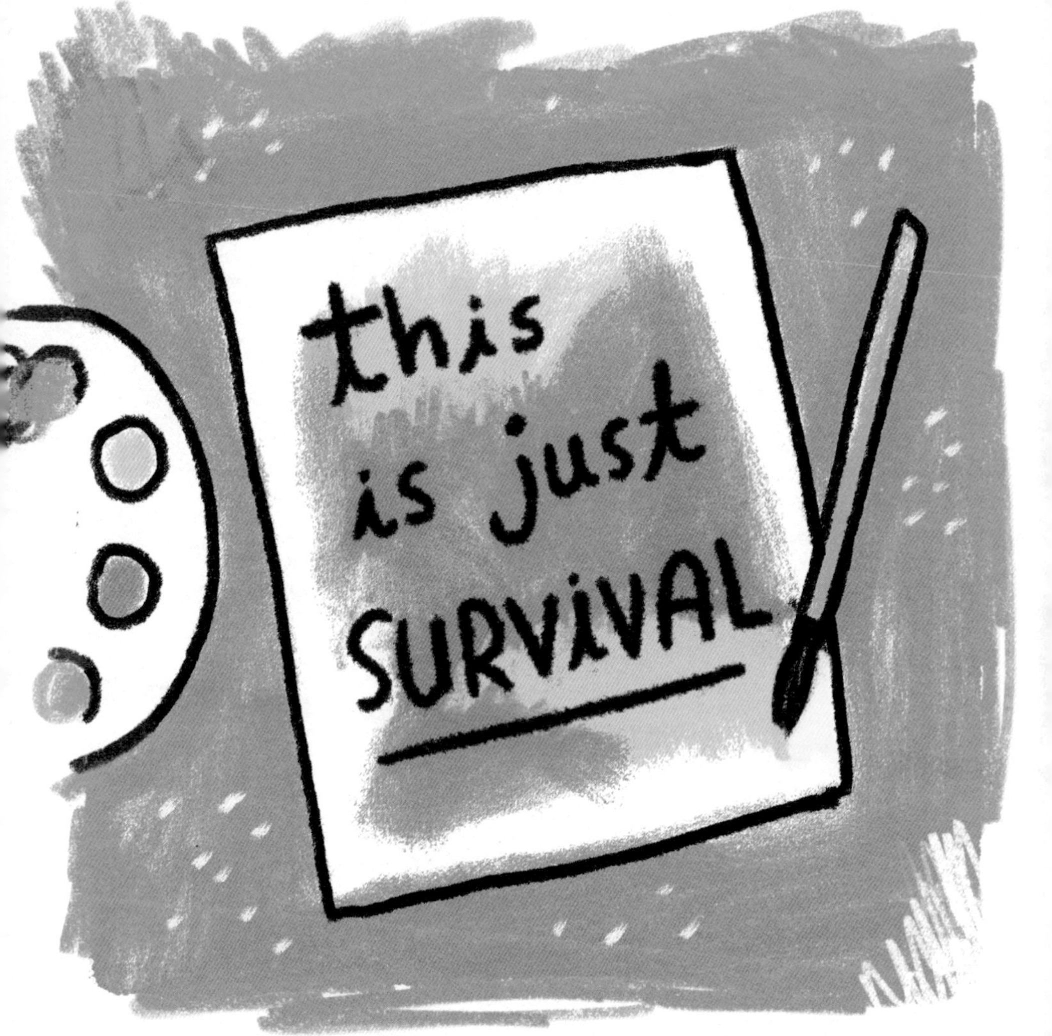
this
is just
SURVIVAL

I thought I always saw the glass
BOTH

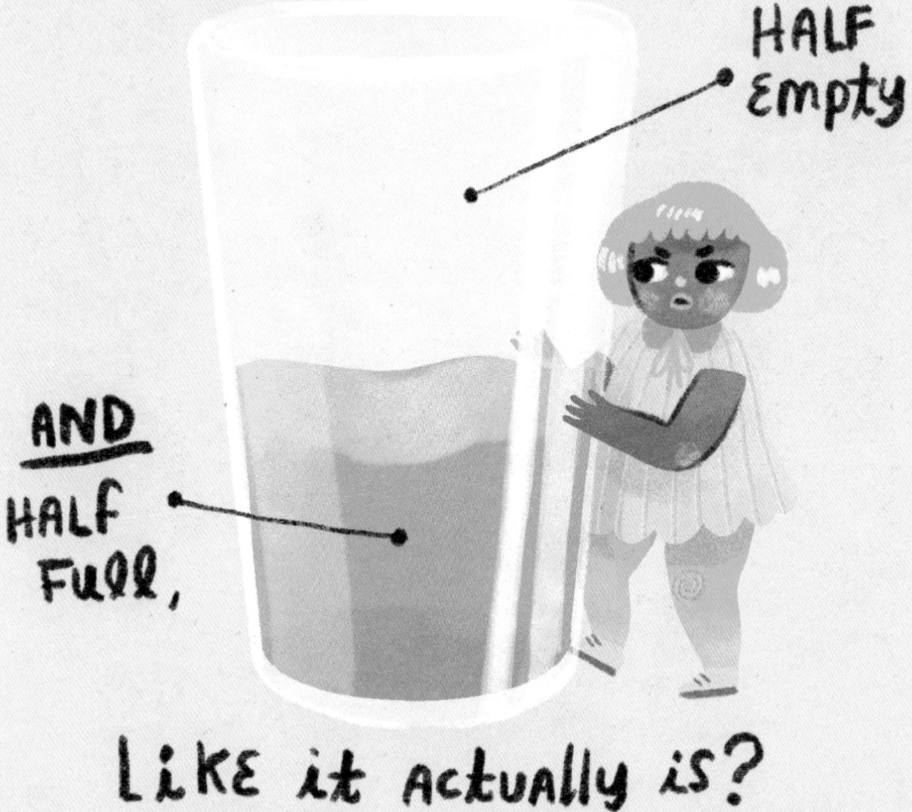
HALF
Empty
AND
HALF
FULL,

LIKE it actually is?

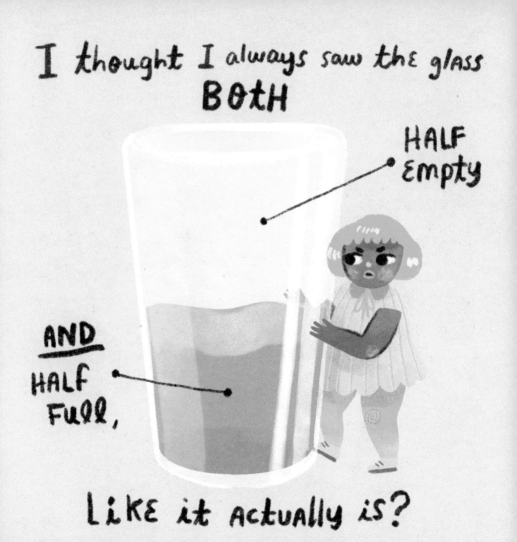

But maybe i was just pretending to be "realistic and logical".

I probably see it

HALF Empty

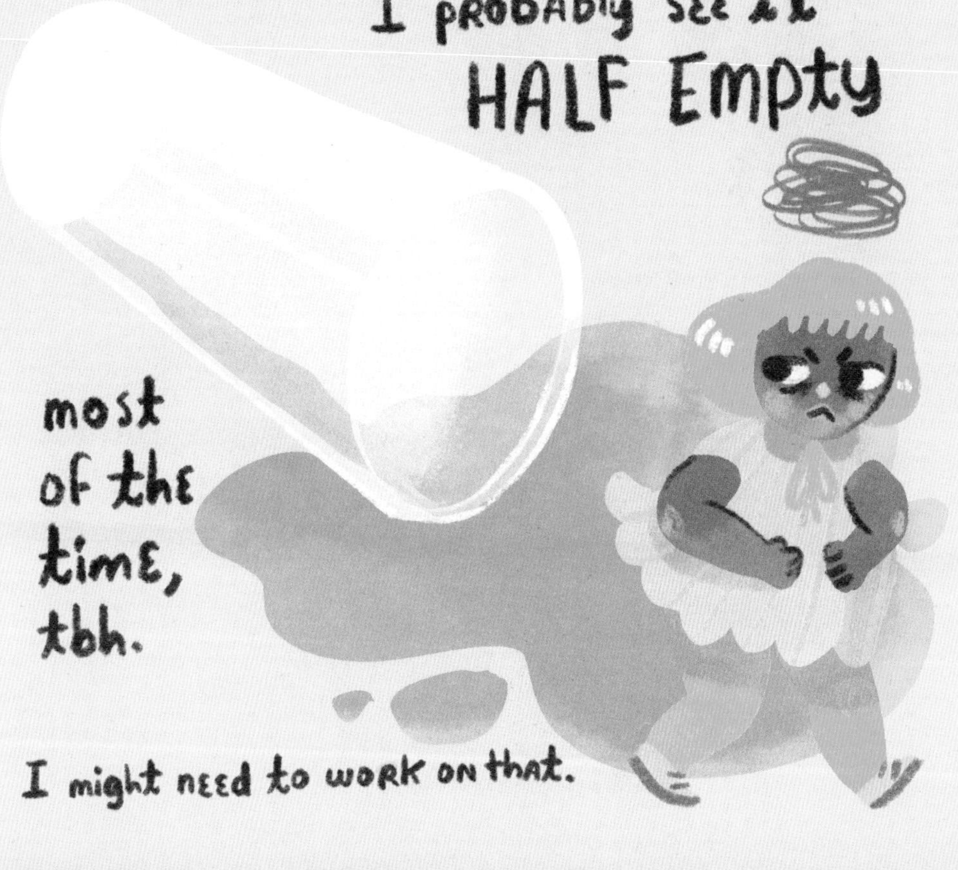

most of the time, tbh.

I might need to work on that.

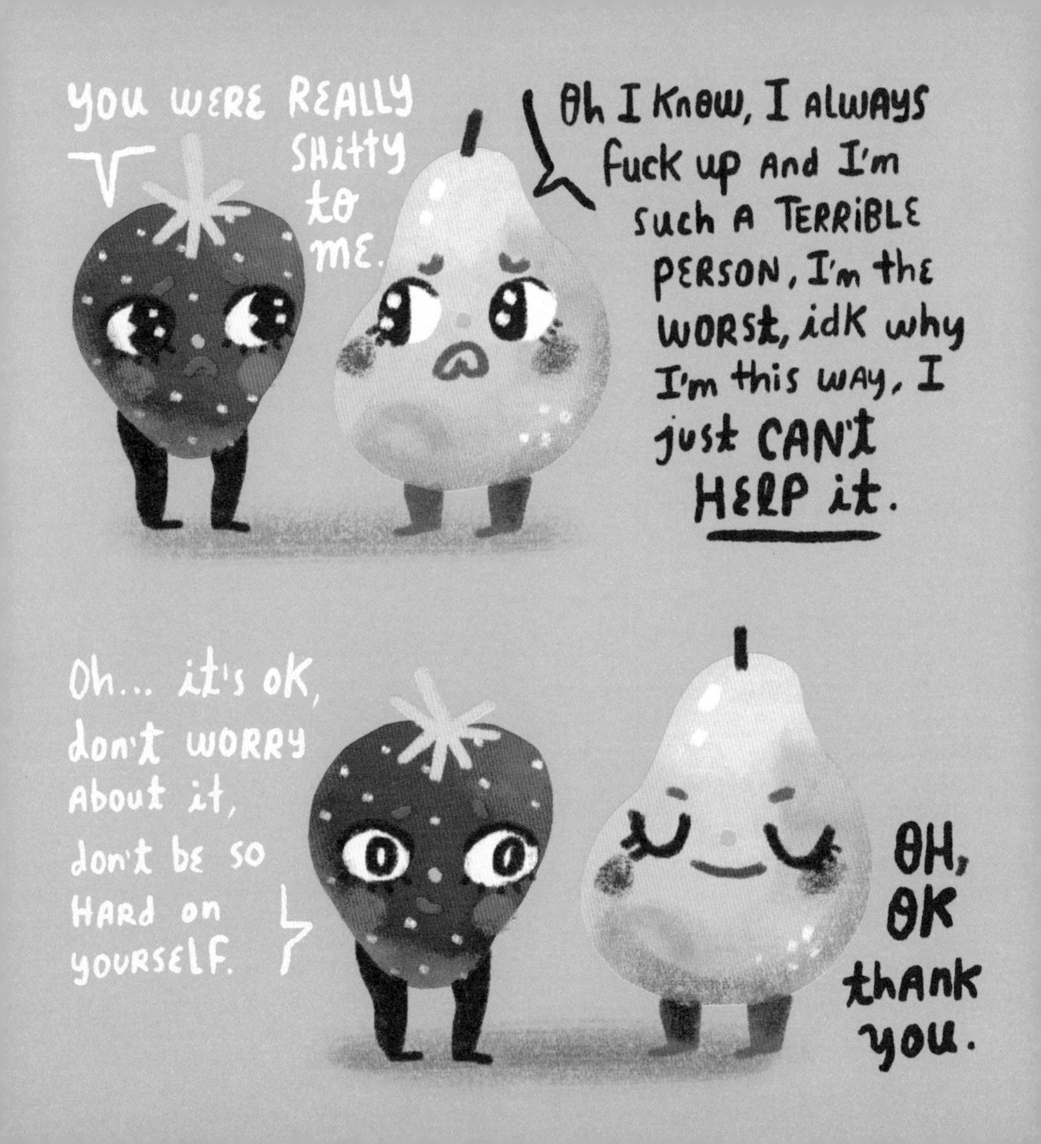
YOU WERE REALLY SHITTY TO ME.
Oh I KNOW, I ALWAYS fuck up AND I'm such A TERRIBLE PERSON, I'm the WORST, idK why I'm this WAY, I just CAN'T HELP it.
Oh... it's OK, don't WORRY About it, don't be SO HARD on yourSELF.
OH, OK thank you.

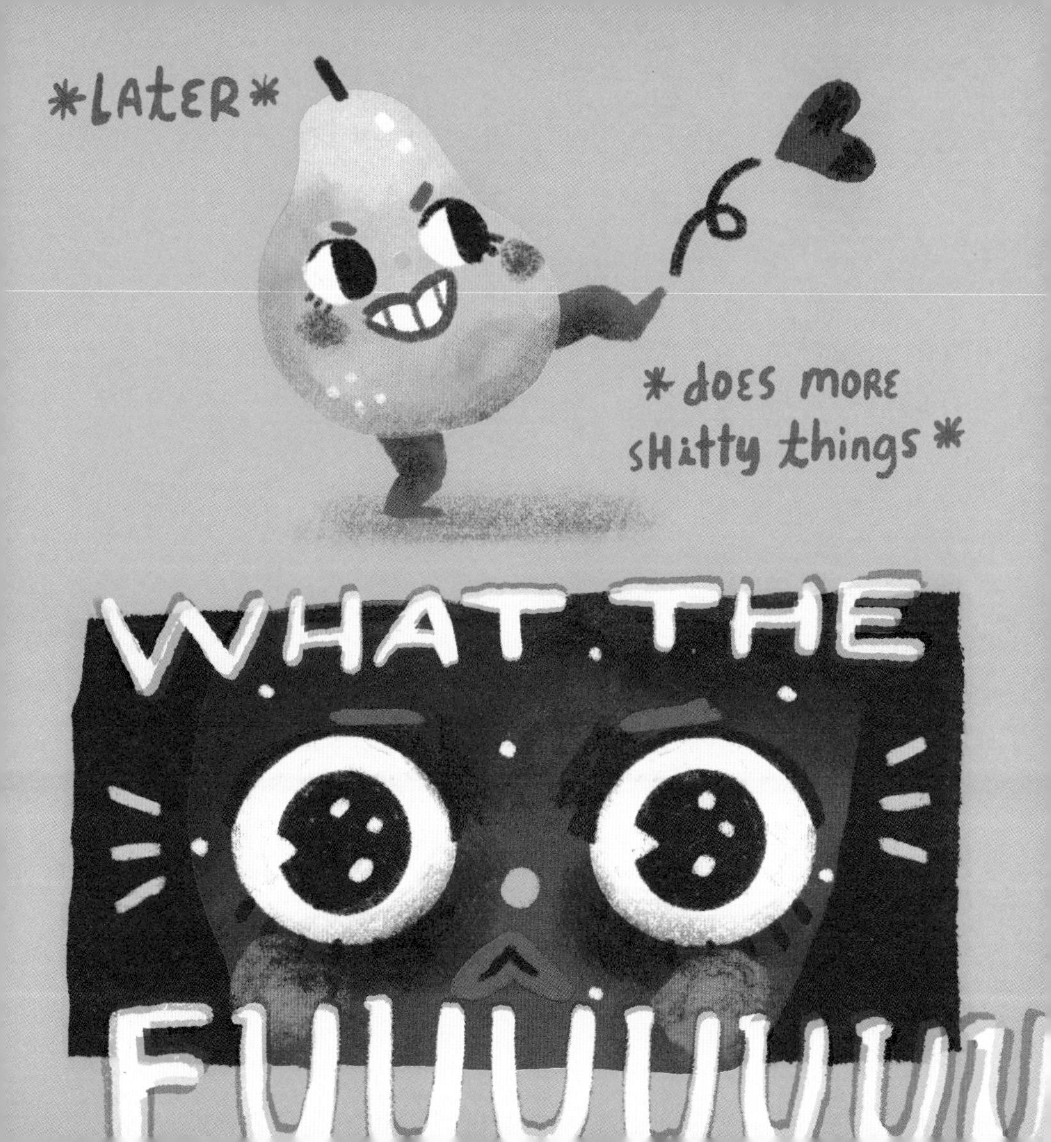
LATER
does more shitty things
WHAT THE
FUUUUUUU

WORKING FROM HOME

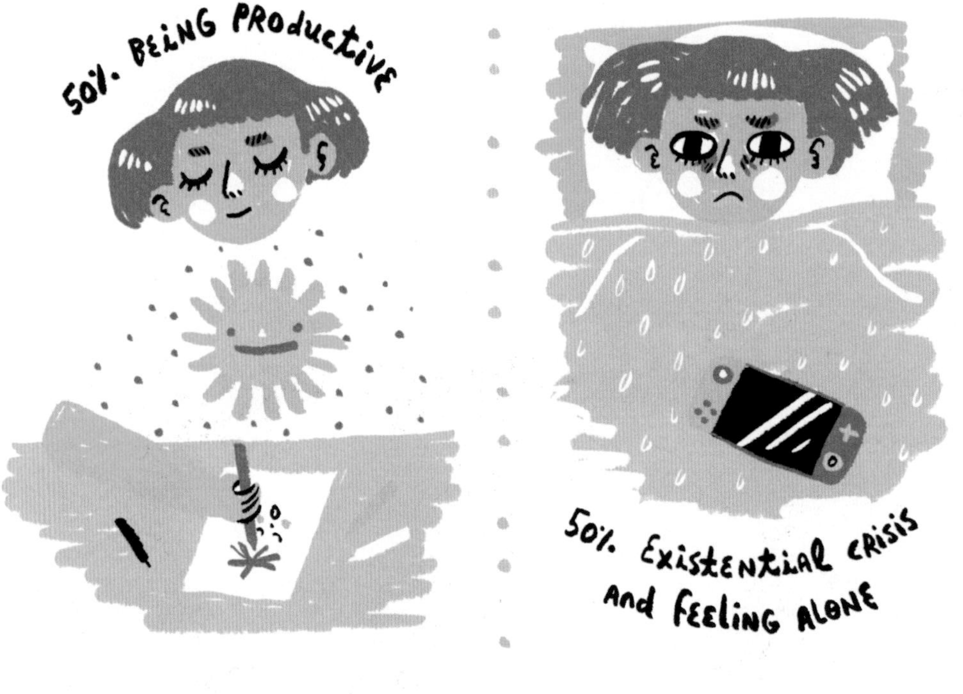

50% BEING PRODUCTIVE
50% EXISTENTIAL CRISIS AND FEELING ALONE

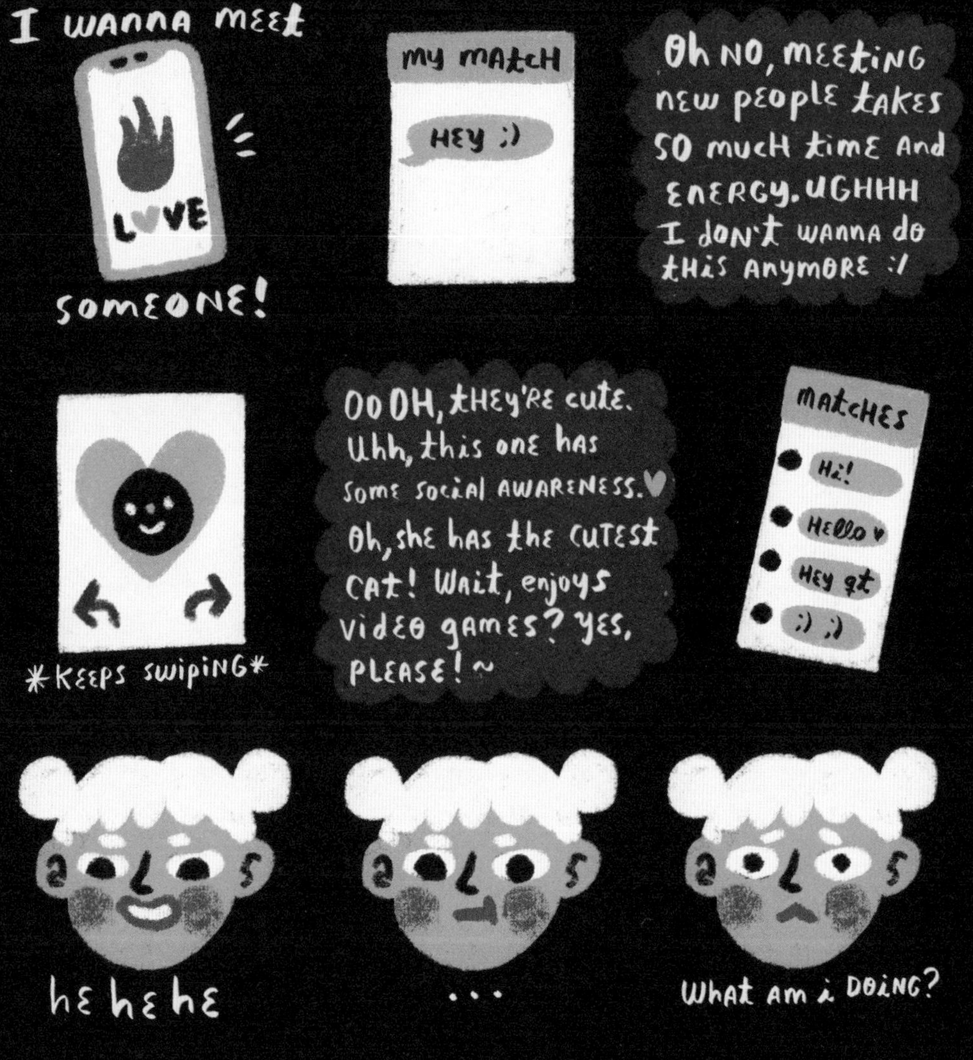
I wanna meet
LOVE
someone!
my match
HEY ;)
Oh no, meeting new people takes so much time and energy. UGHHH I don't wanna do this anymore :/
KEEPS SWIPING
OOOH, they're cute. Uhh, this one has some social awareness. Oh, she has the cutest cat! Wait, enjoys video games? Yes, please! ~
matches
Hi!
Hello
Hey qt
;) ;)
hehehe
...
What am i doing?

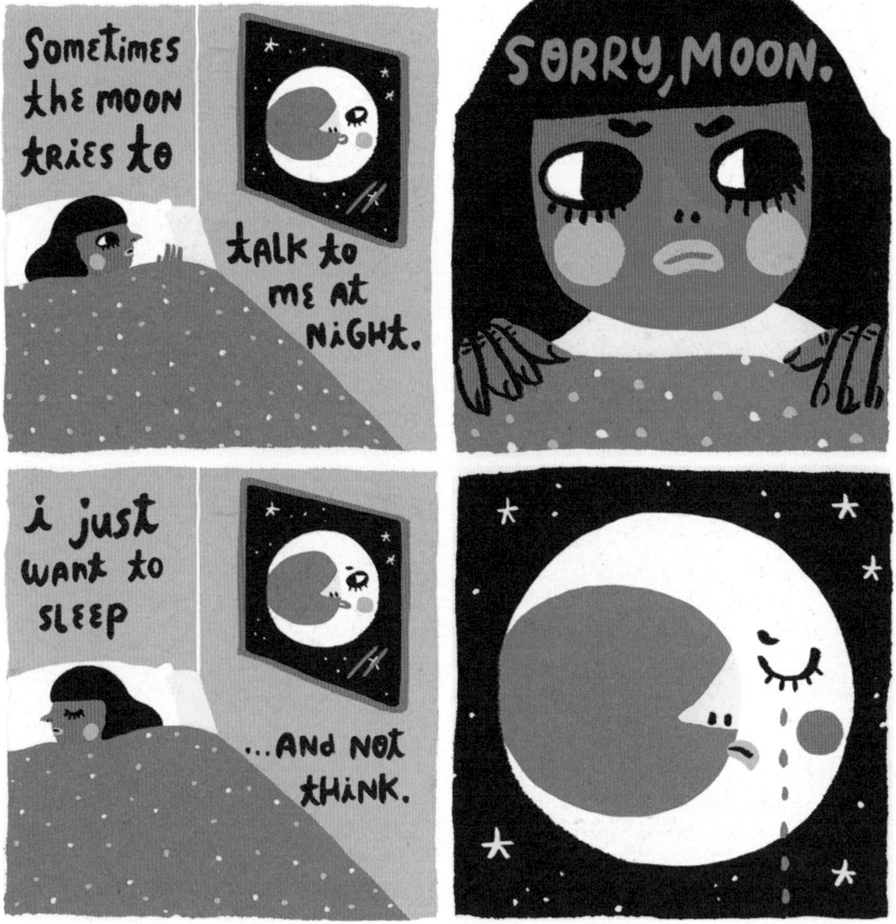
Sometimes the moon tries to
talk to me at night.
SORRY, MOON.
i just want to sleep
...AND NOT THINK.

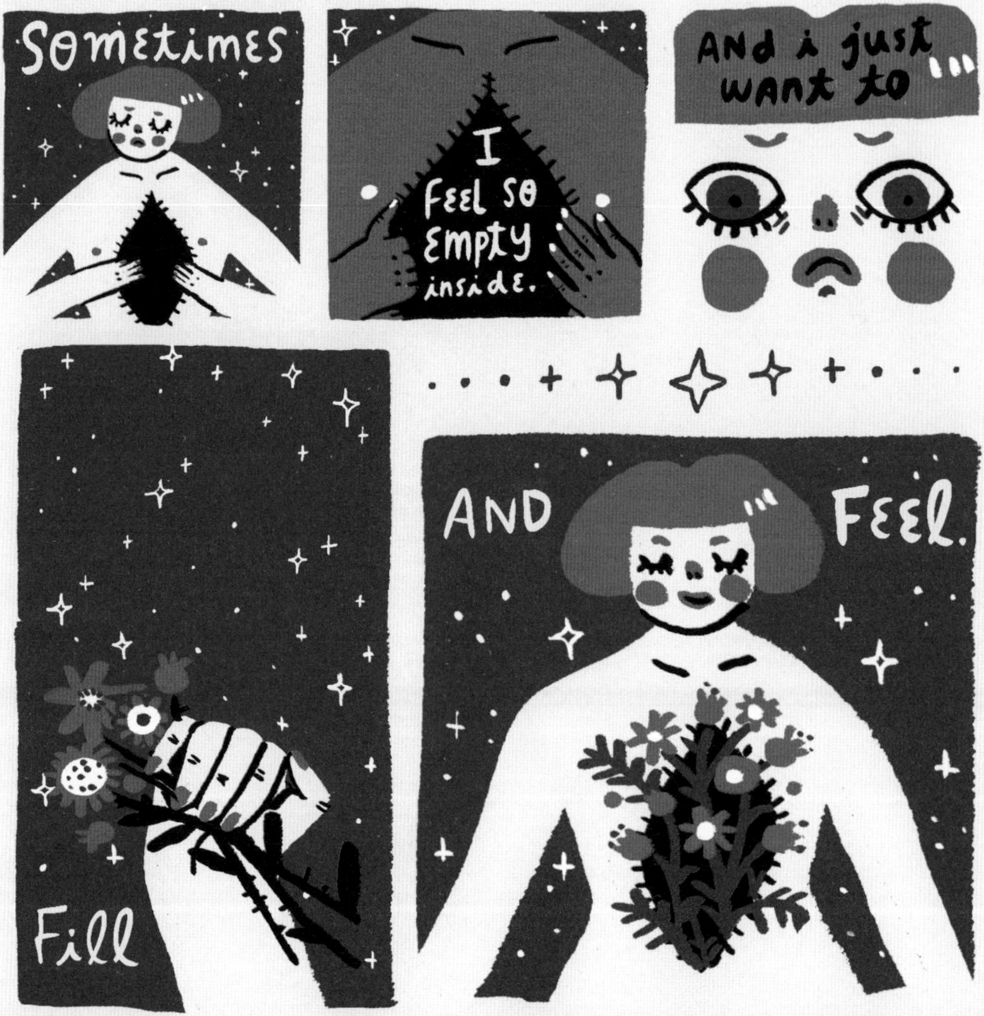
Sometimes
I feel so empty inside.
And i just want to...
Fill
AND
Feel.

REMINDER

THE UNIVERSE

DOES NOT

REVOLVE AROUND

>ME<

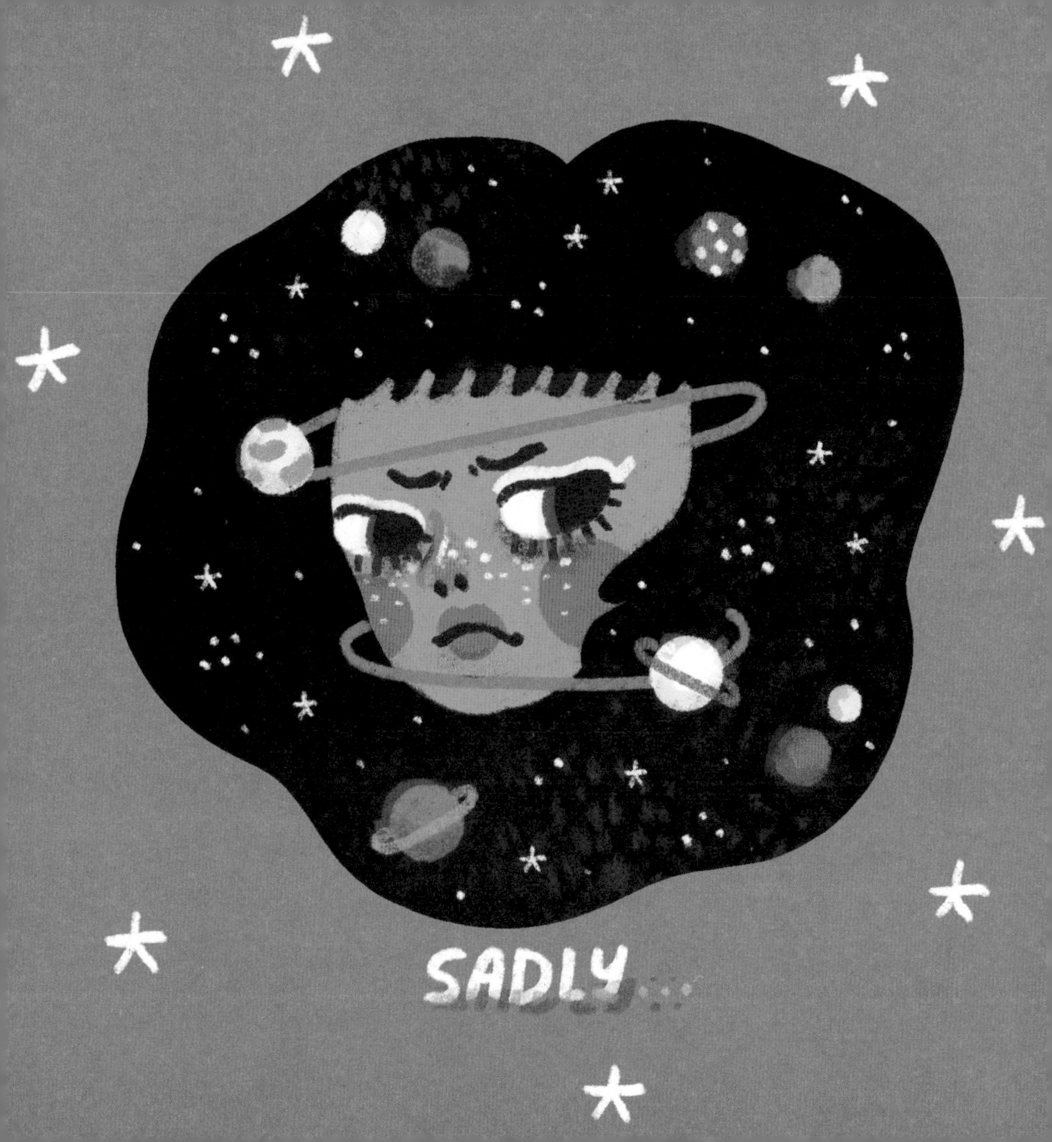
SADLY...

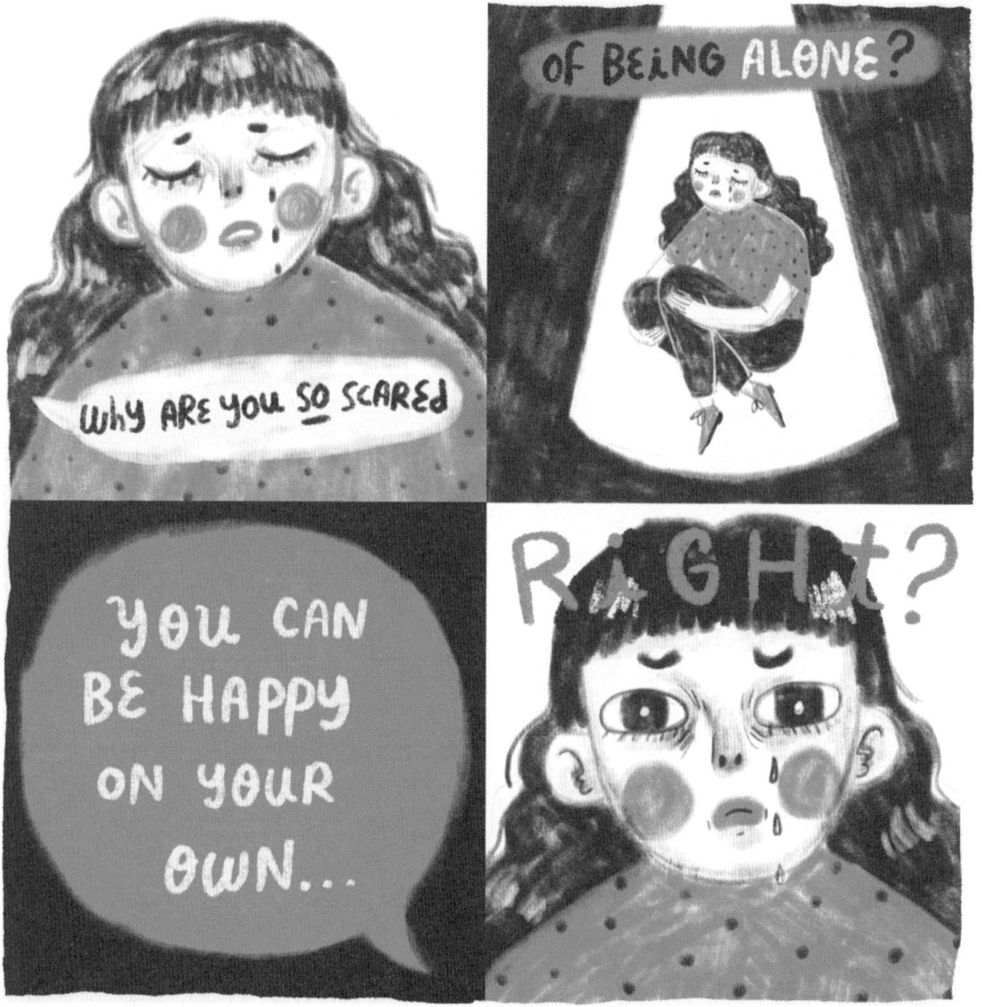
WHY ARE YOU SO SCARED
OF BEING ALONE?
YOU CAN BE HAPPY ON YOUR OWN...
RIGHT?

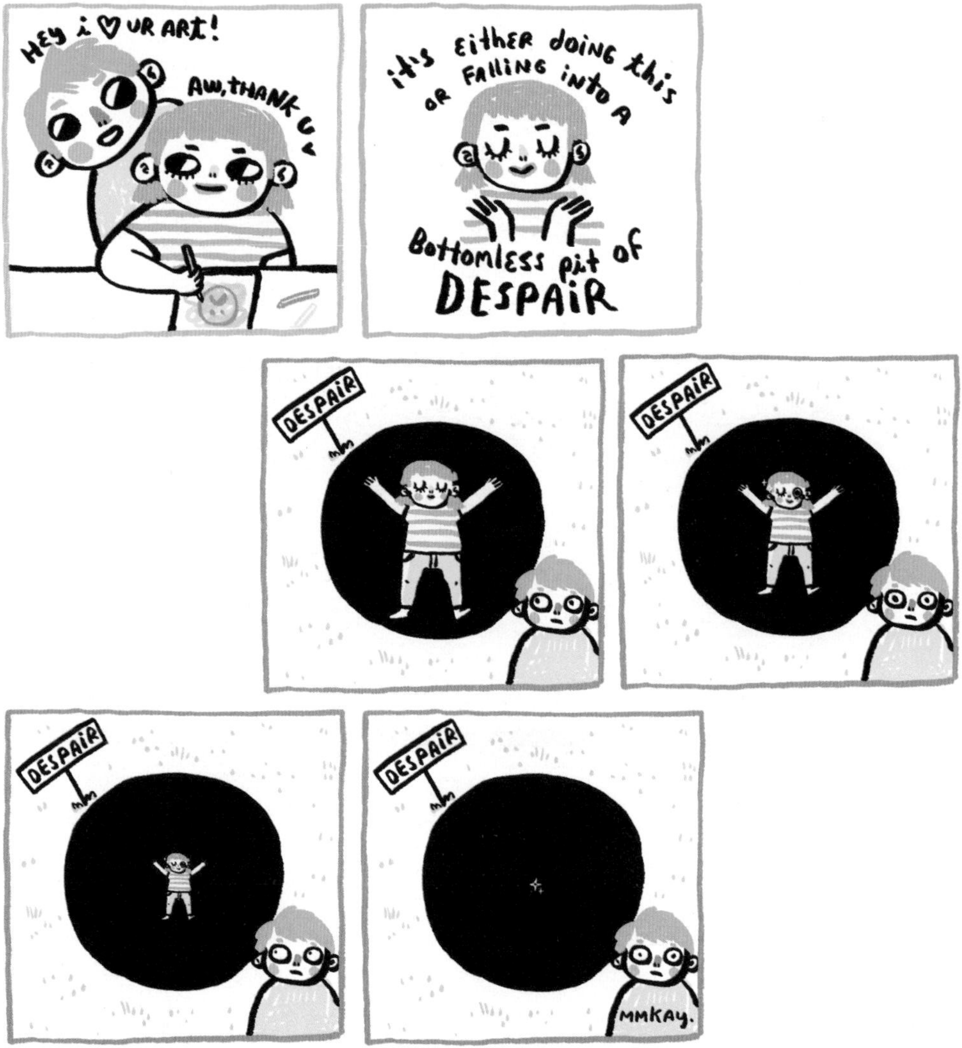
HEY i ♡ UR ART!
AW, THANK U ♡
it's either doing this or FALLING into a
Bottomless pit of
DESPAIR
DESPAIR
DESPAIR
DESPAIR
DESPAIR
MMKAY.

A list of things that AREN'T my problem and that i shouldn't CARE about:

men's* perception of women

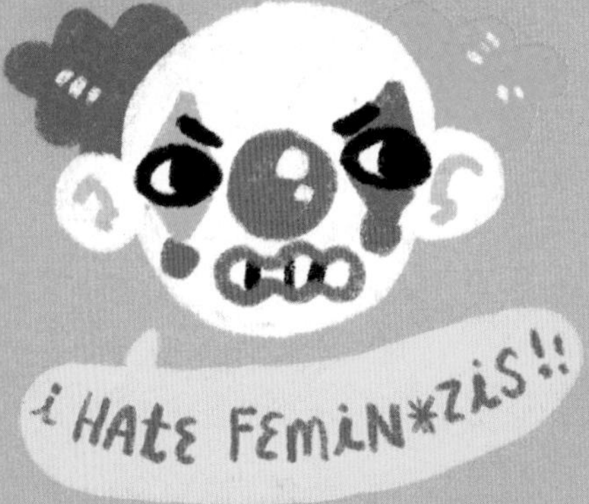
i HATE FEMIN*ZIS!!

* cishet men

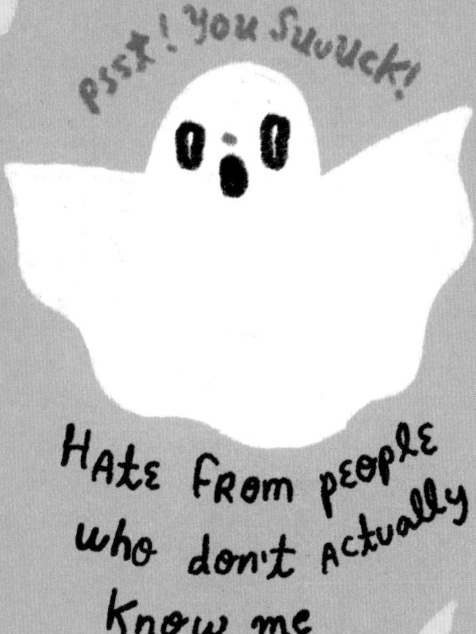
psst! You Suuuck!

Hate from people who don't actually know me

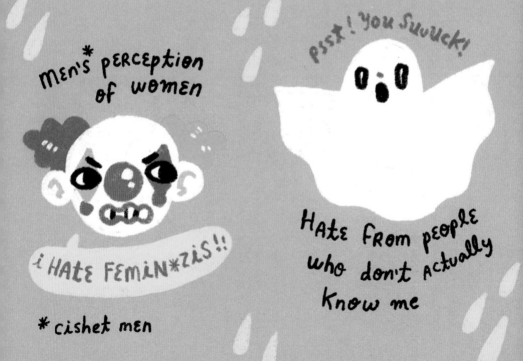

the opinion of homophobes, RACists, sexists, and TERFs.

i mean i just don't think that being trans i" NOPE.

that one cat that lives down the street And whose FACE is just TOO human FOR SOME REASON and I can NEVER get close enough to take a photo

MEOW!

YOU'LL NEVER CATCH ME.

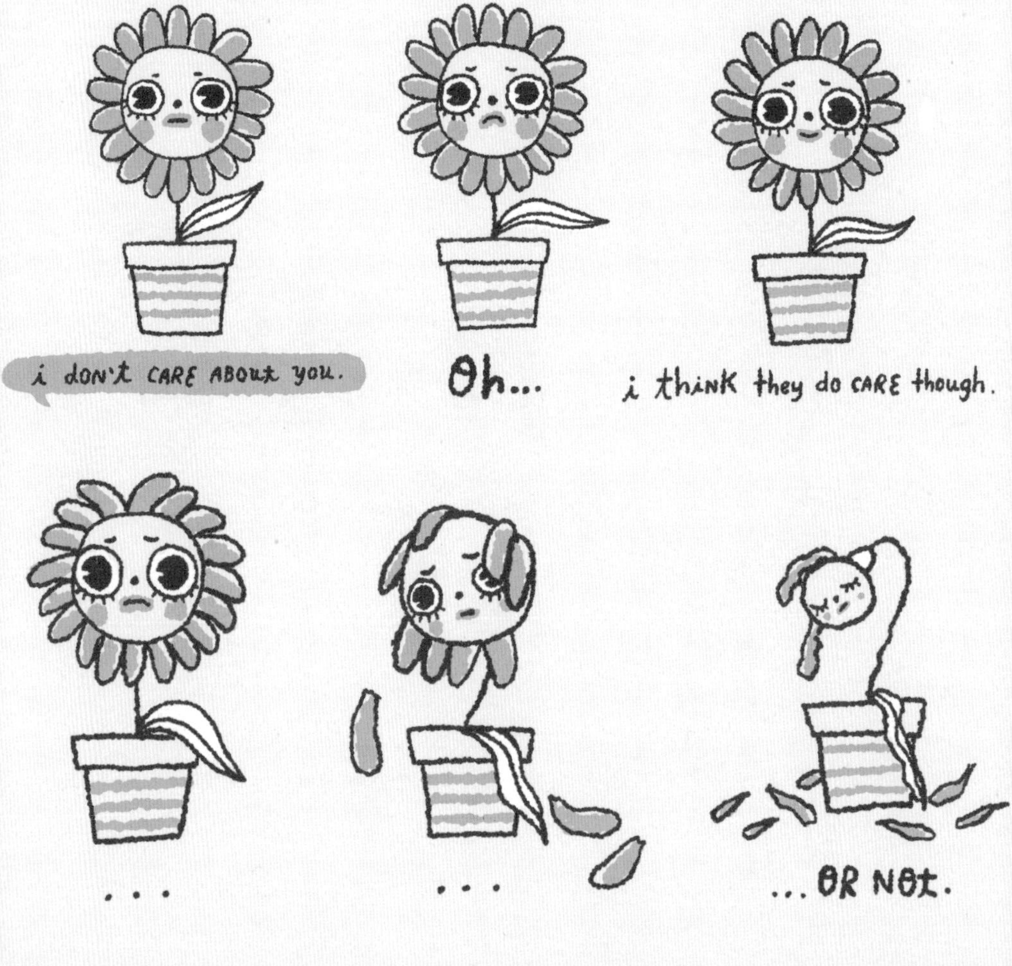

i don't CARE ABOUT you.
Oh...
i think they do CARE though.
...
...
...OR NOT.

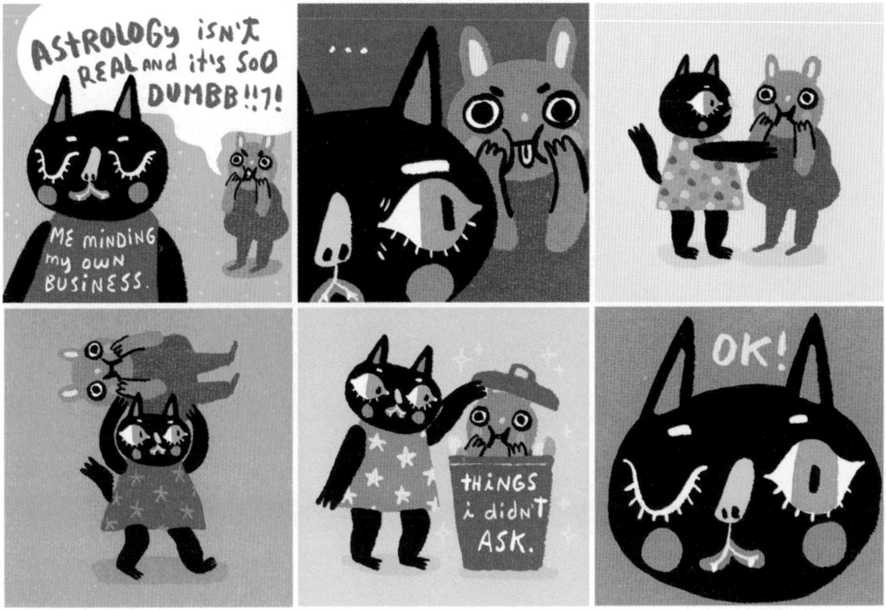
ASTROLOGY isN'T REAL and it's SoO DUMBB!!?!
ME minding my own BUSINESS.
...
thiNGS i didn'T ASK.
OK!

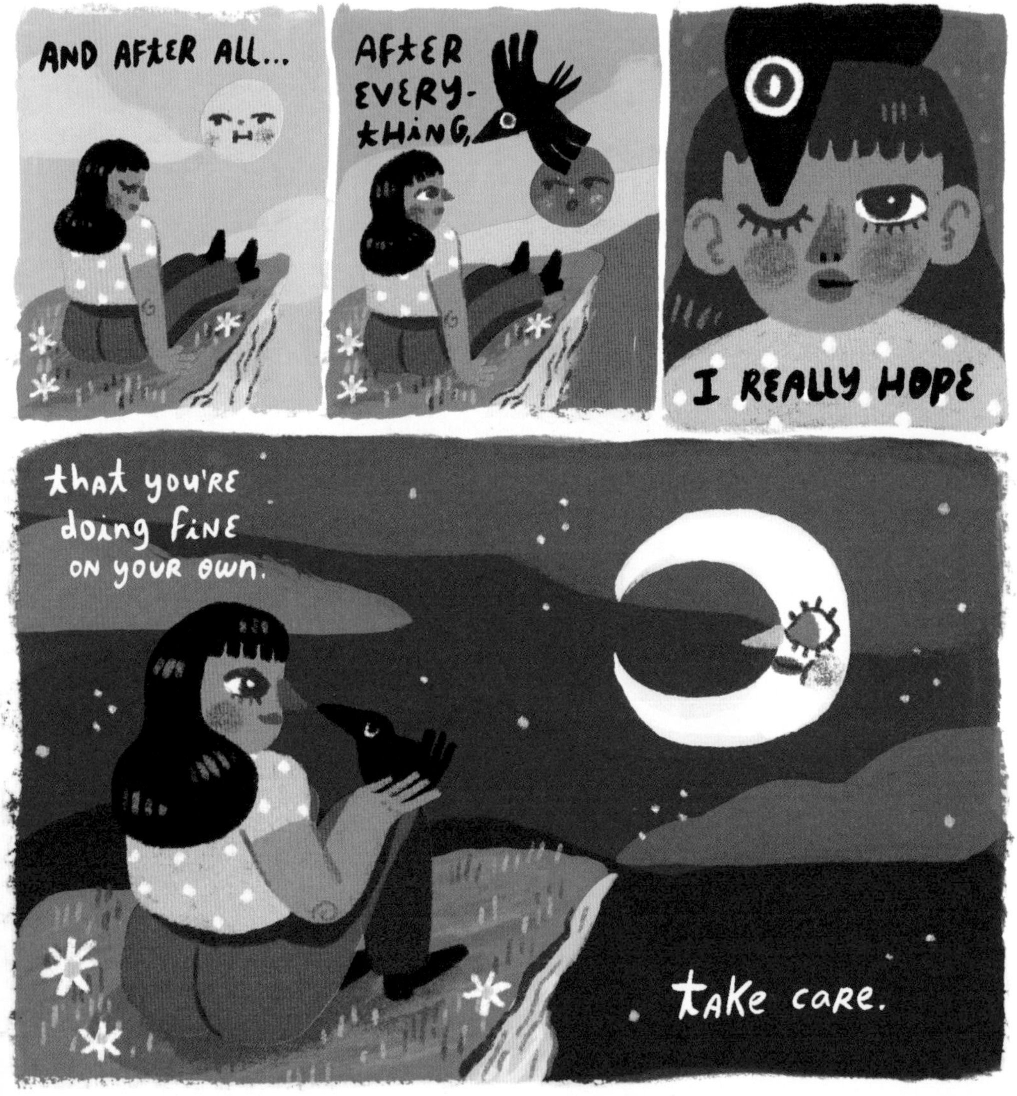
AND AFTER ALL...
AFTER EVERY-THING,
I REALLY HOPE
that you're doing fine on your own.
take care.

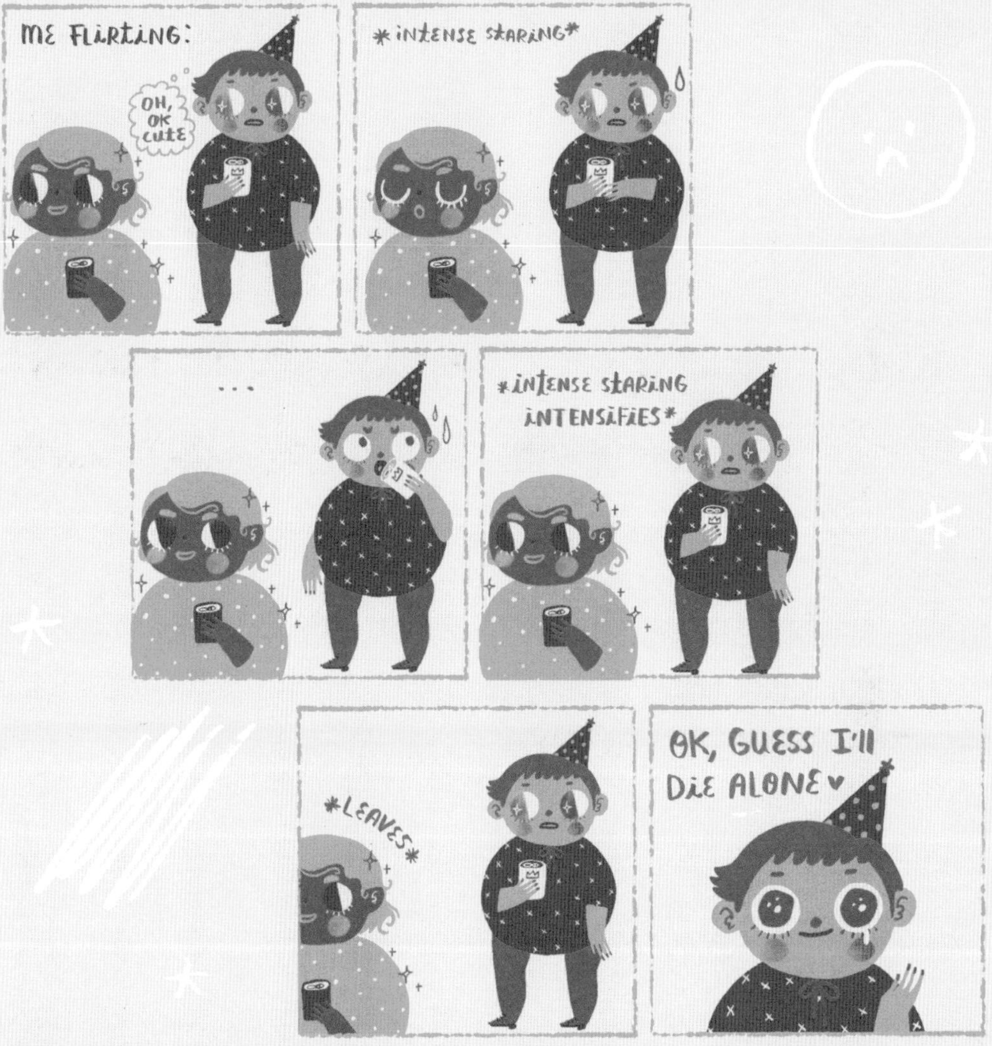
ME FLIRTING:
OH, OK CUTE
INTENSE STARING
...
INTENSE STARING INTENSIFIES
LEAVES
OK, GUESS I'LL DIE ALONE ♥

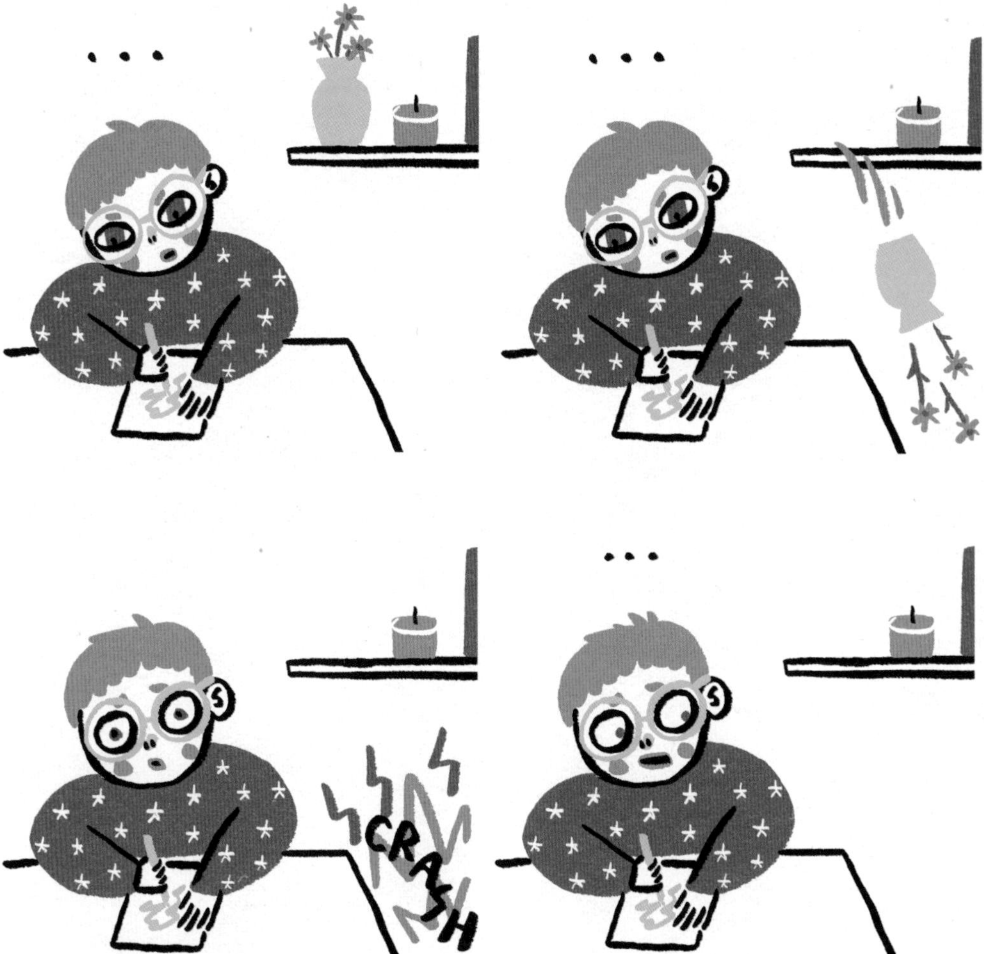
CRASH

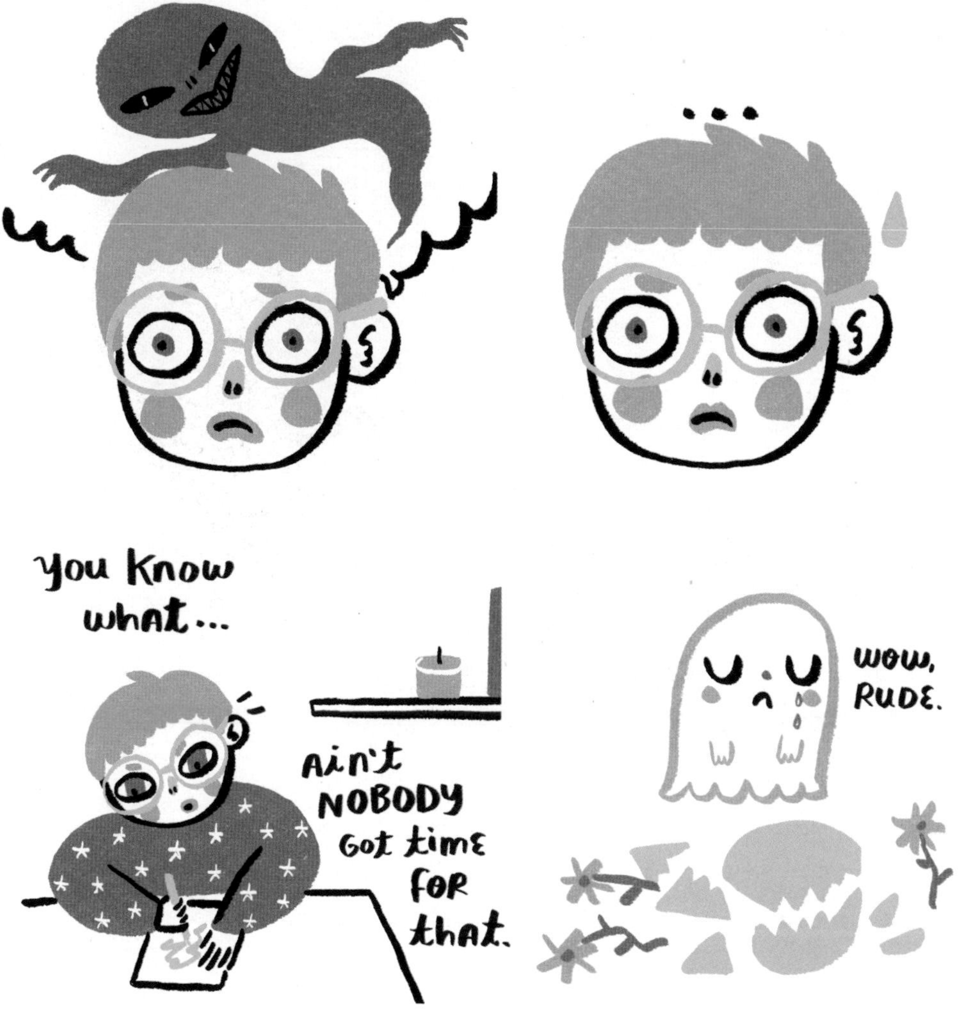
you know what...
Ain't NOBODY Got time FOR that.
wow, RUDE.

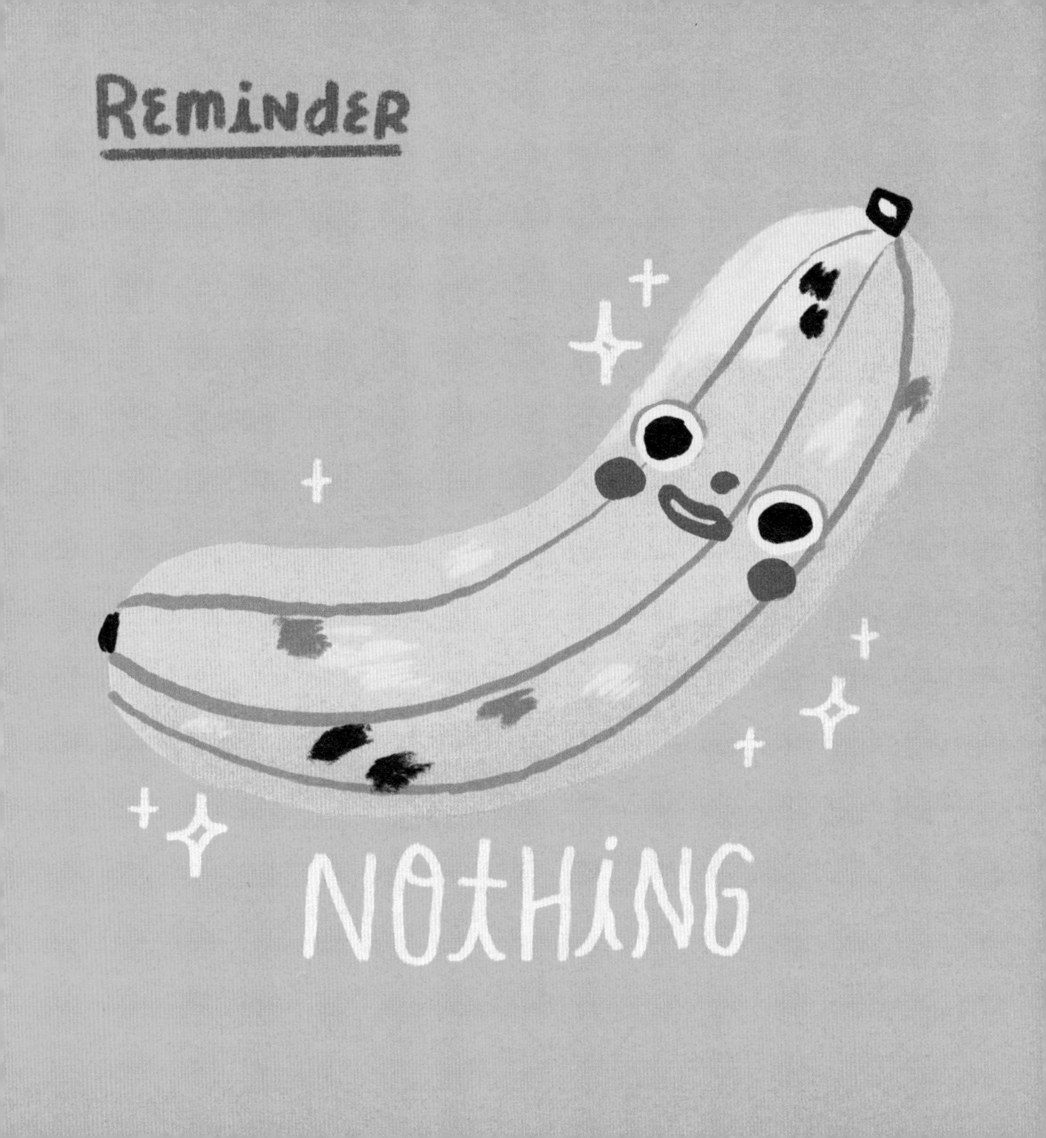
Reminder
Nothing

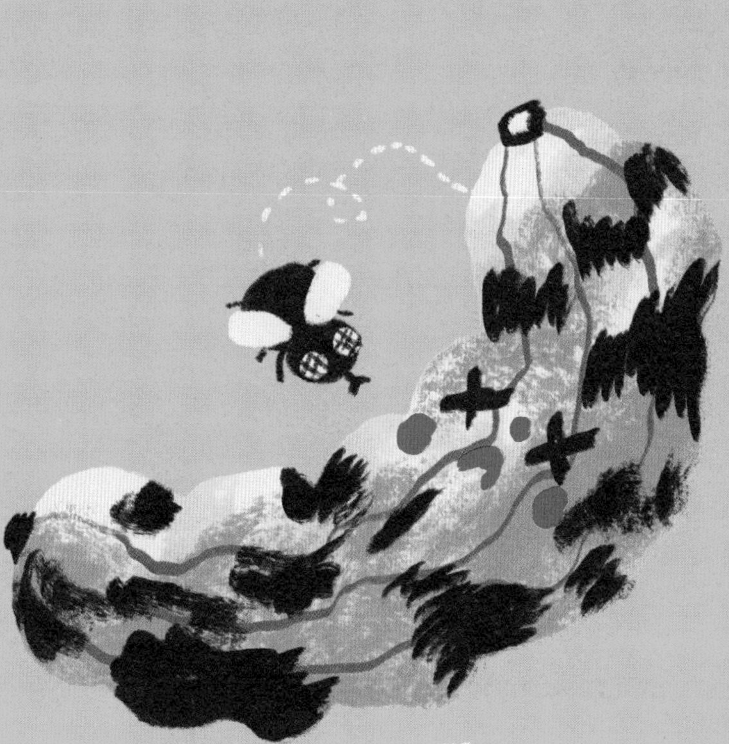

iS FOREVER.

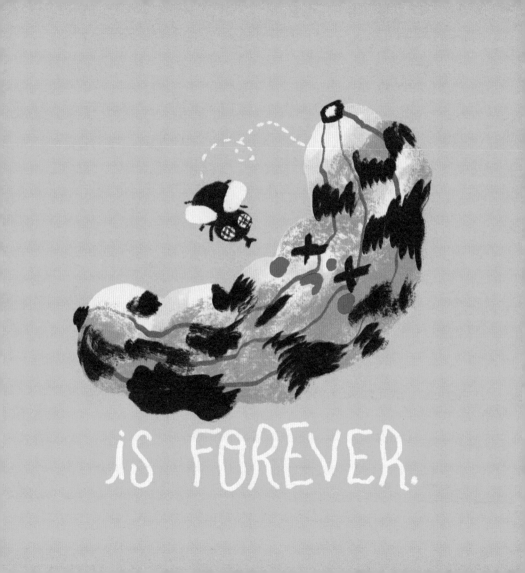

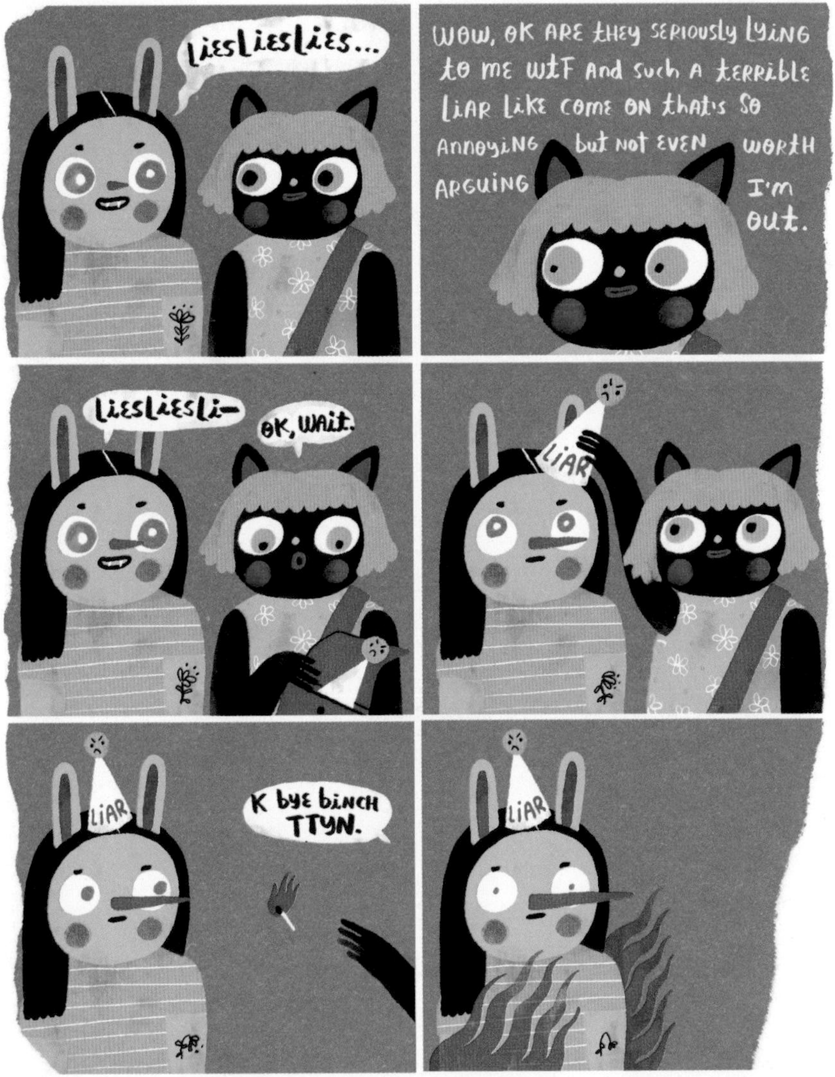
LiesLiesLies...
WOW, OK ARE THEY SERIOUSLY LYING TO ME WTF AND SUCH A TERRIBLE LIAR LIKE COME ON THAT'S SO ANNOYING
BUT NOT EVEN WORTH ARGUING
I'M OUT.
LiesLiesLi–
OK, WAIT.
LIAR
LIAR
K BYE BINCH TTYN.
LIAR

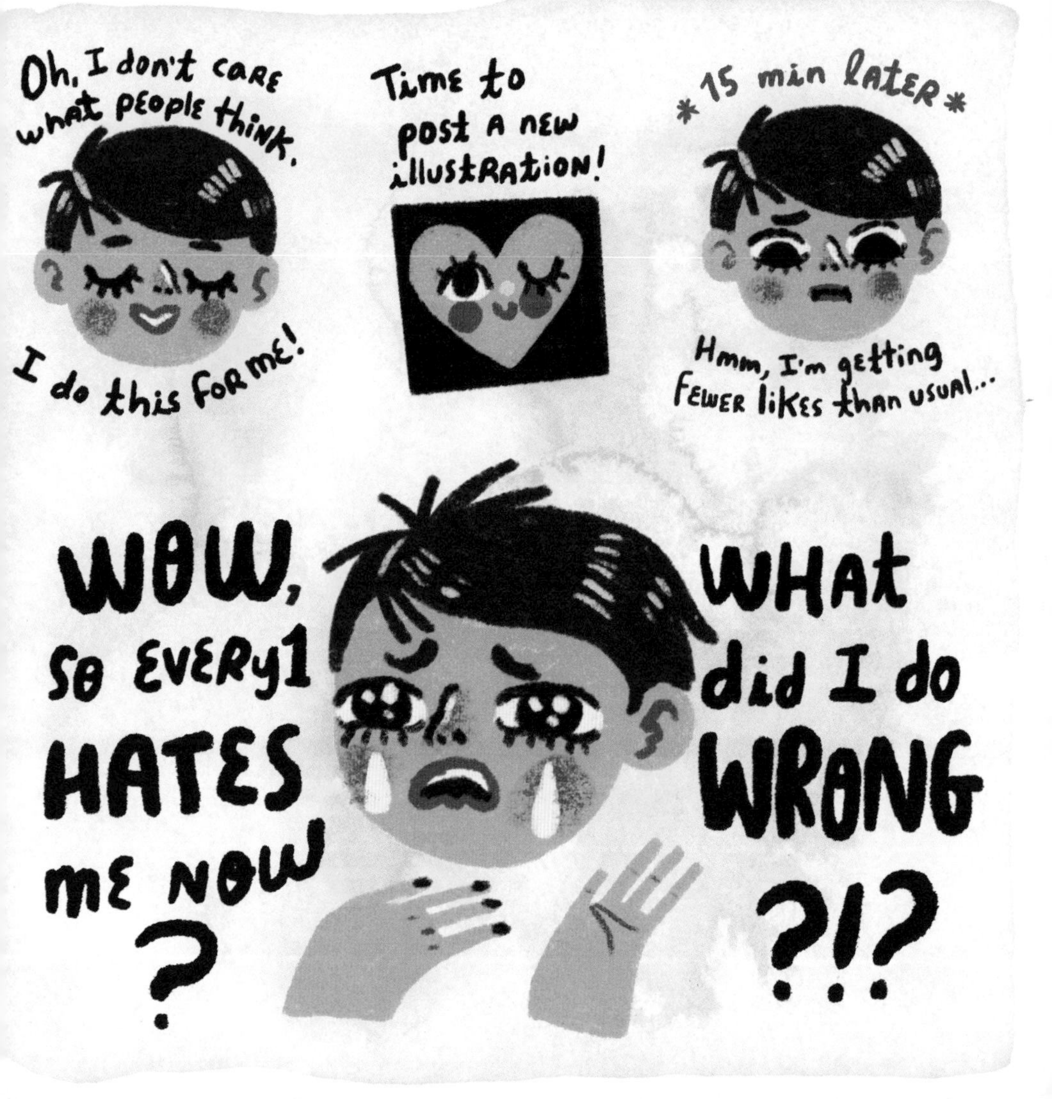
Oh, I don't care what people think.
I do this for me!
Time to post a new illustration!
15 min later
Hmm, I'm getting fewer likes than usual...
WOW, so every1 HATES me now?
WHAT did I do WRONG?!?

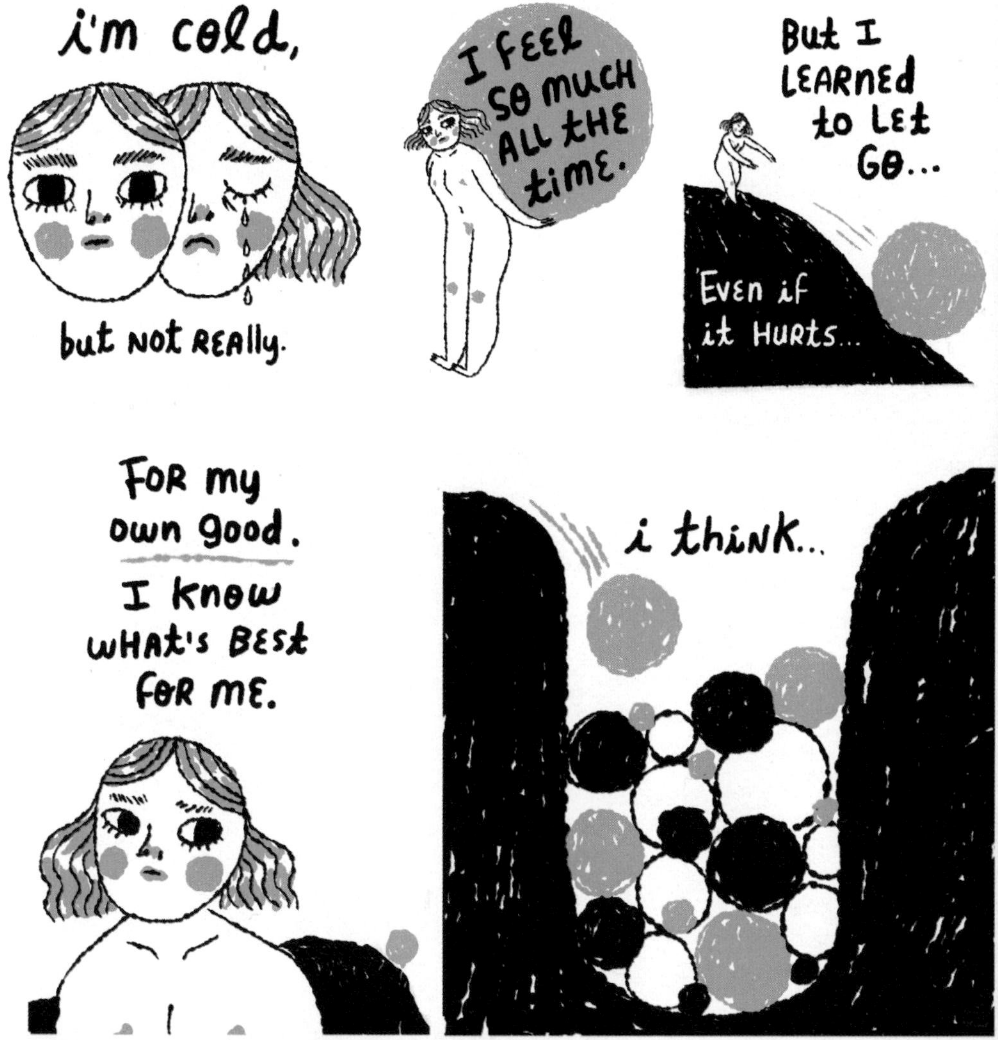

i'm cold,
but not really.
I feel so much all the time.
But I learned to let go...
Even if it hurts...
For my own good.
I know what's best for me.
i think...

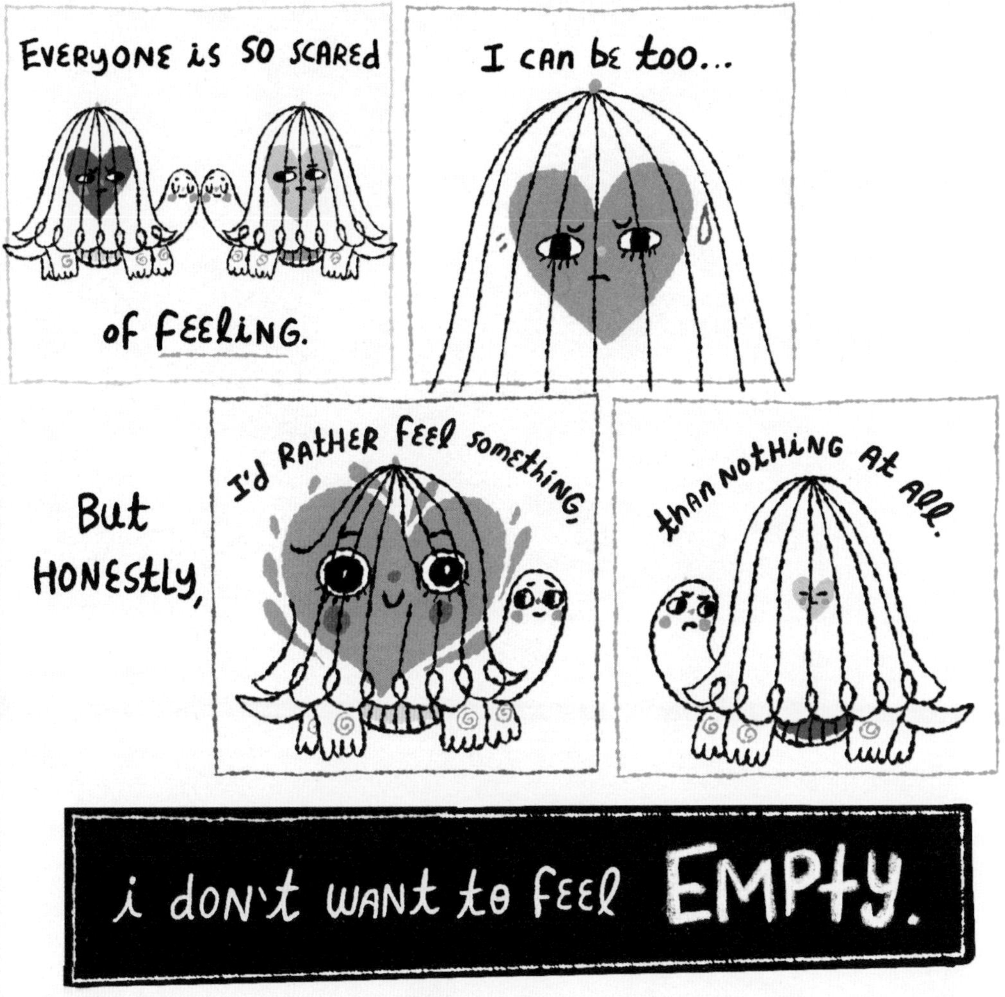
EVERYONE IS SO SCARED
of FEELING.
I can be too...
But
HONESTLY,
I'd RATHER FEEL SOMETHING,
than NOTHING AT ALL.
i don't WANT to FEEL EMPTY.

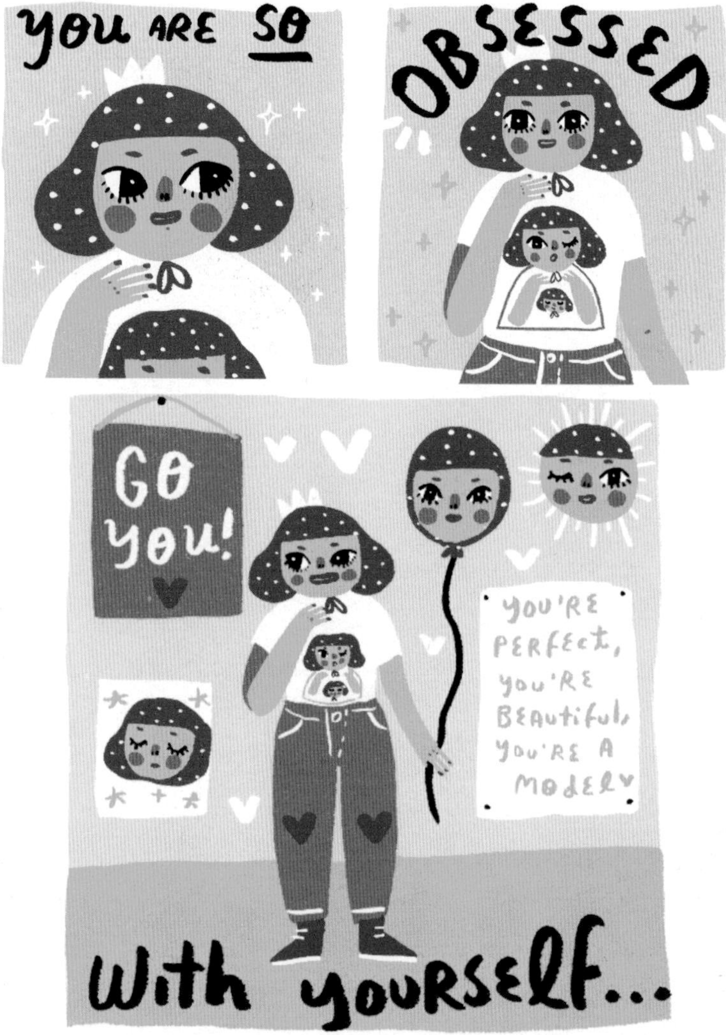
YOU ARE SO
OBSESSED
GO YOU!
YOU'RE PERFECT, YOU'RE BEAUTIFUL, YOU'RE A MODEL
With yourself...

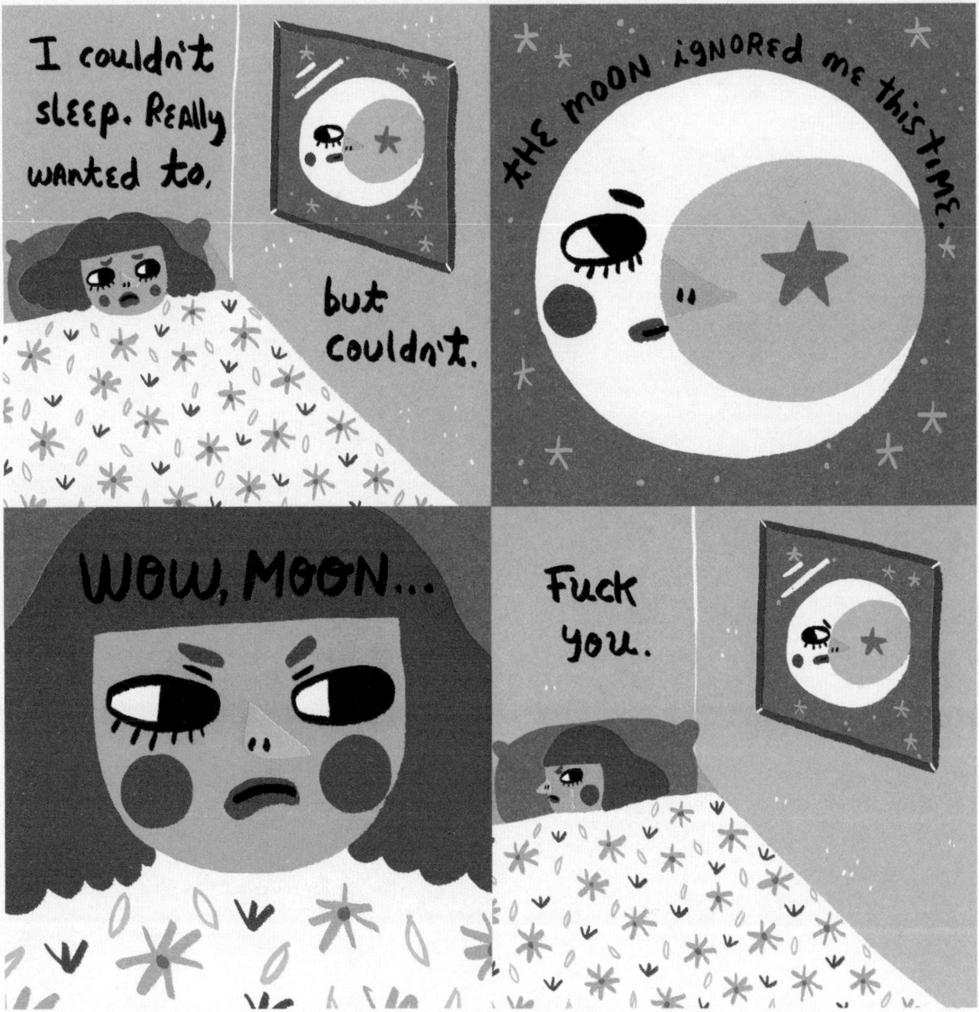
I couldn't sleep. Really wanted to,
but couldn't.
THE MOON ignored me this time.
WOW, MOON...
Fuck you.

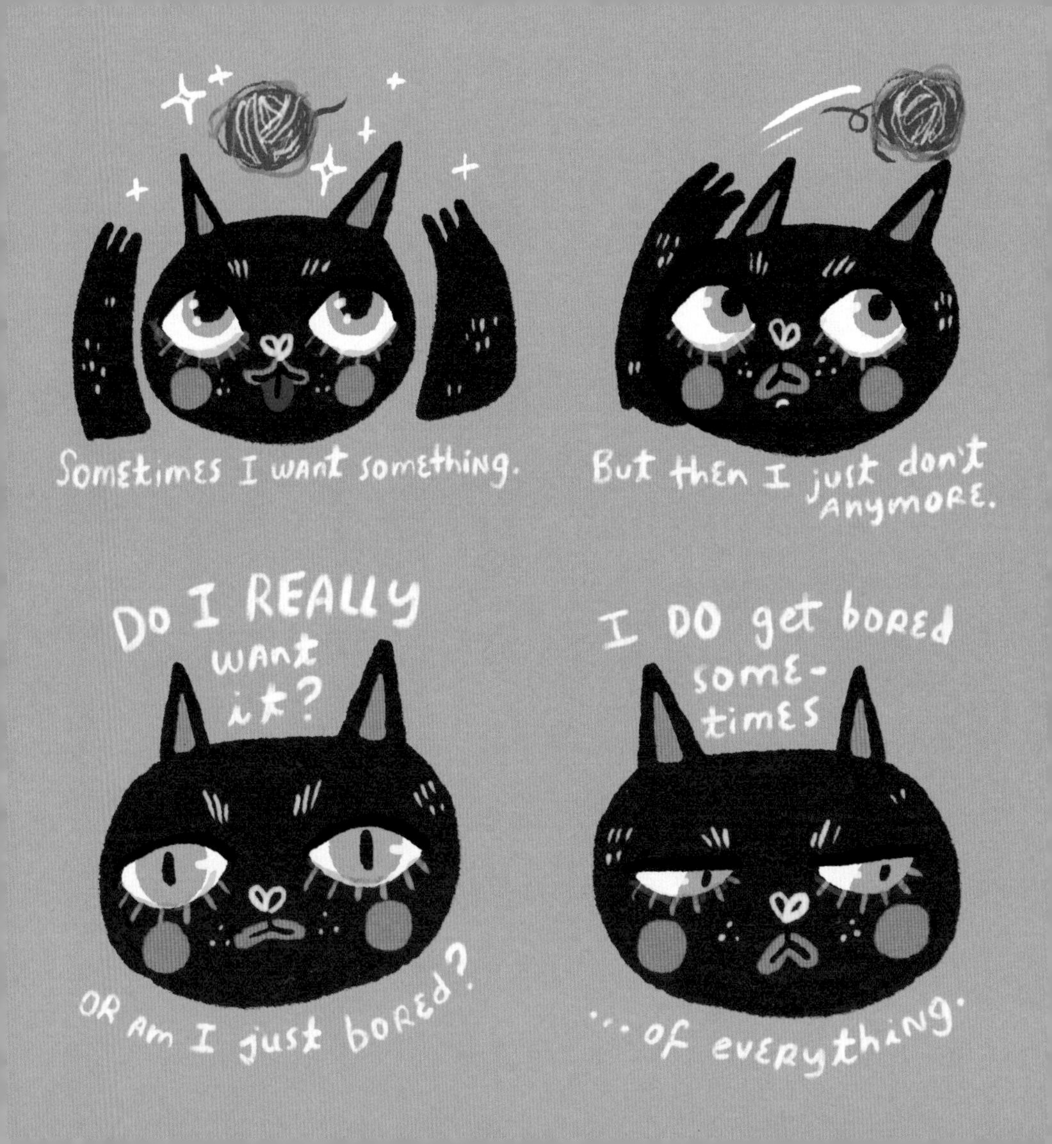
Sometimes I want something.
But then I just don't anymore.
Do I REALLY want it?
OR am I just bored?
I DO get bored some-times
...of everything.

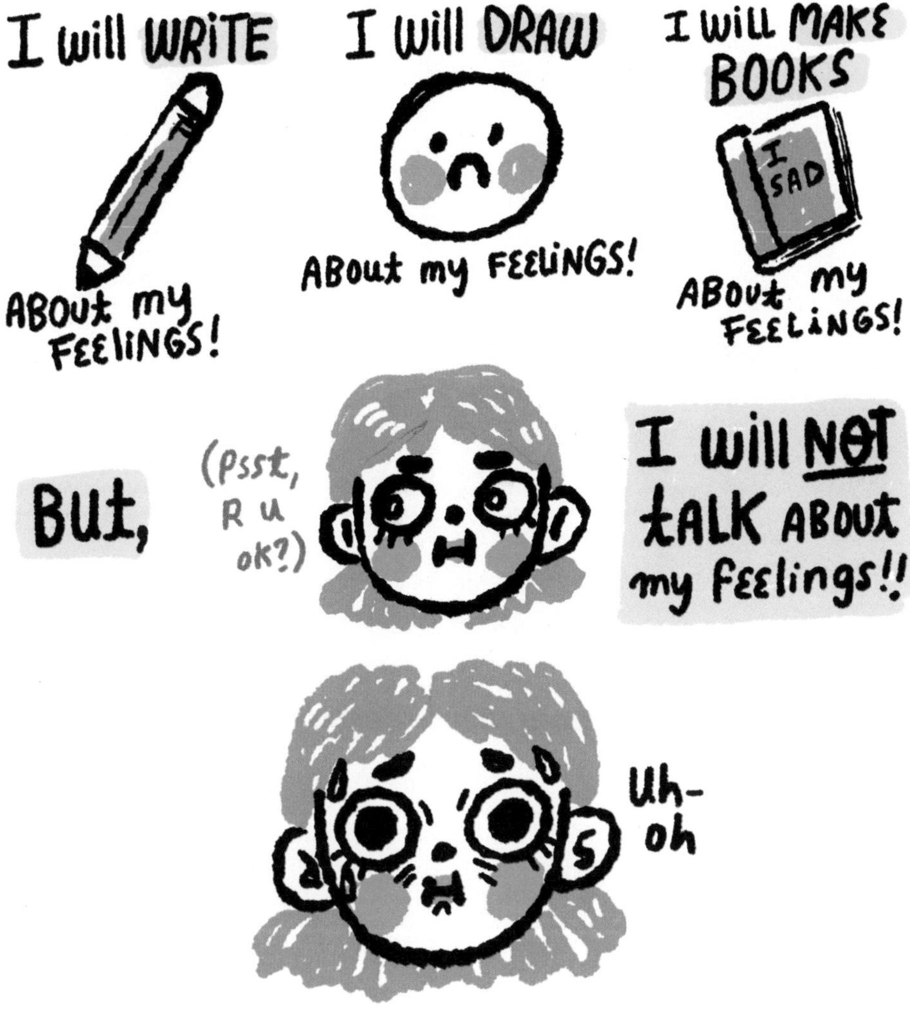
I will WRITE
ABOUT my FEELINGS!
I will DRAW
ABOUT my FEELINGS!
I WILL MAKE BOOKS
I SAD
ABOUT my FEELINGS!
But,
(Psst, R u ok?)
I will NOT TALK ABOUT my feelings!!
Uh-oh

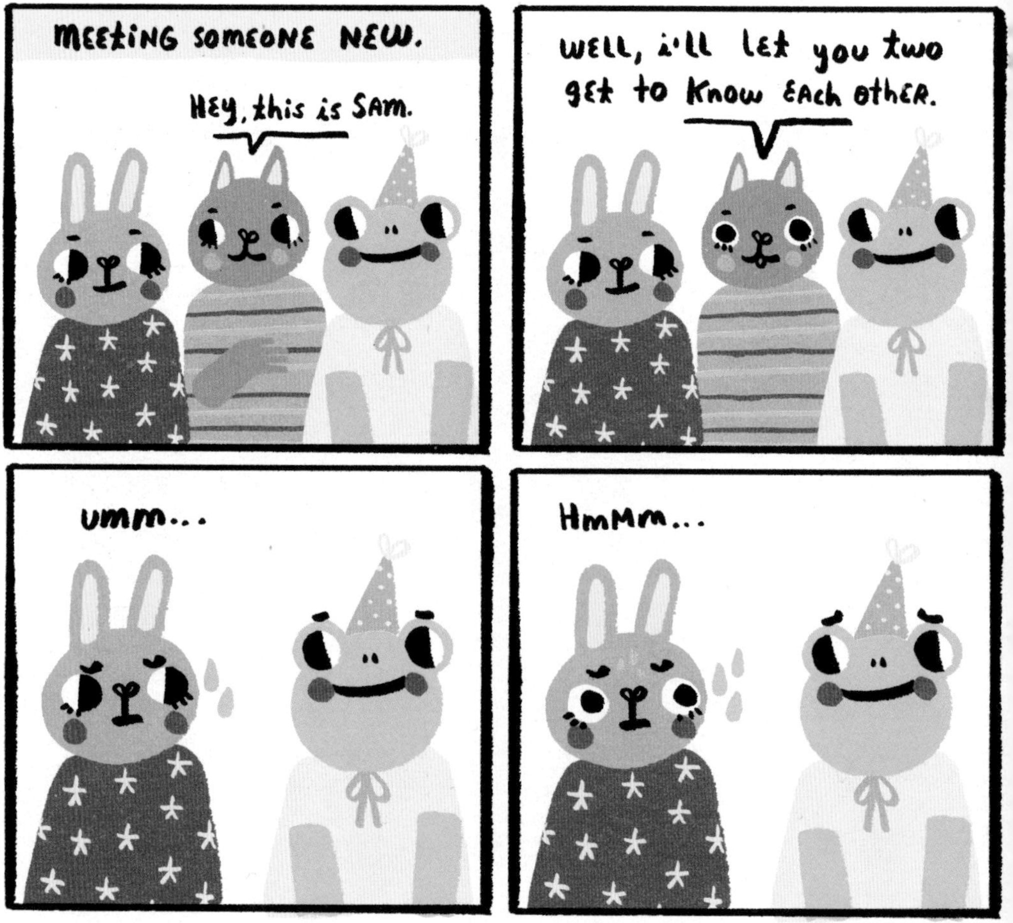
MEETING SOMEONE NEW.
HEY, this is SAM.
WELL, i'll let you two get to know each other.
umm...
HmMm...

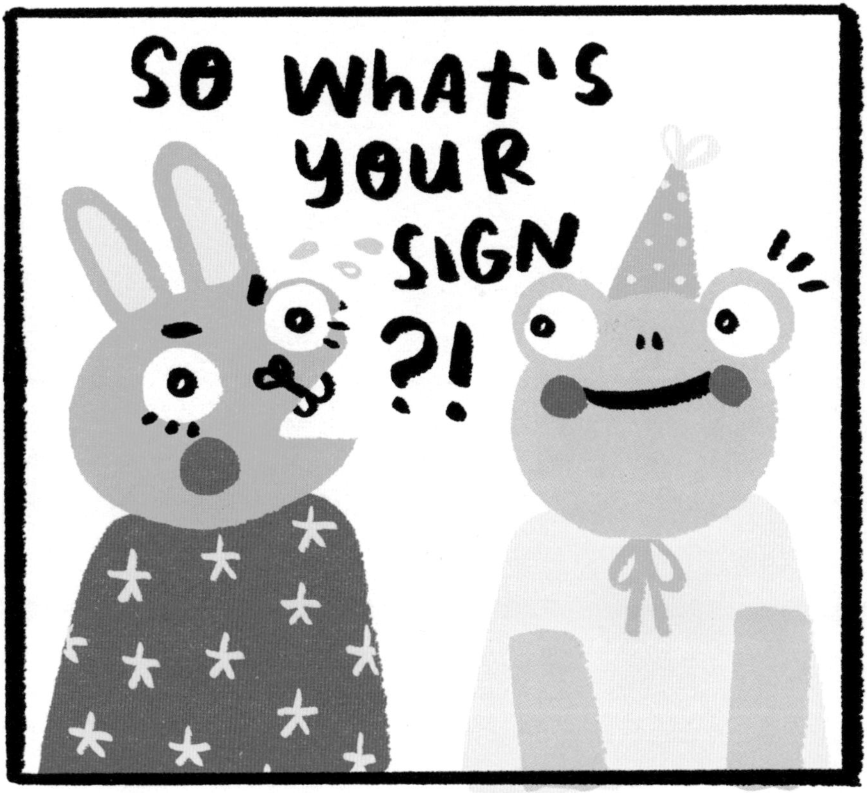
SO WHAT'S YOUR SIGN ?!

REMINDER

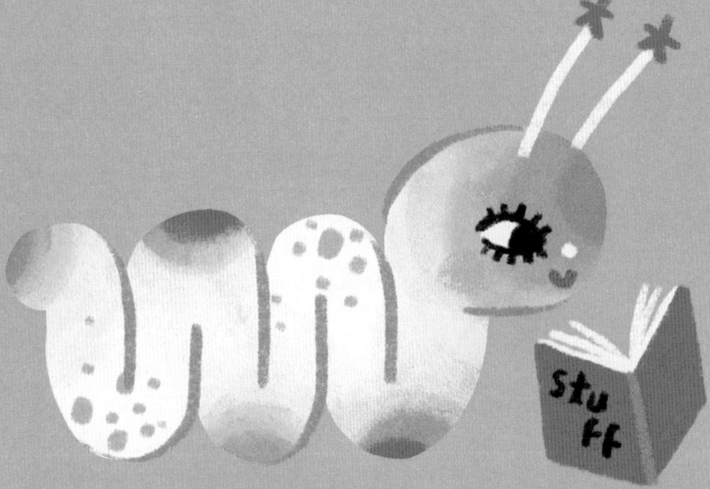
STUFF

I DO NOT KNOW EVERYTHING.

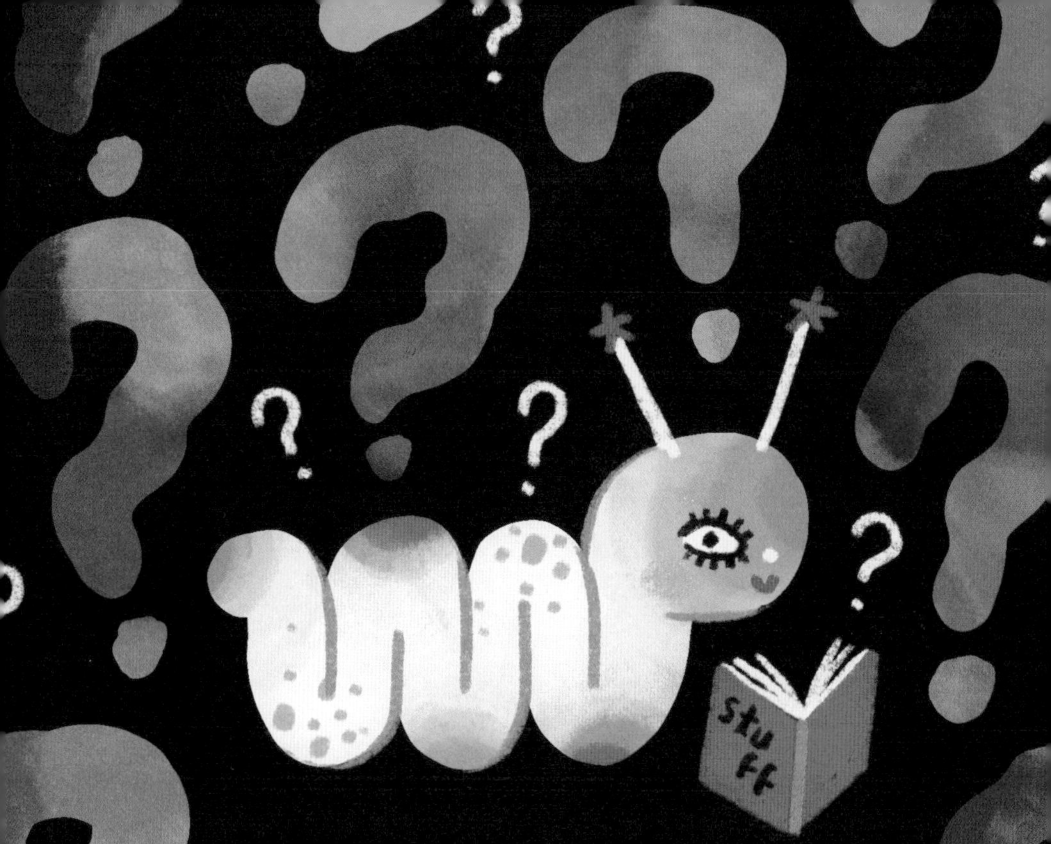
STUFF

IN FACT, I DON'T KNOW MUCH ABOUT ANYTHING, AT ALL!

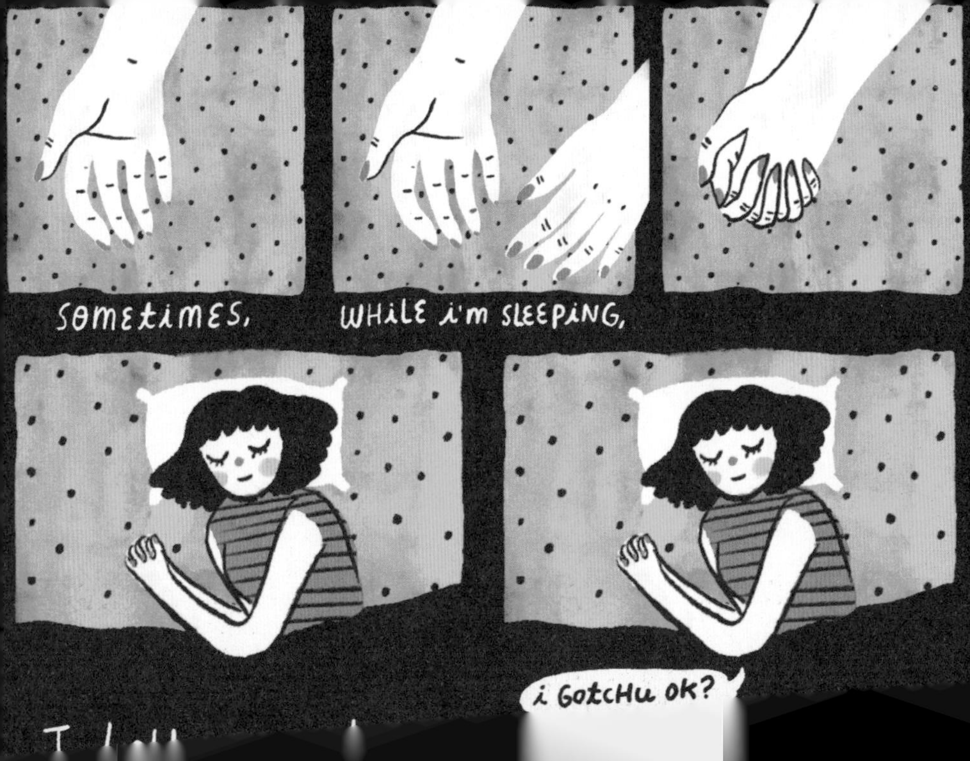
SOMETIMES,
WHILE i'M SLEEPING,
i GOTCHU OK?

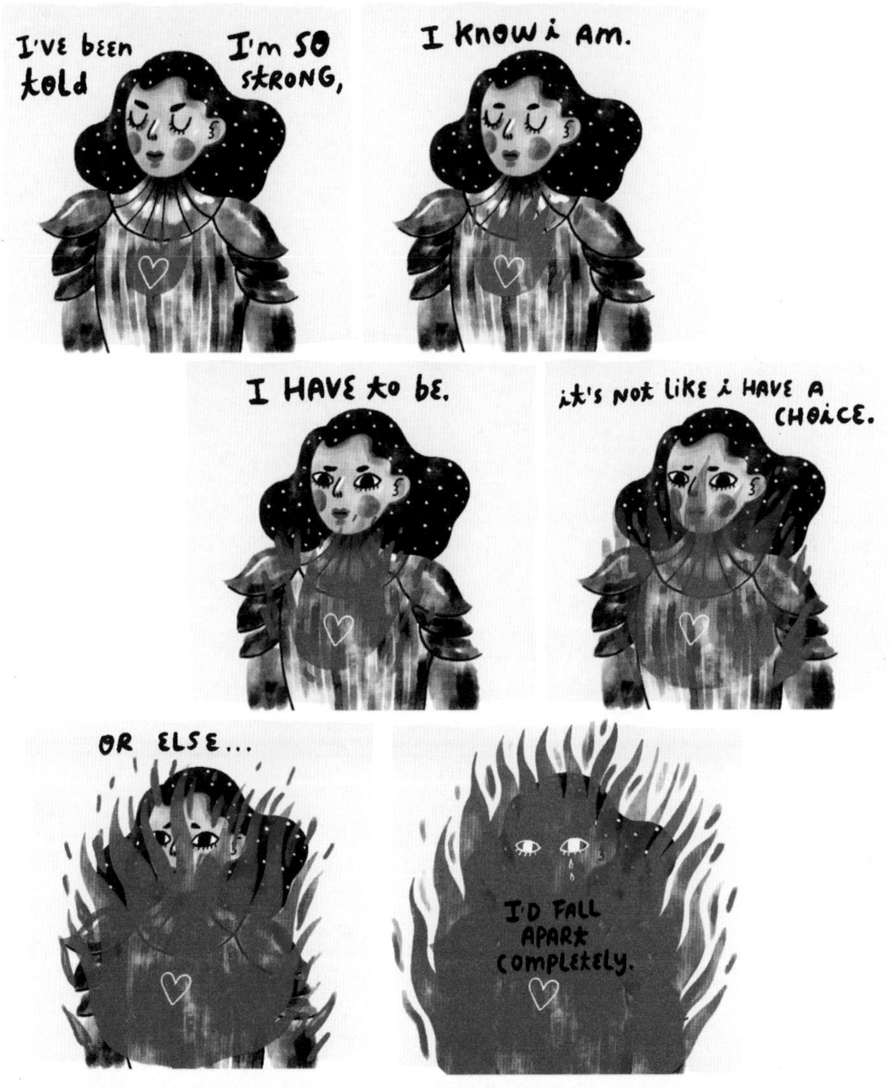
I'VE been told
I'm SO STRONG,
I know i AM.
I HAVE to be.
it's not like i HAVE A CHOiCE.
OR ELSE...
I'D FALL APART COMPLETELY.

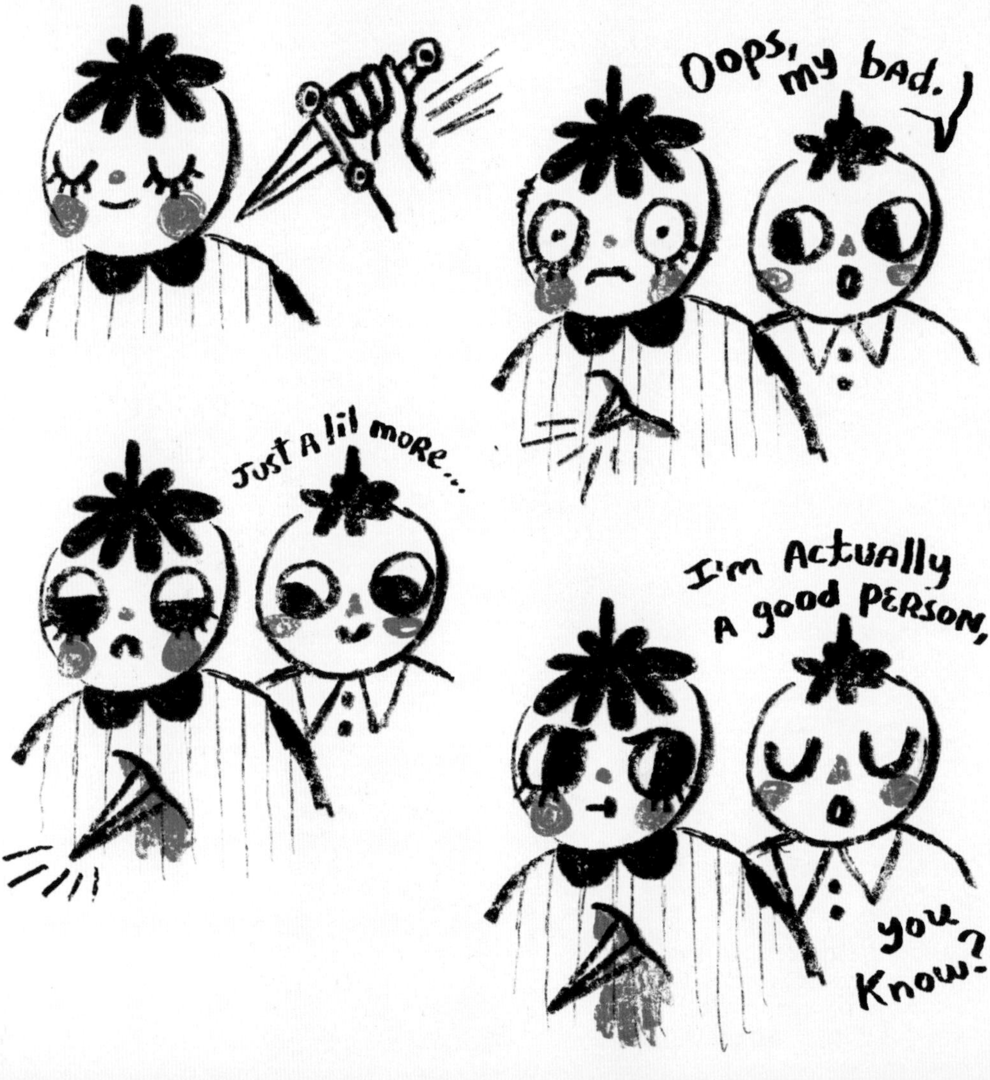
Oops, my bad.
Just a lil more...
I'm actually a good person,
you know?

The moon and I are friends now; we decided to resolve our differences and get along.

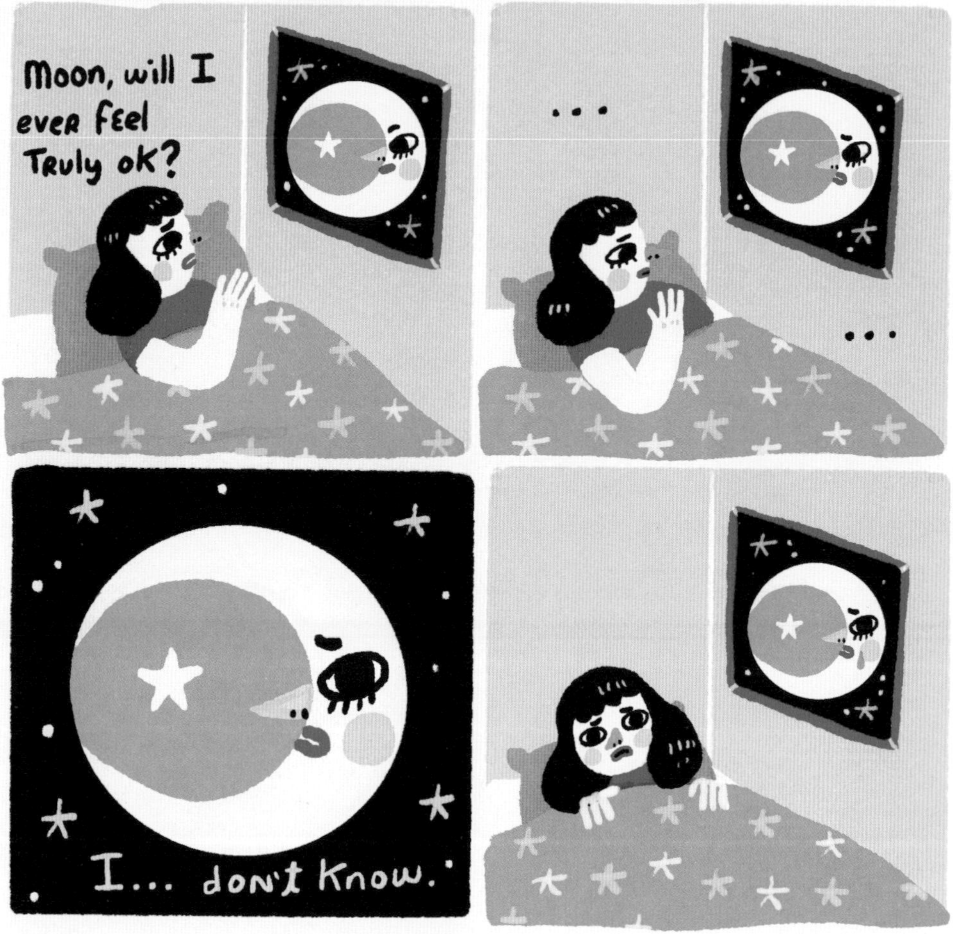
Moon, will I ever feel truly ok?
...
...
I... don't know.

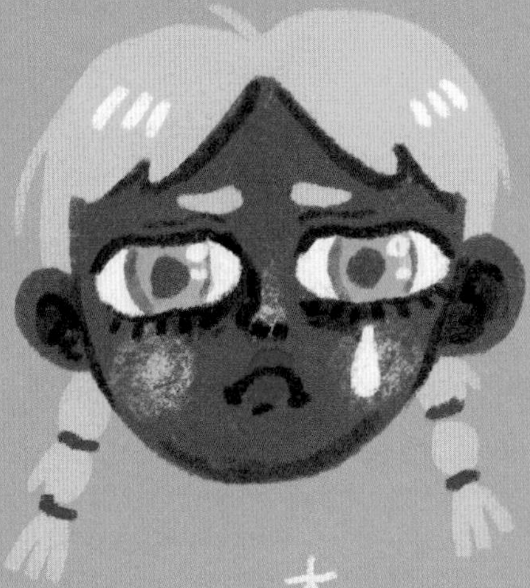

People think crybabies are weak. But honestly, I feel like crying is VERY helpful.

And when I'm sad or upset, I cry and let it all out.

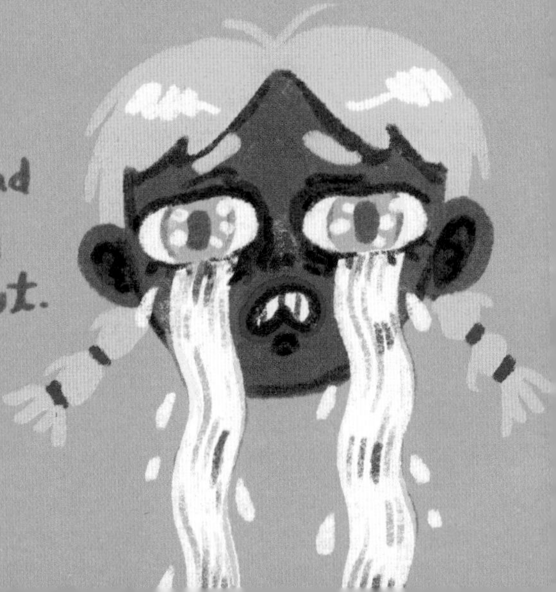

And everything's good again. It makes it easier to move on.

You were my tears, but they're gone now.

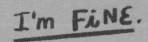

I'm FINE.

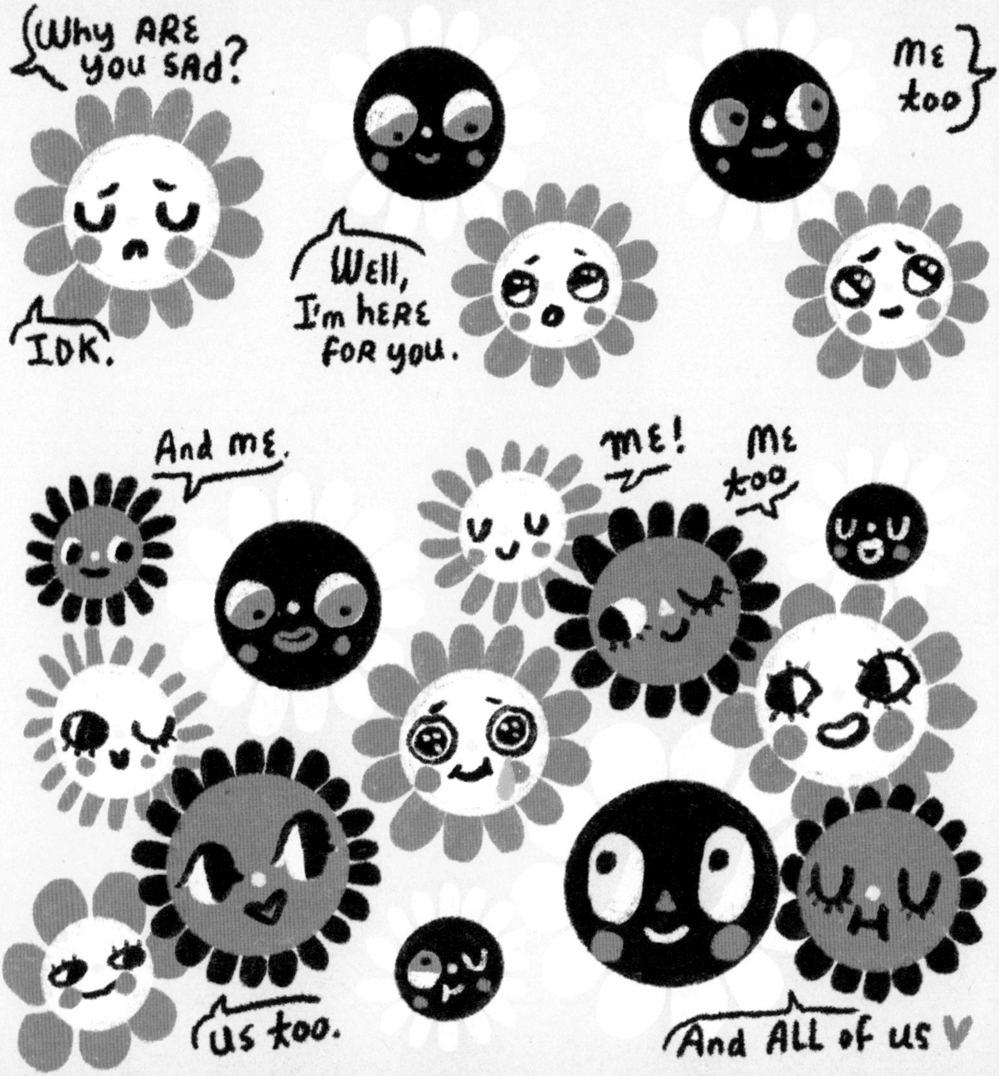
Why ARE you SAd?
IDK.
Well, I'm hERE FOR you.
mE too
And mE.
mE!
mE too
us too.
And ALL of us

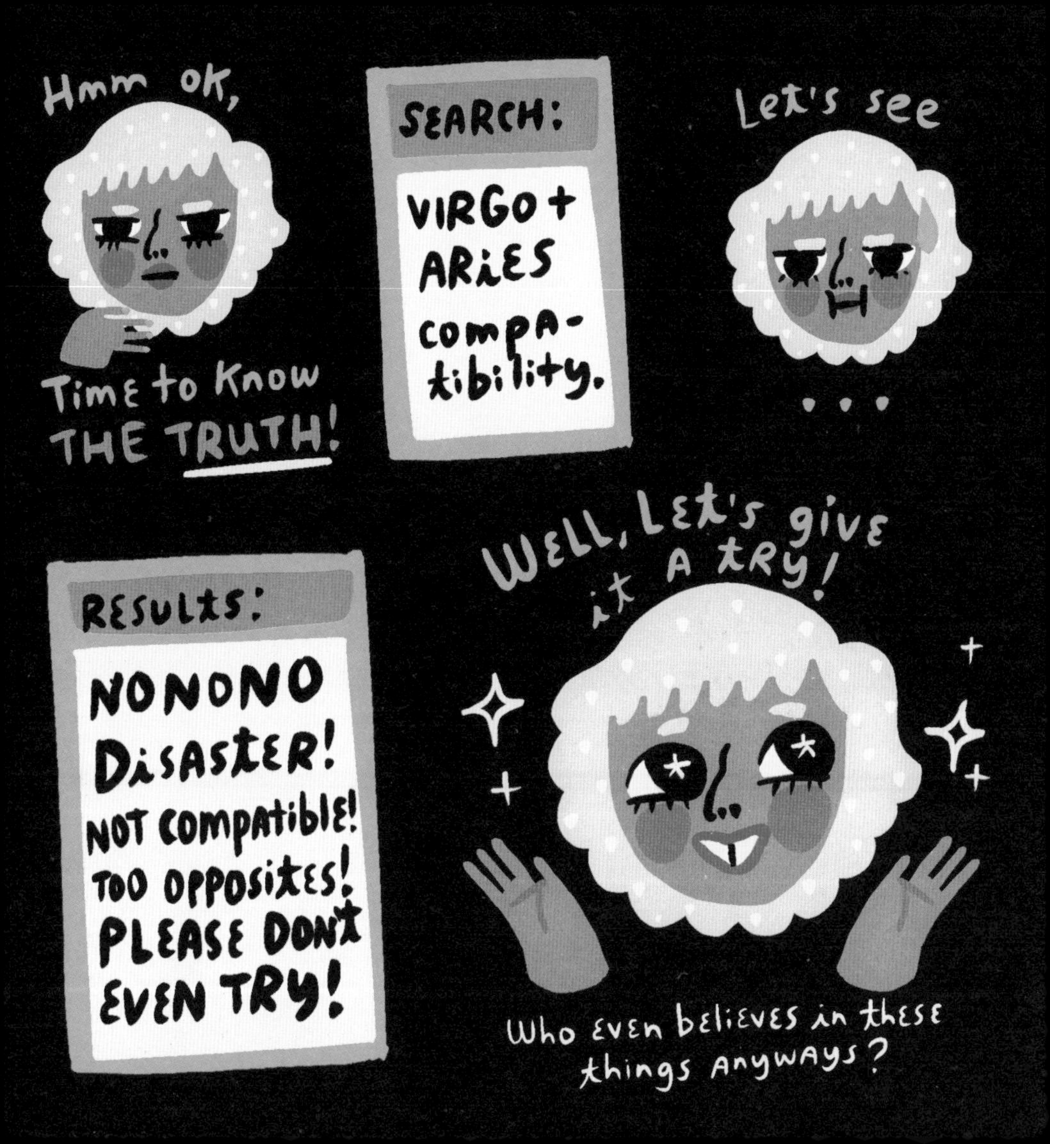
Hmm ok,
Time to Know THE TRUTH!
SEARCH:
VIRGO + ARIES compa-tibility.
Let's see
...
RESULTS:
NONONO Disaster! NOT COMPATIBLE! TOO OPPOSITES! PLEASE DON'T EVEN TRY!
WELL, Let's give it A TRY!
Who even believes in these things anyways?

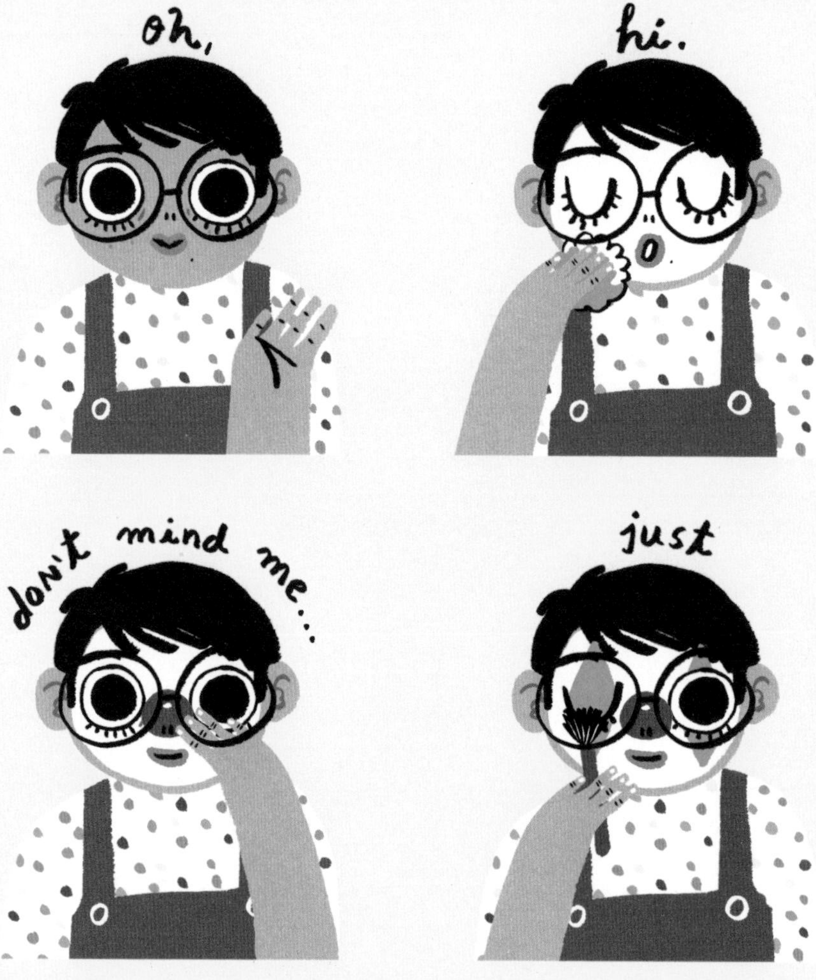
oh,
hi.
don't mind me...
just

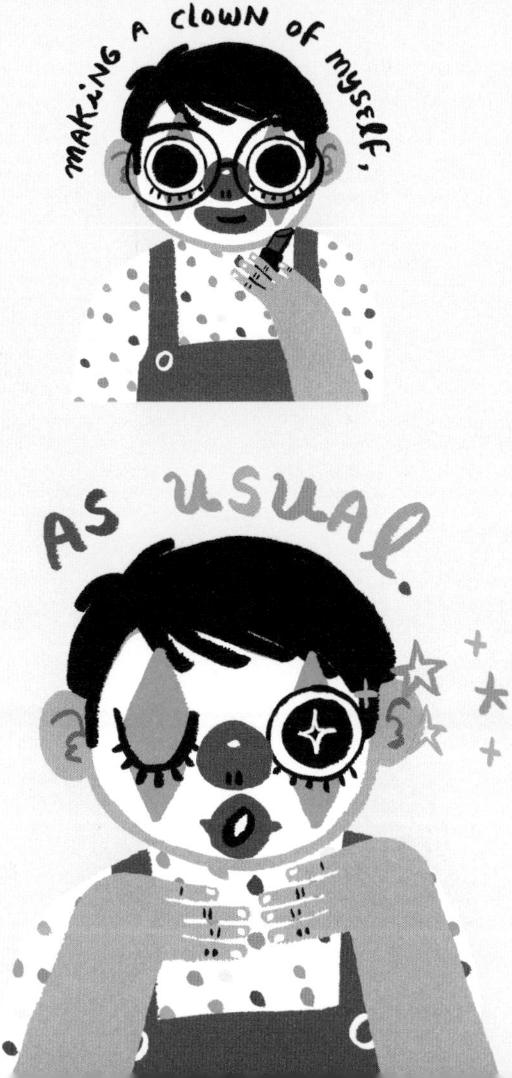
MAKiNG A CLOWN OF MYSELF,
AS USUAL.

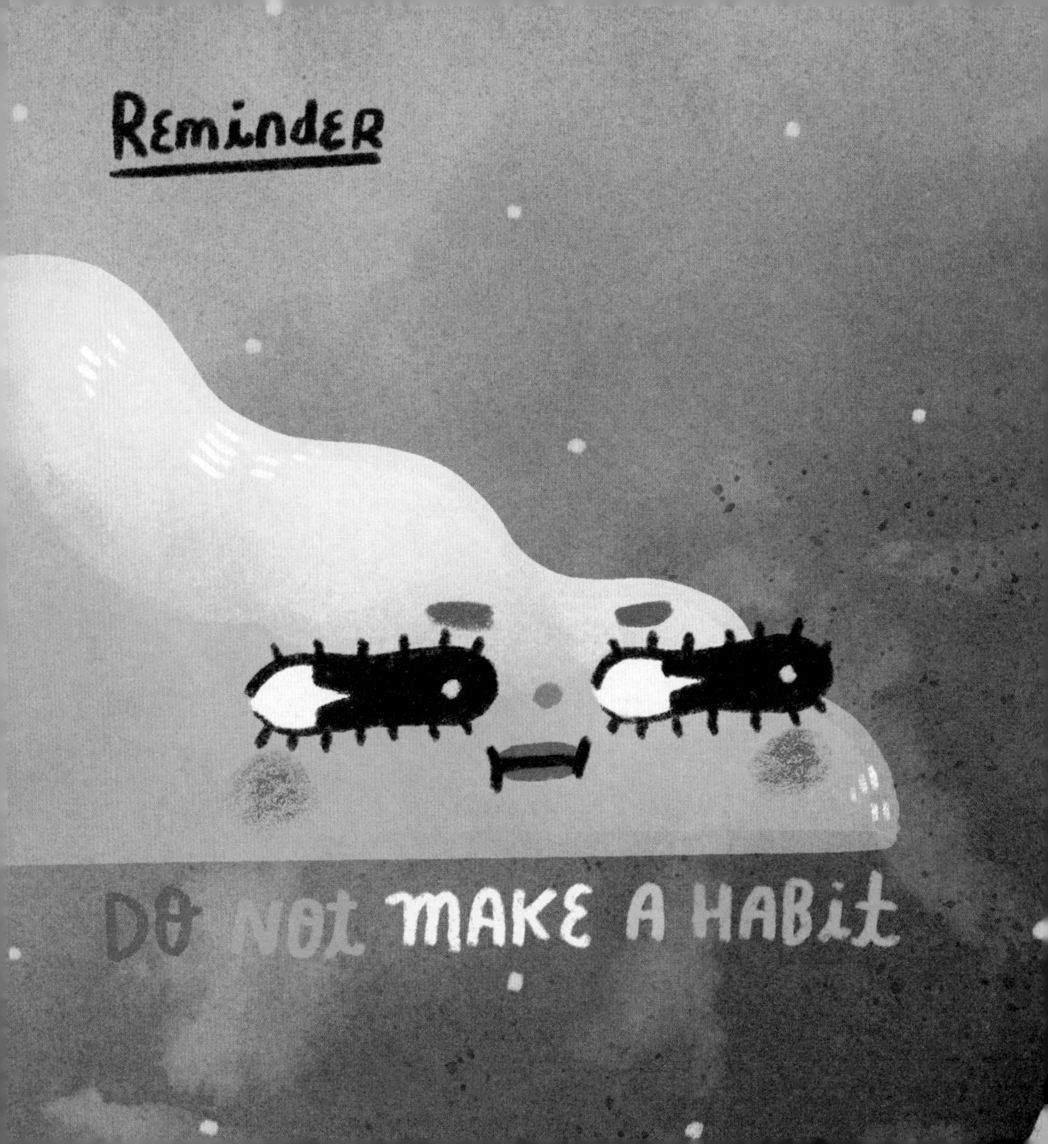
REMINDER
DO NOT MAKE A HABIT

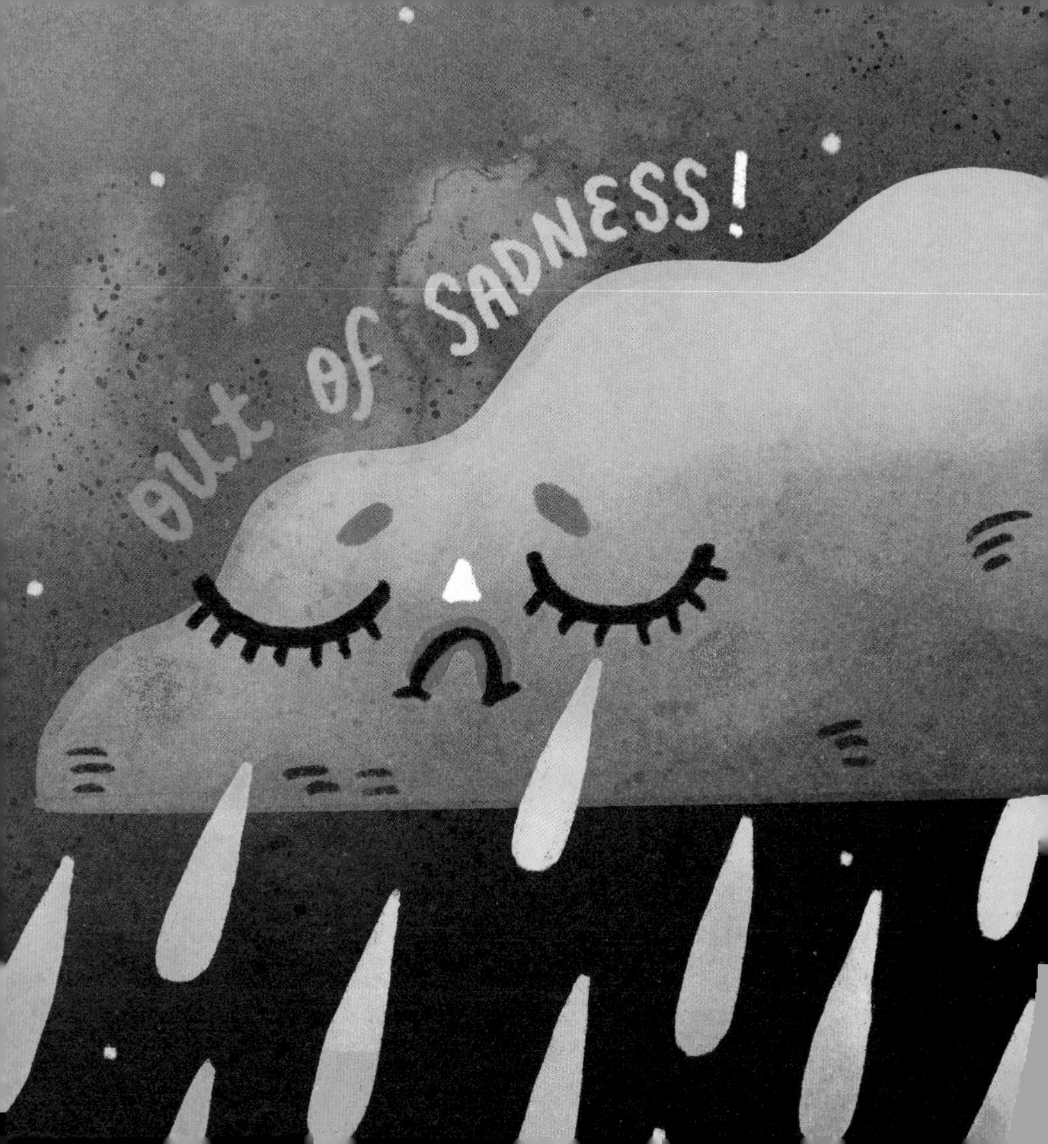
OUT OF SADNESS!

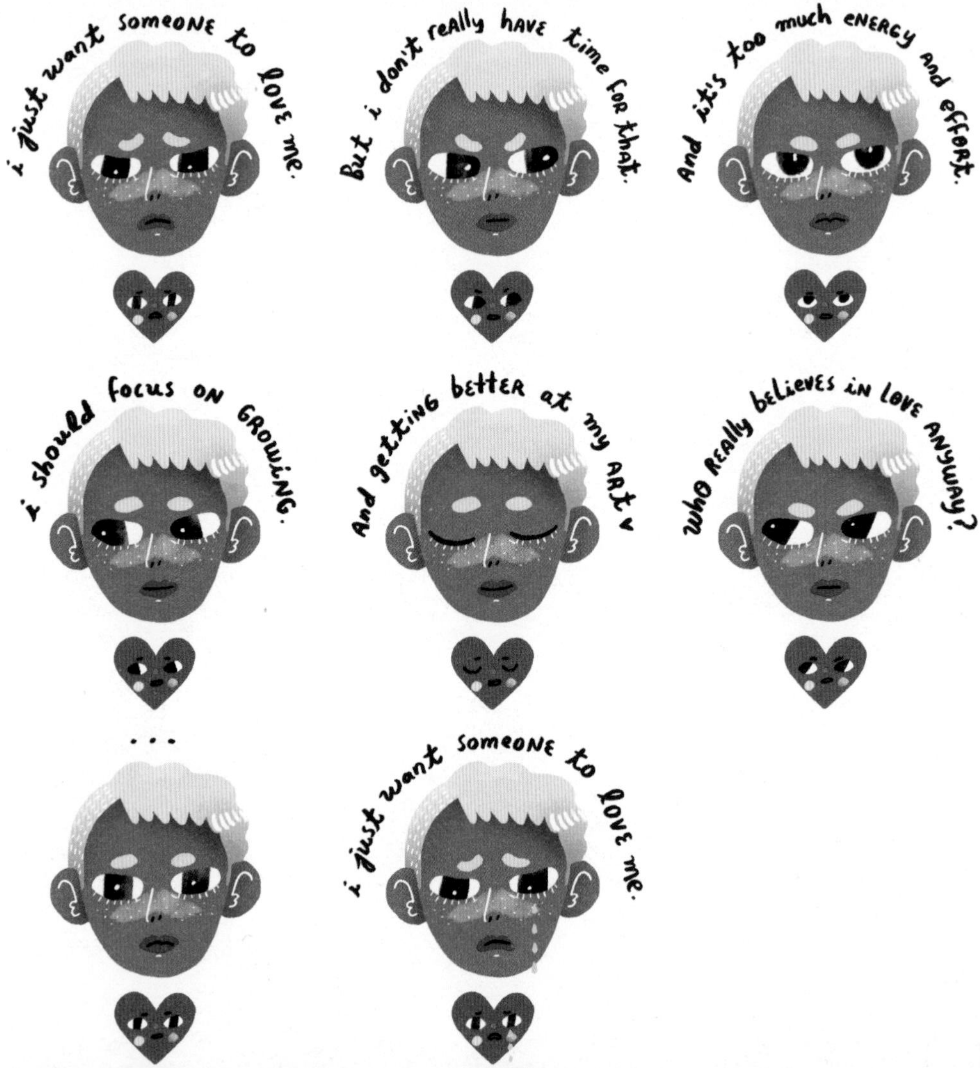
i just want someone to love me.
But i don't really have time for that.
And it's too much energy and effort.
i should focus on growing.
And getting better at my art
Who really believes in love anyway?
...
i just want someone to love me.

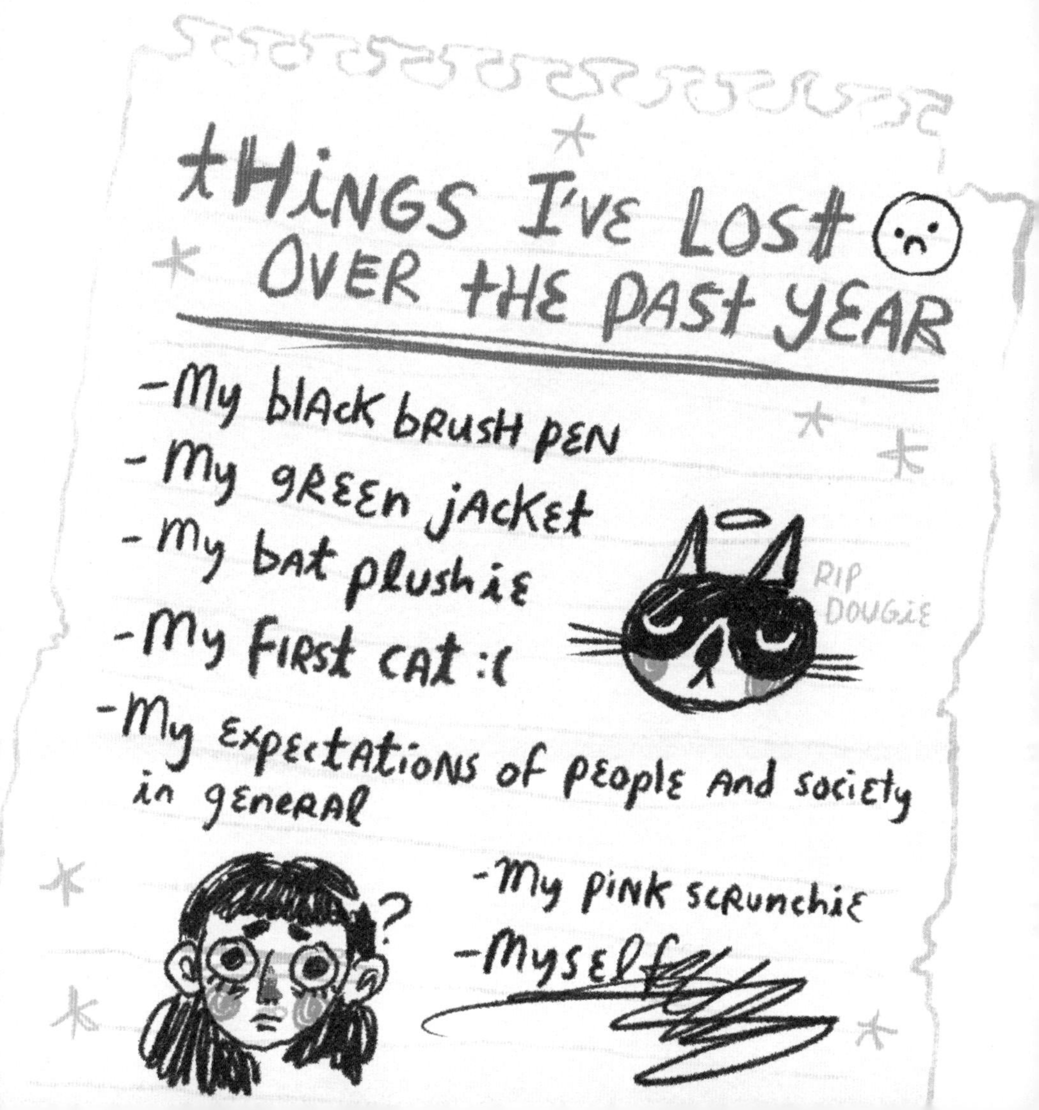
THINGS I'VE LOST OVER THE PAST YEAR
-My black brush pen
-My green jacket
-My bat plushie
-My first cat :(
RIP DOUGIE
-My expectations of people and society in general
?
-My pink scrunchie
-Myself

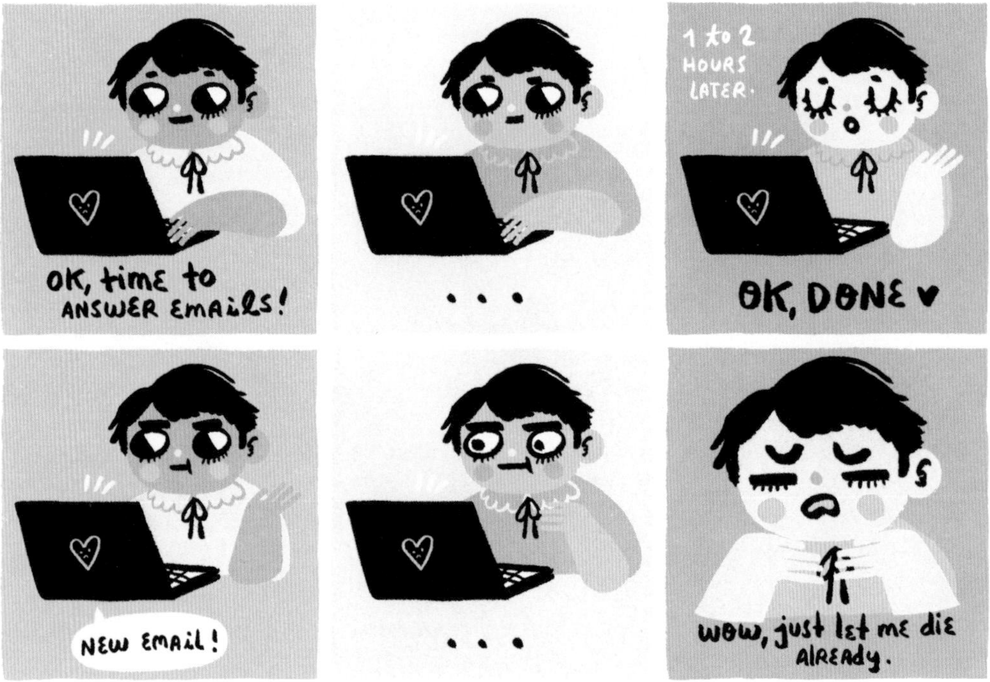
OK, time to ANSWER EMAILS!
...
1 to 2 HOURS LATER.
OK, DONE ♥
NEW EMAIL!
...
wow, just let me die already.

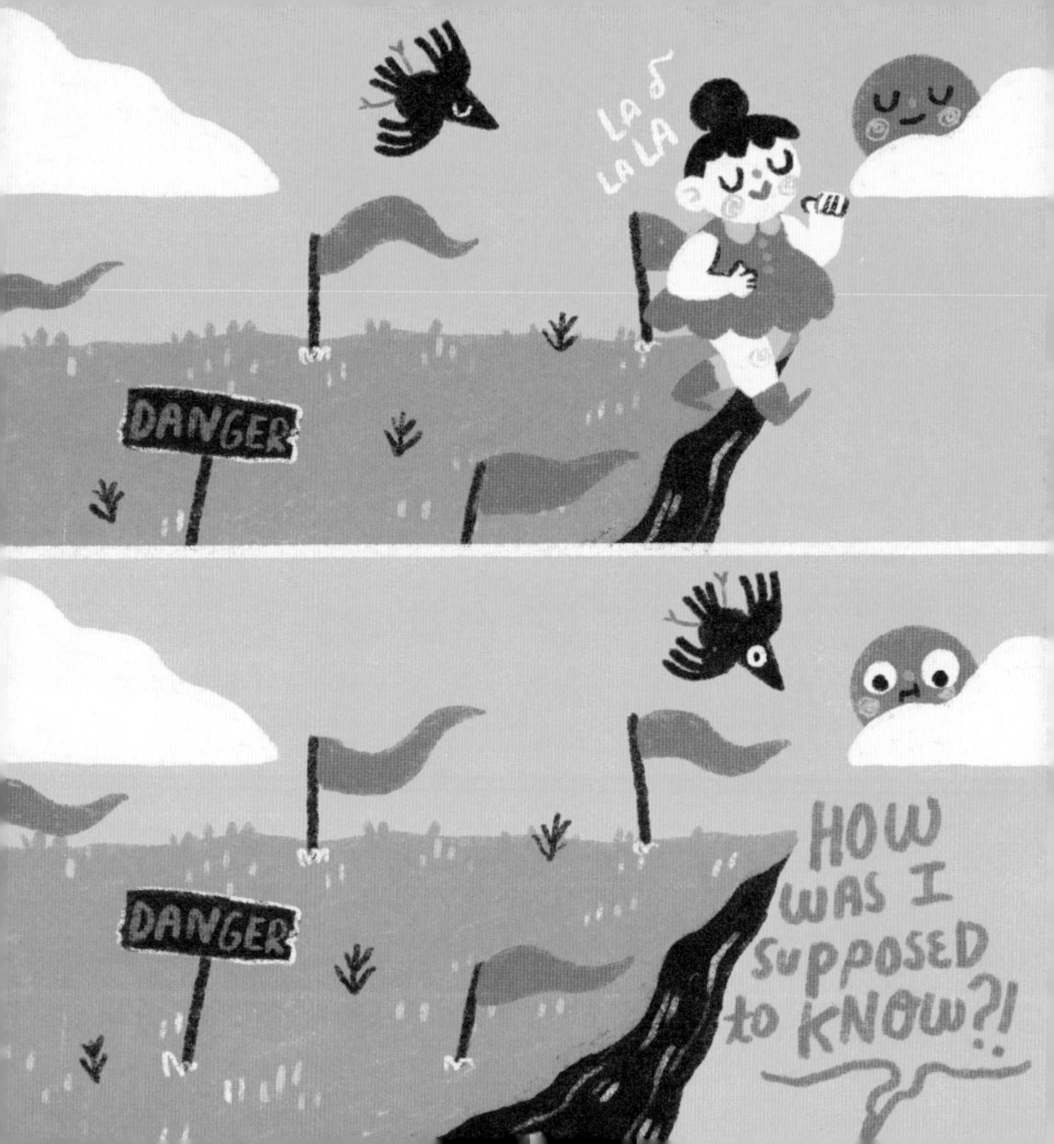
LA LA LA
DANGER
DANGER
HOW WAS I SUPPOSED TO KNOW?!

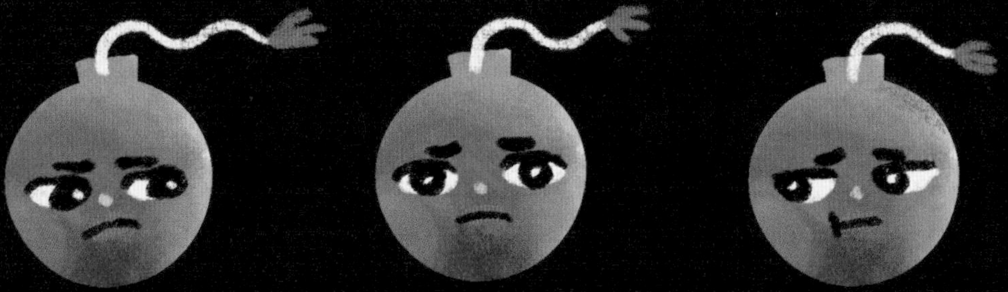

I feel so much ANGER. What AM I supposed to do with it?

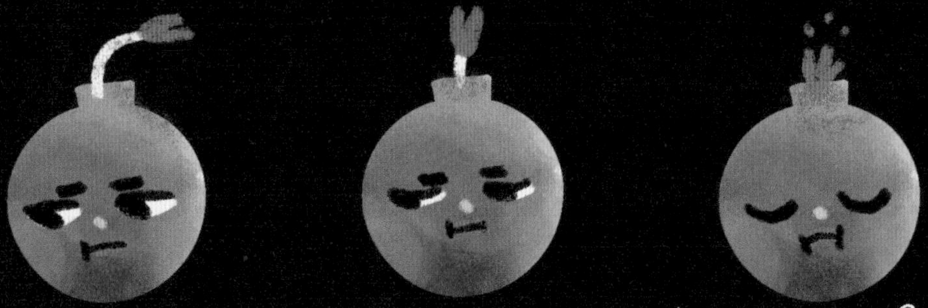

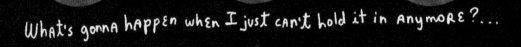

What's gonna happen when I just can't hold it in anymore?...

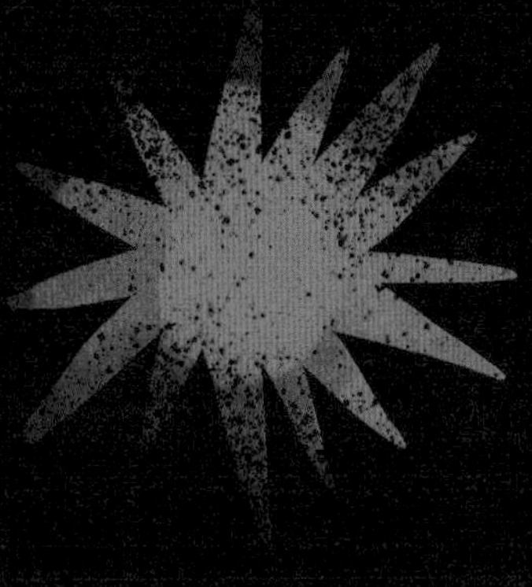

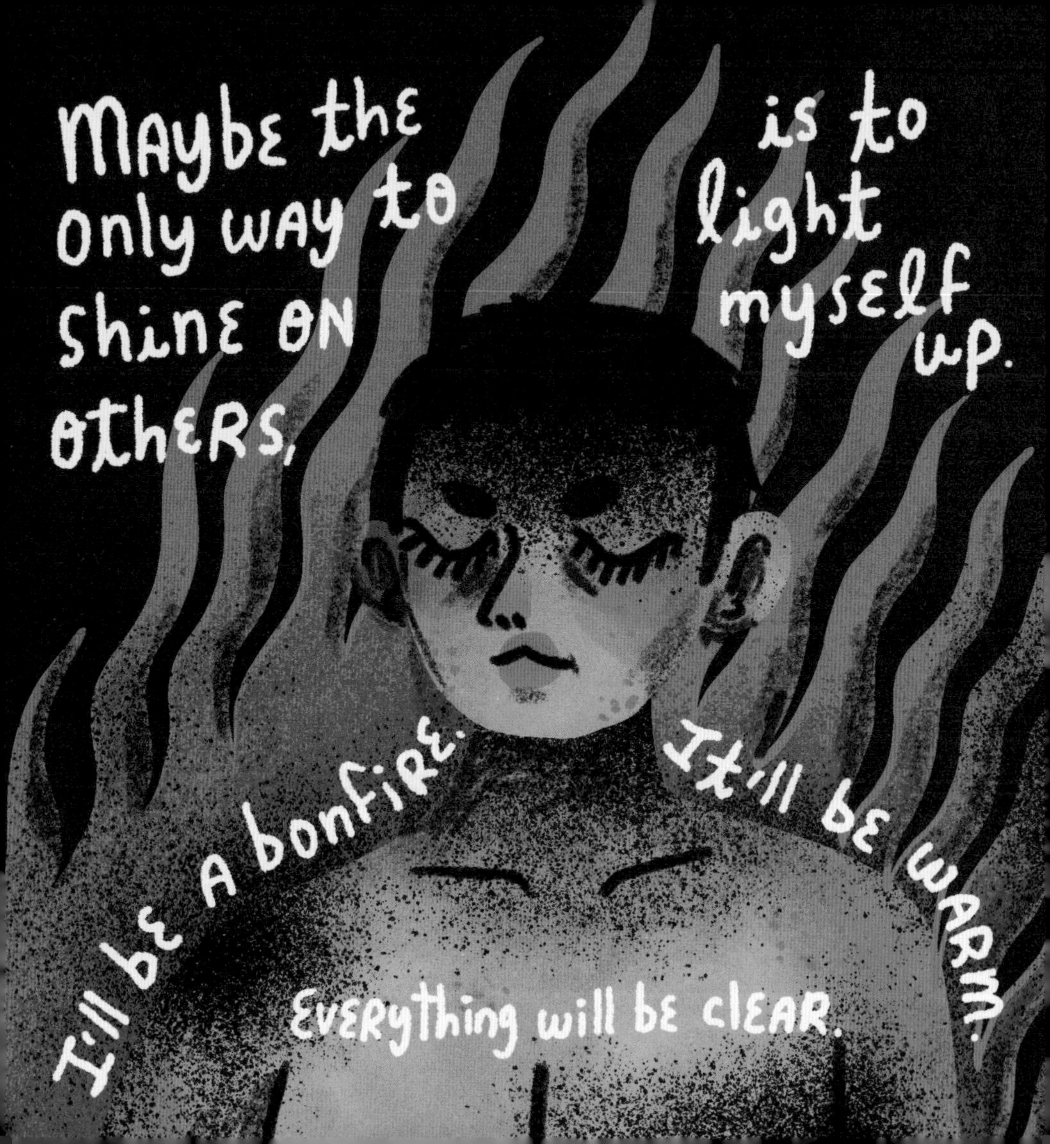
Maybe the only way to shine on others, is to light myself up.
I'll be a bonfire.
It'll be warm.
Everything will be clear.

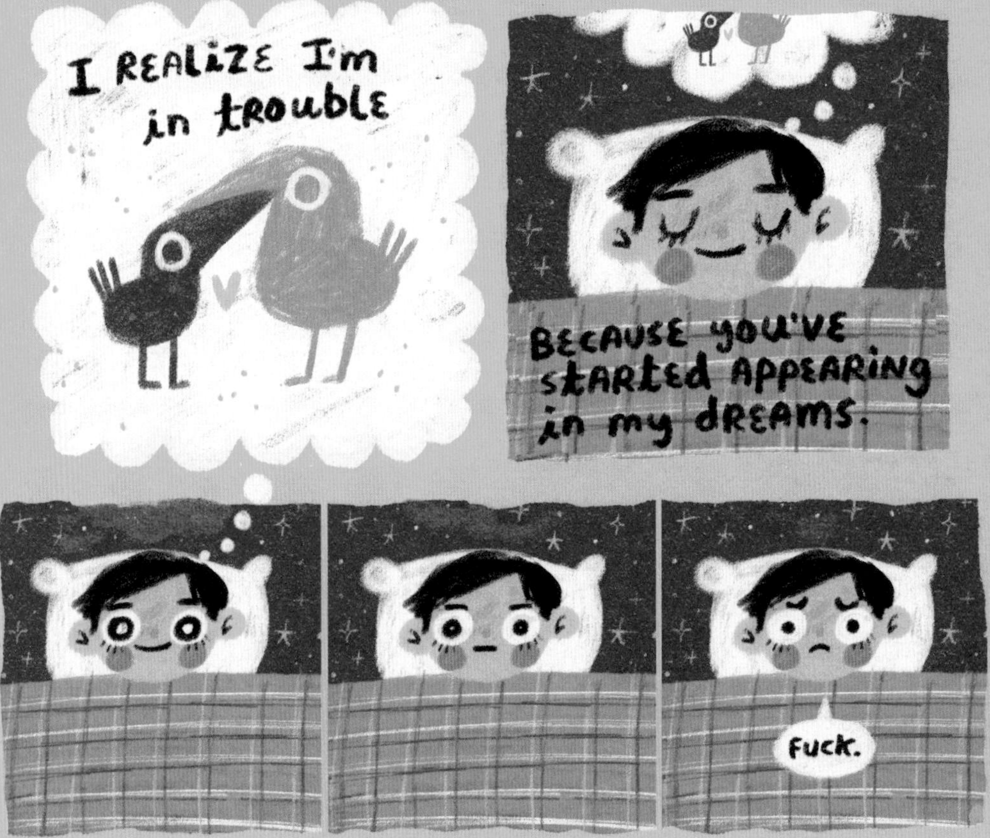
I REALIZE I'm in trouble
BECAUSE you'VE started APPEARING in my dREAMS.
Fuck.

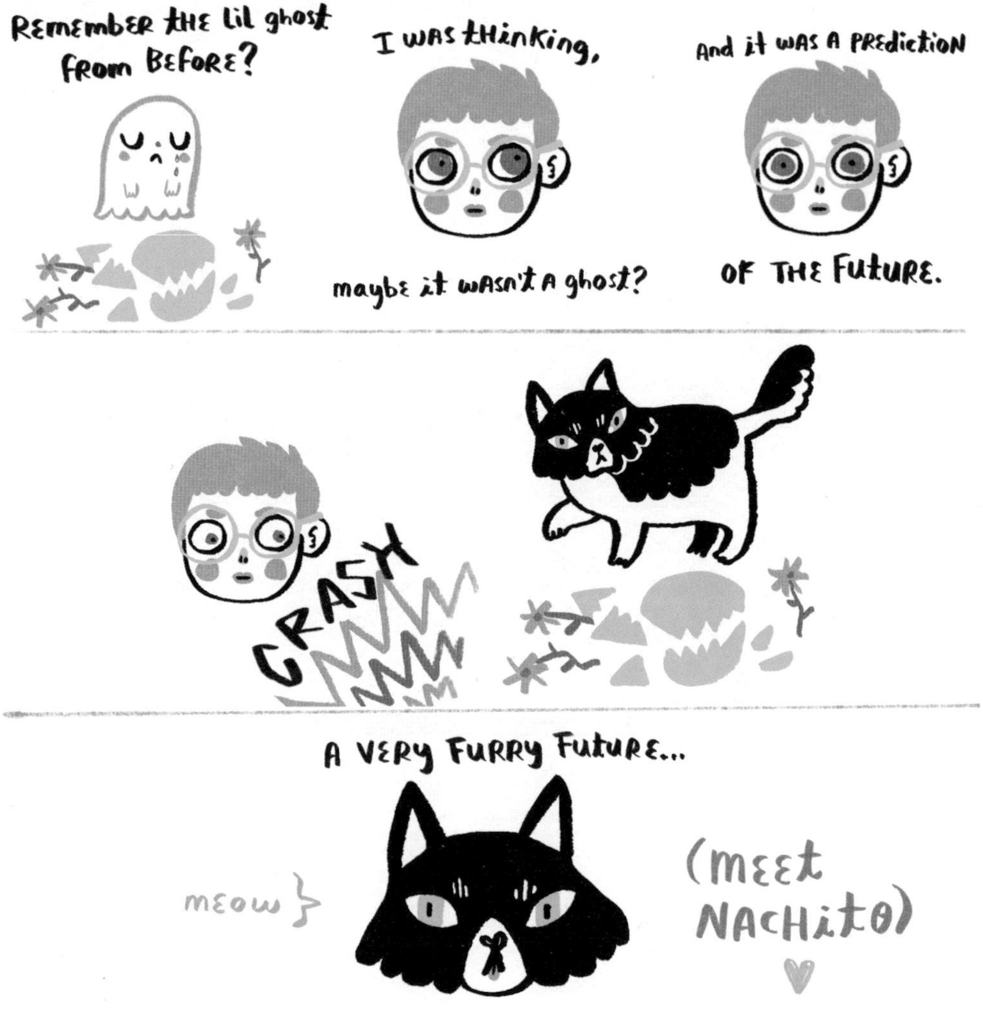
REMEMBER THE LIL GHOST FROM BEFORE?
I WAS THINKING,
MAYBE IT WASN'T A GHOST?
AND IT WAS A PREDICTION
OF THE FUTURE.
CRASH
A VERY FURRY FUTURE...
MEOW
(MEET NACHITO)

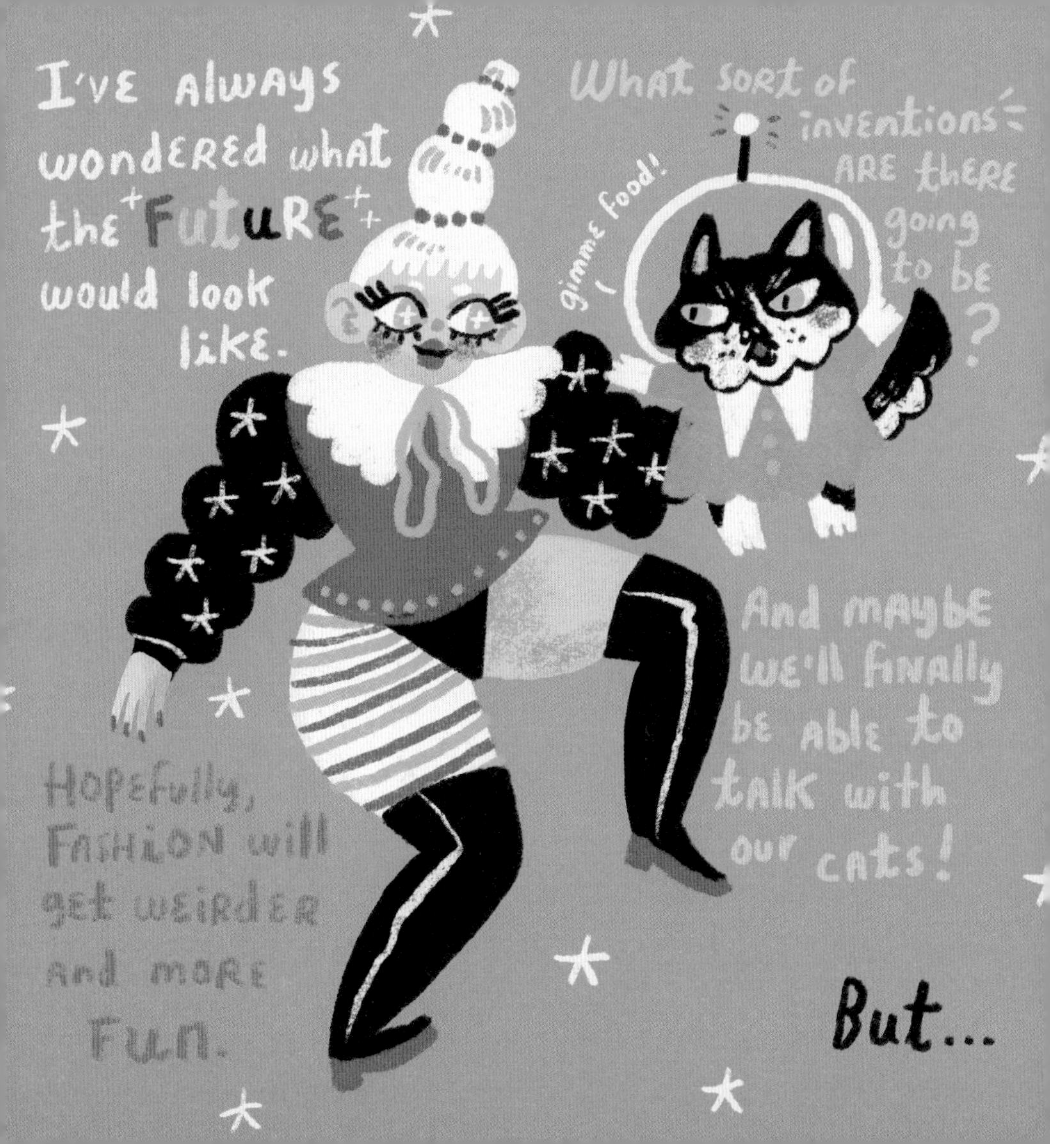
I've always wondered what the FUTURE would look like.
What sort of inventions are there going to be?
gimme food!
And maybe we'll finally be able to talk with our cats!
Hopefully, fashion will get weirder and more fun.
But...

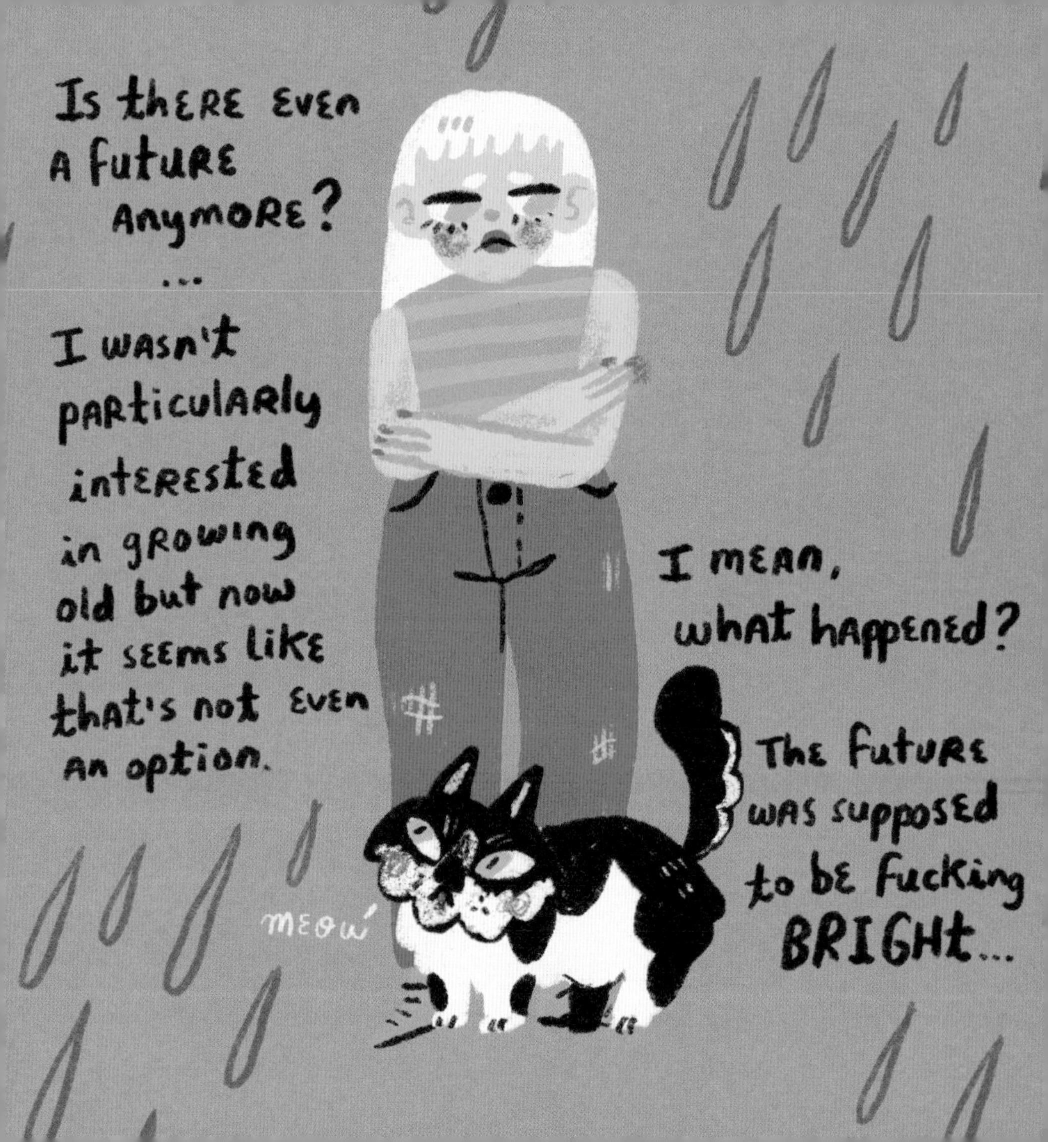
Is there even a future anymore?
...
I wasn't particularly interested in growing old but now it seems like that's not even an option.
I mean, what happened?
The future was supposed to be fucking BRIGHT...
MEOW

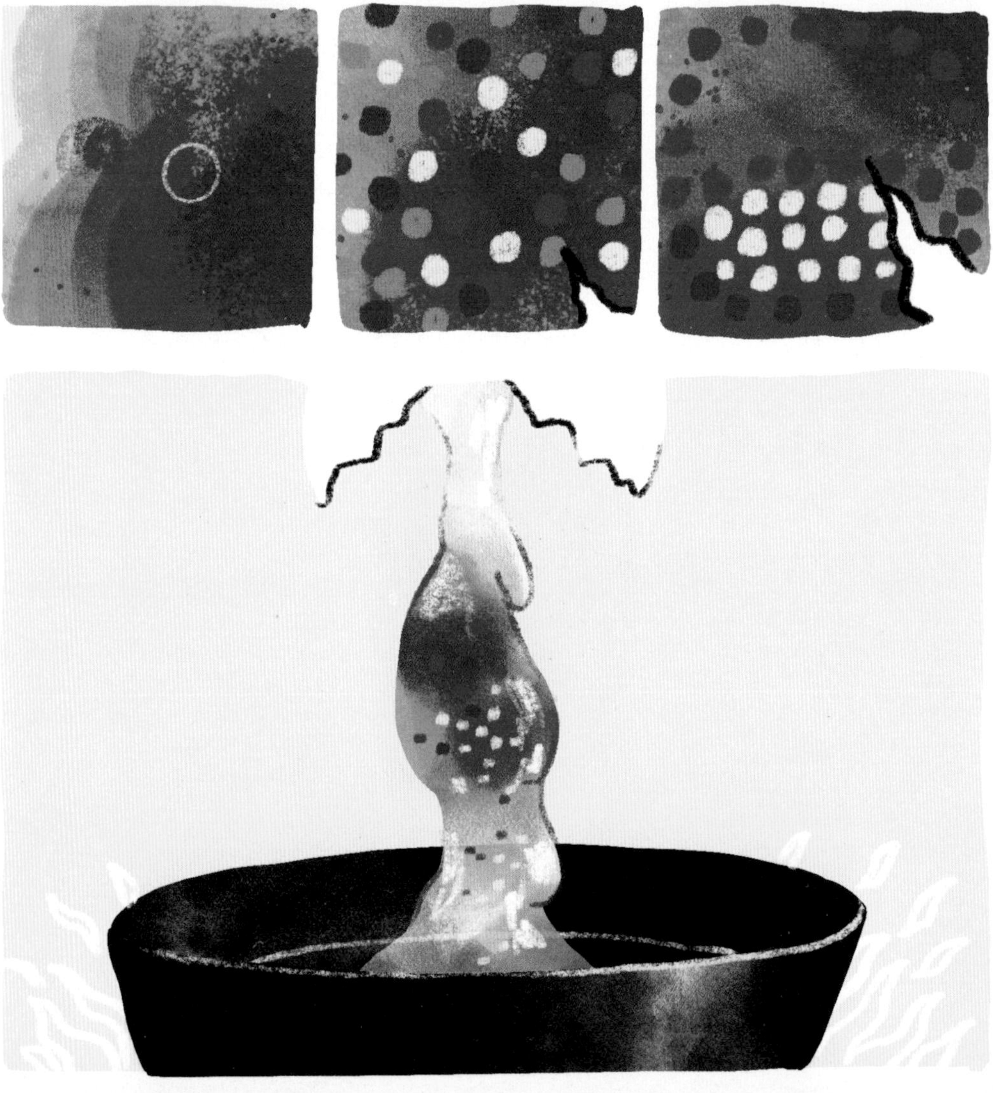

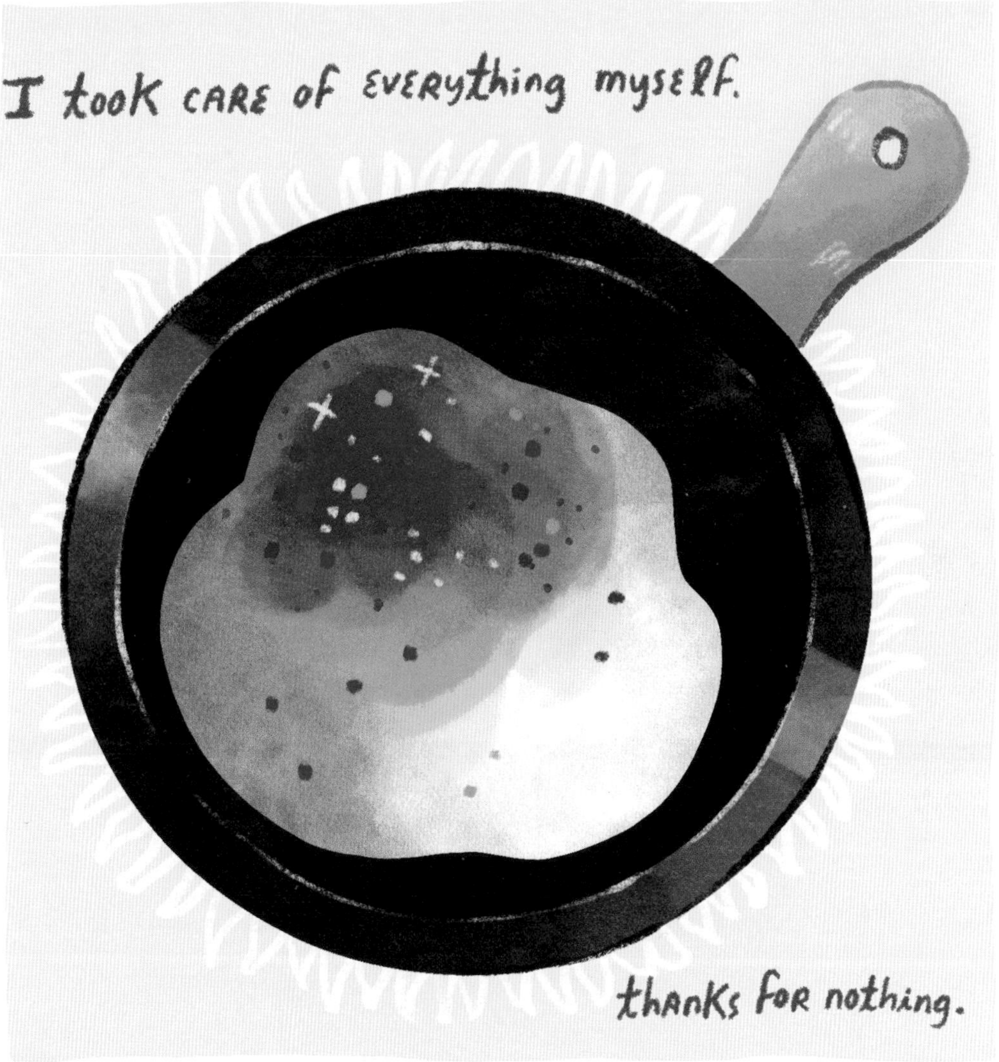
I took care of everything myself.
thanks for nothing.

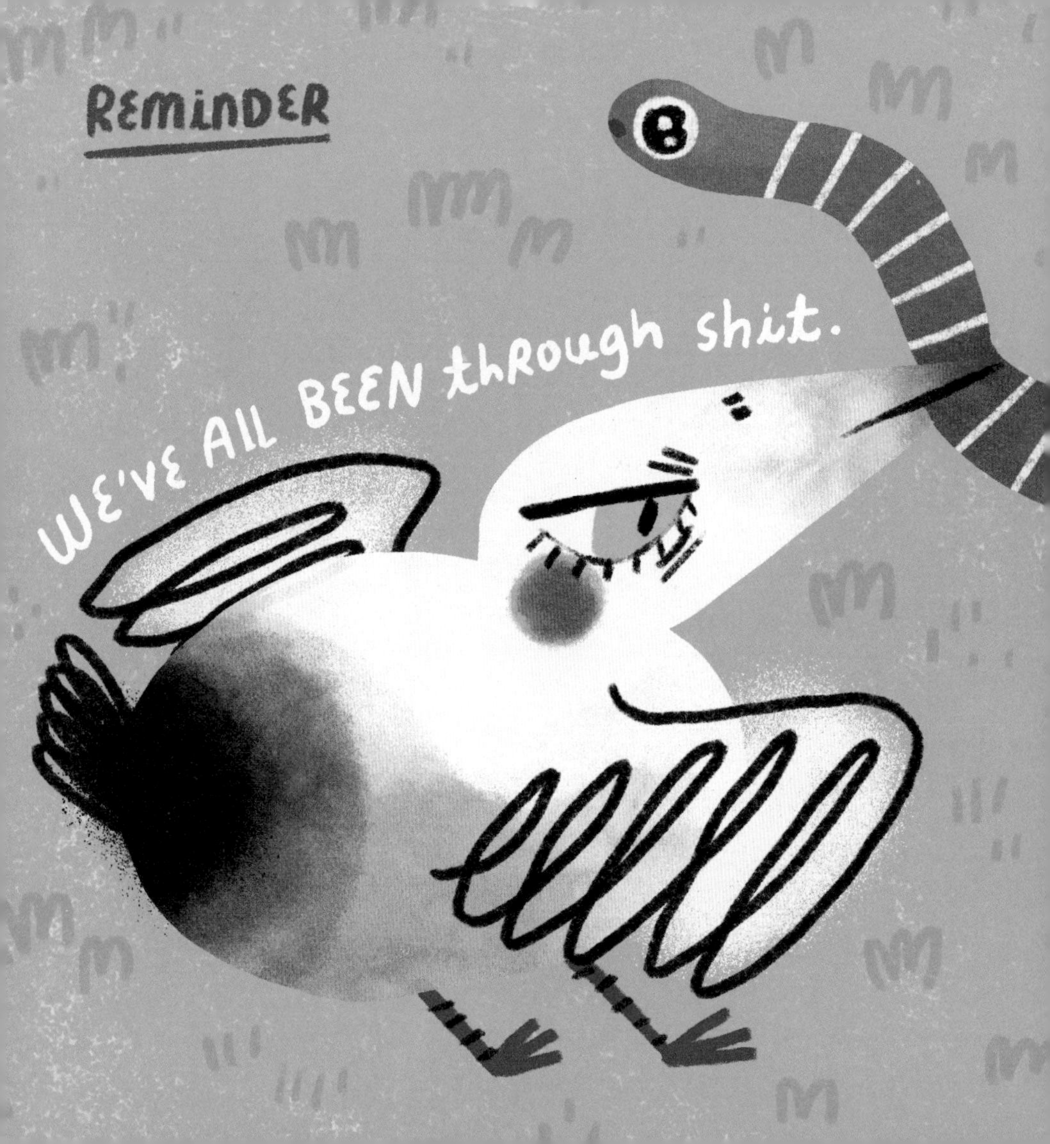
REMINDER
WE'VE ALL BEEN through shit.

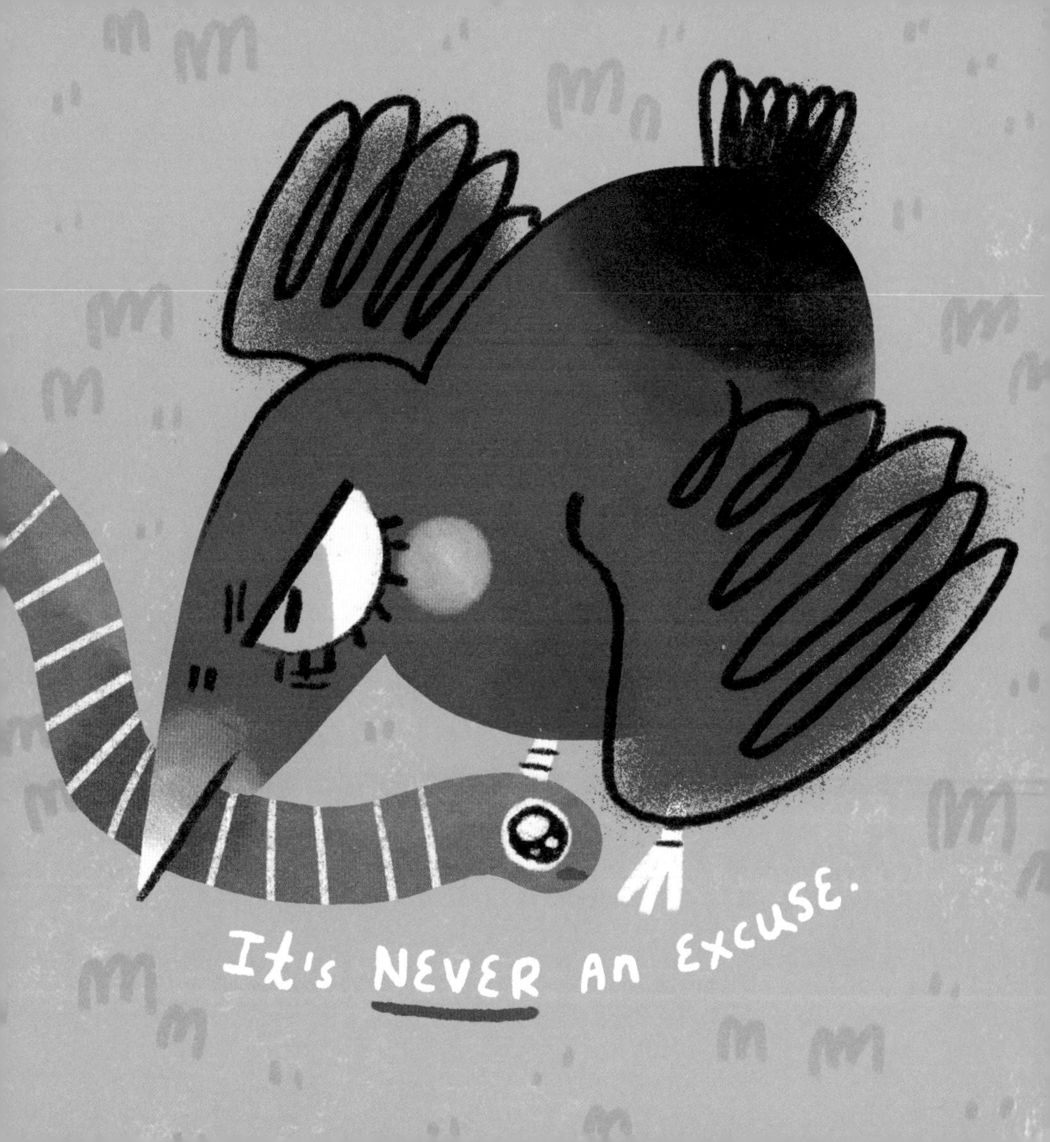
It's NEVER an EXCUSE.

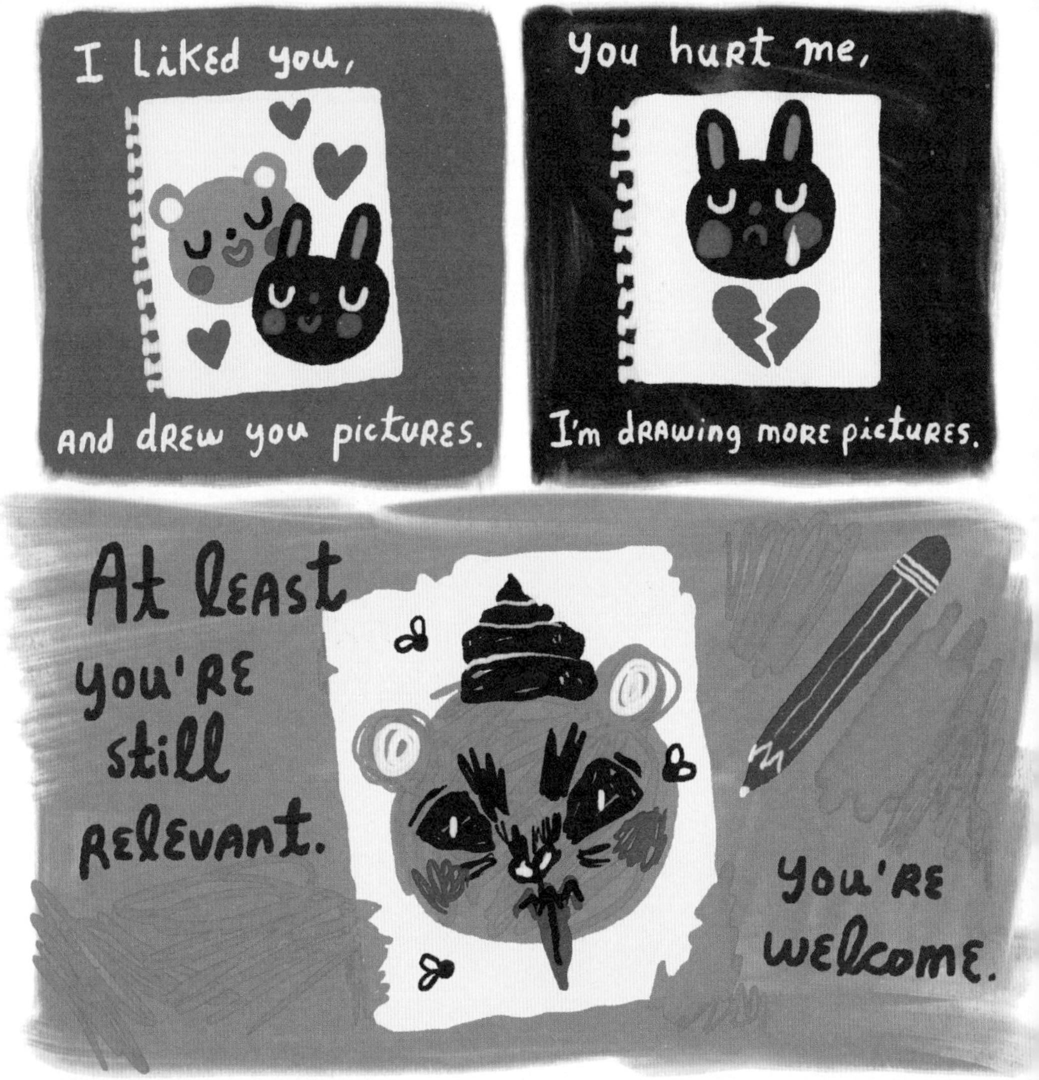
I liked you,
and drew you pictures.
You hurt me,
I'm drawing more pictures.
At least you're still relevant.
You're welcome.

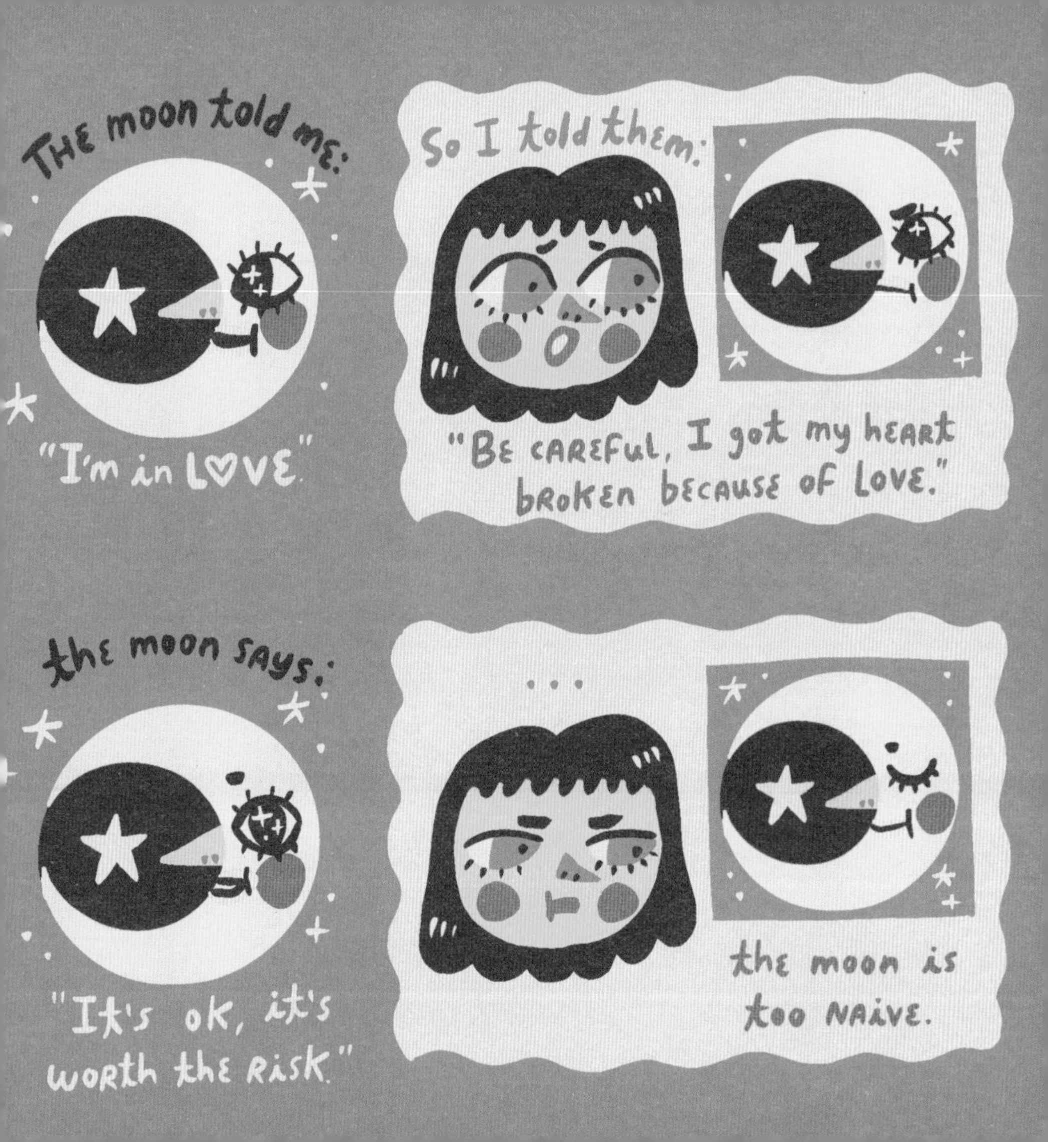

THE moon told me:
"I'm in LOVE"
So I told them:
"BE CAREFUL, I got my heart broken because of LOVE."
the moon says:
"It's ok, it's worth the RISK."
...
the moon is too NAIVE.

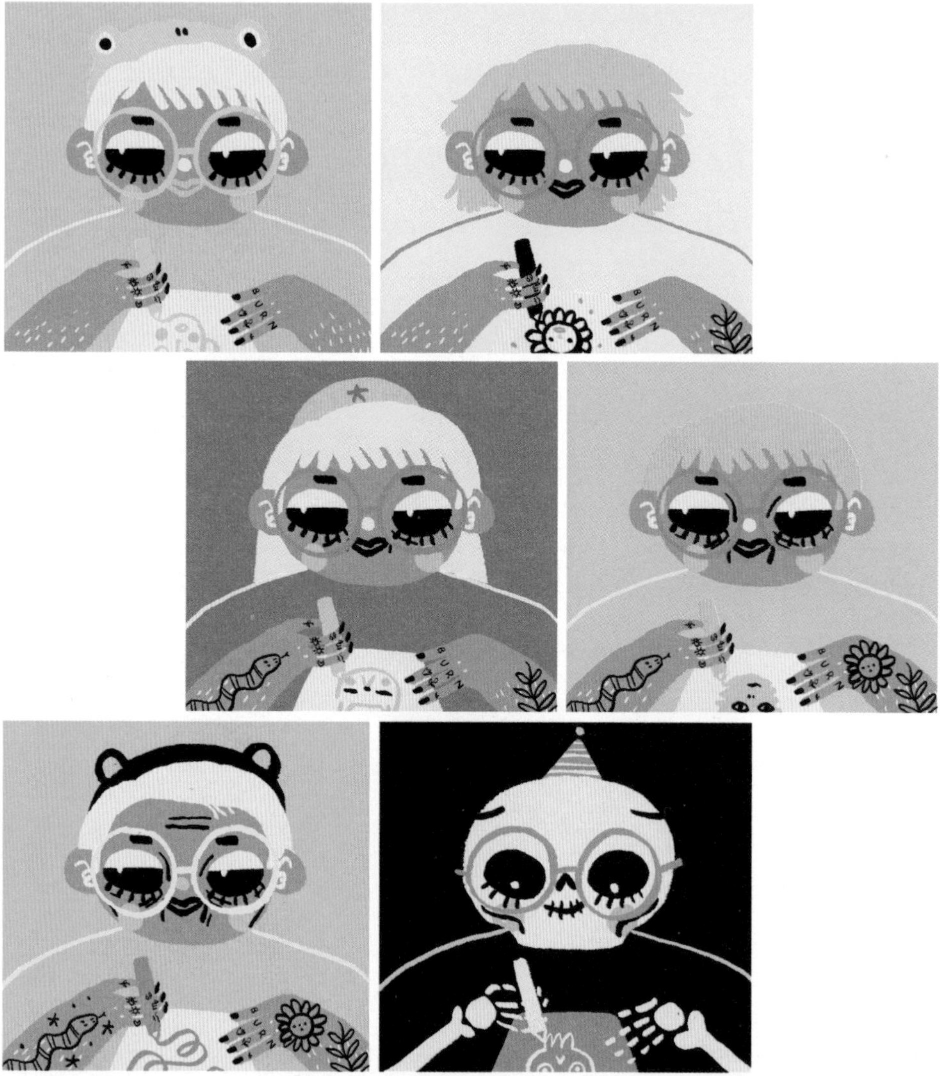
BURN

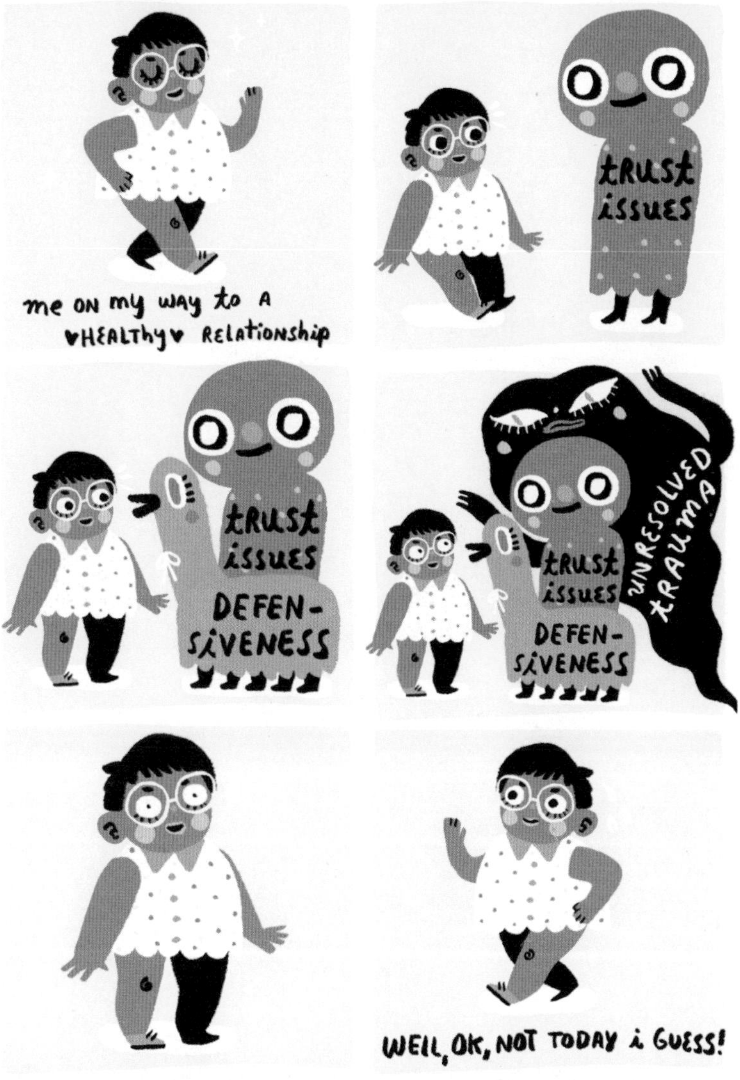
me on my way to a ♥healthy♥ relationship
trust issues
trust issues
DEFEN-
siVENESS
UNRESOLVED TRAUMA
trust issues
DEFEN-
siVENESS
WELL, OK, NOT TODAY i GUESS!

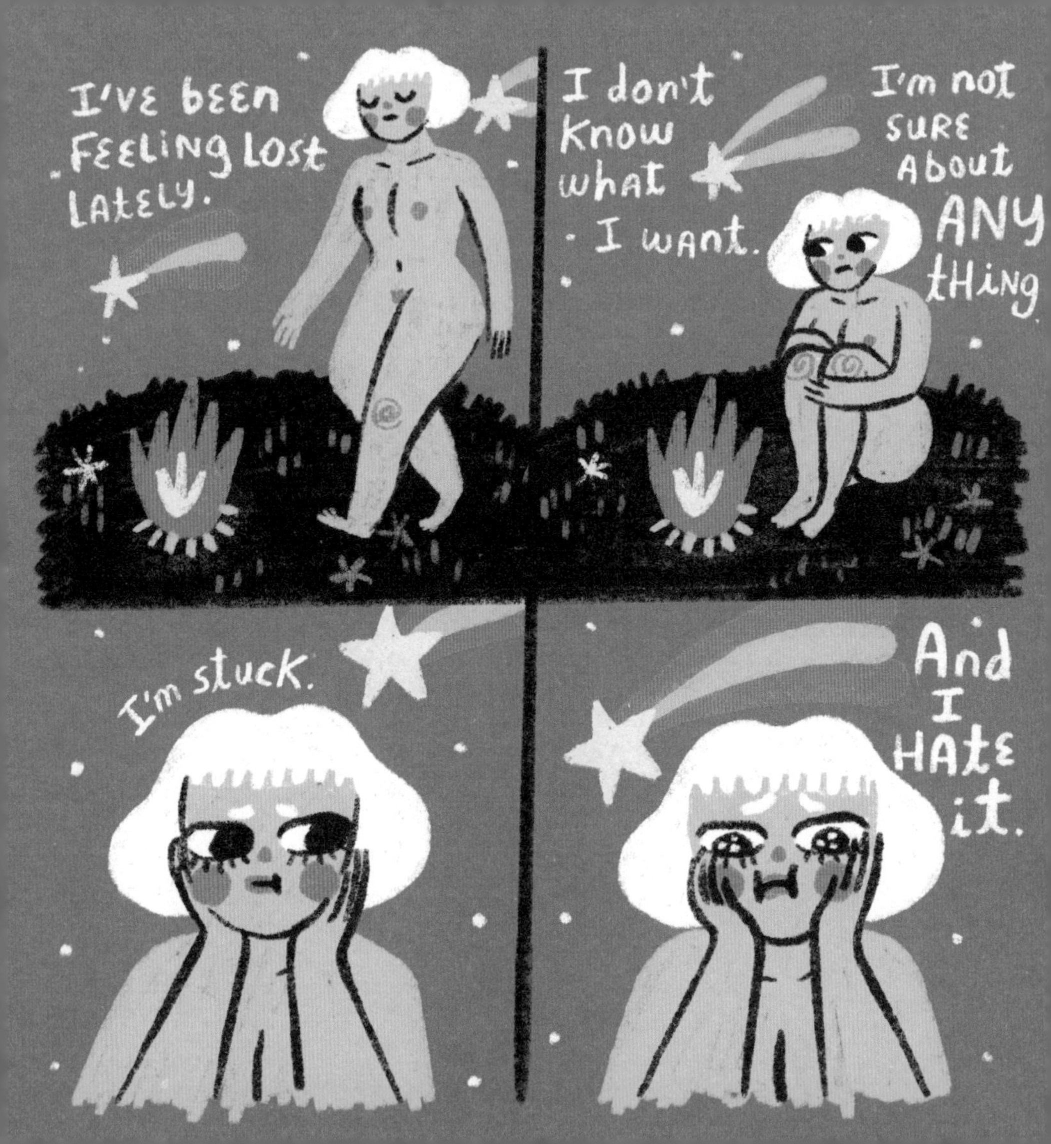
I've been feeling lost lately.
I don't know what I want.
I'm not sure about ANY thing
I'm stuck.
And I HATE it.

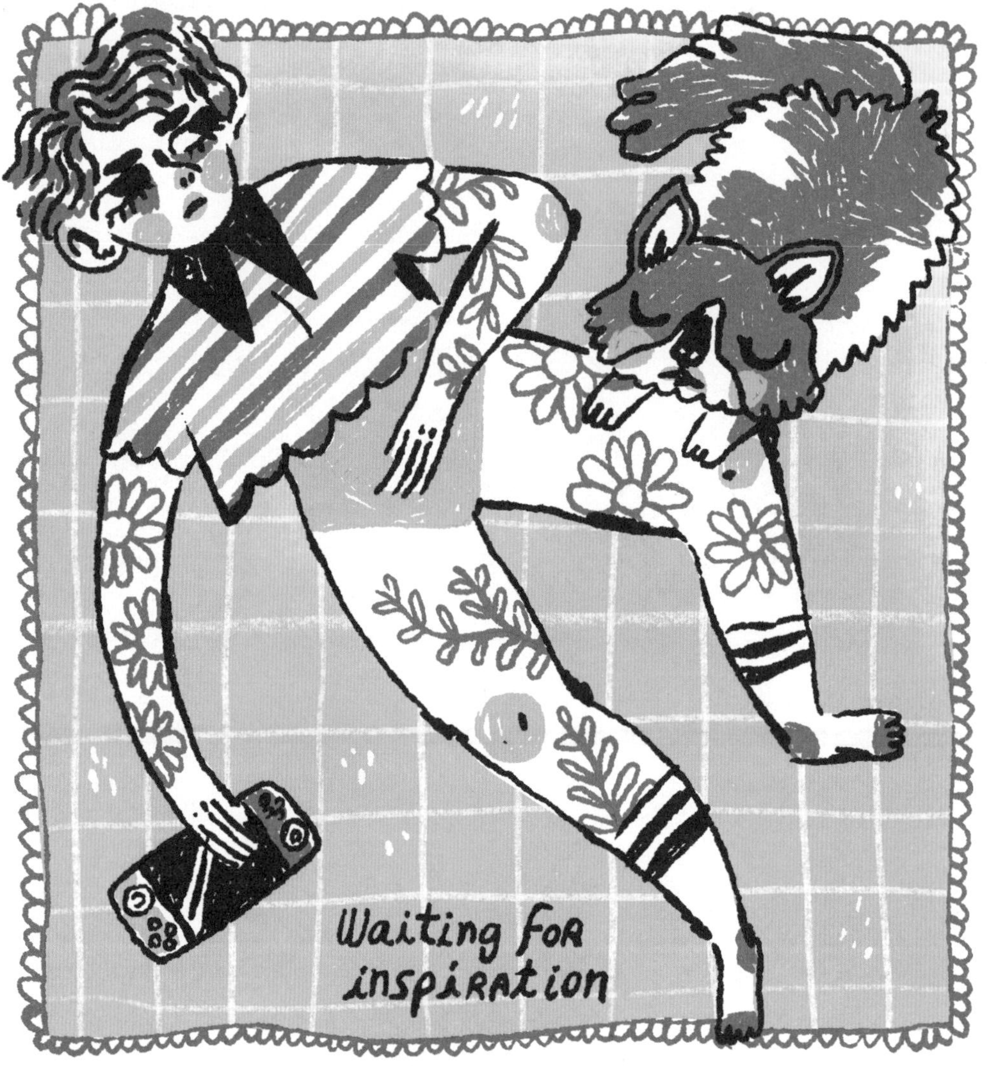
Waiting for inspiration

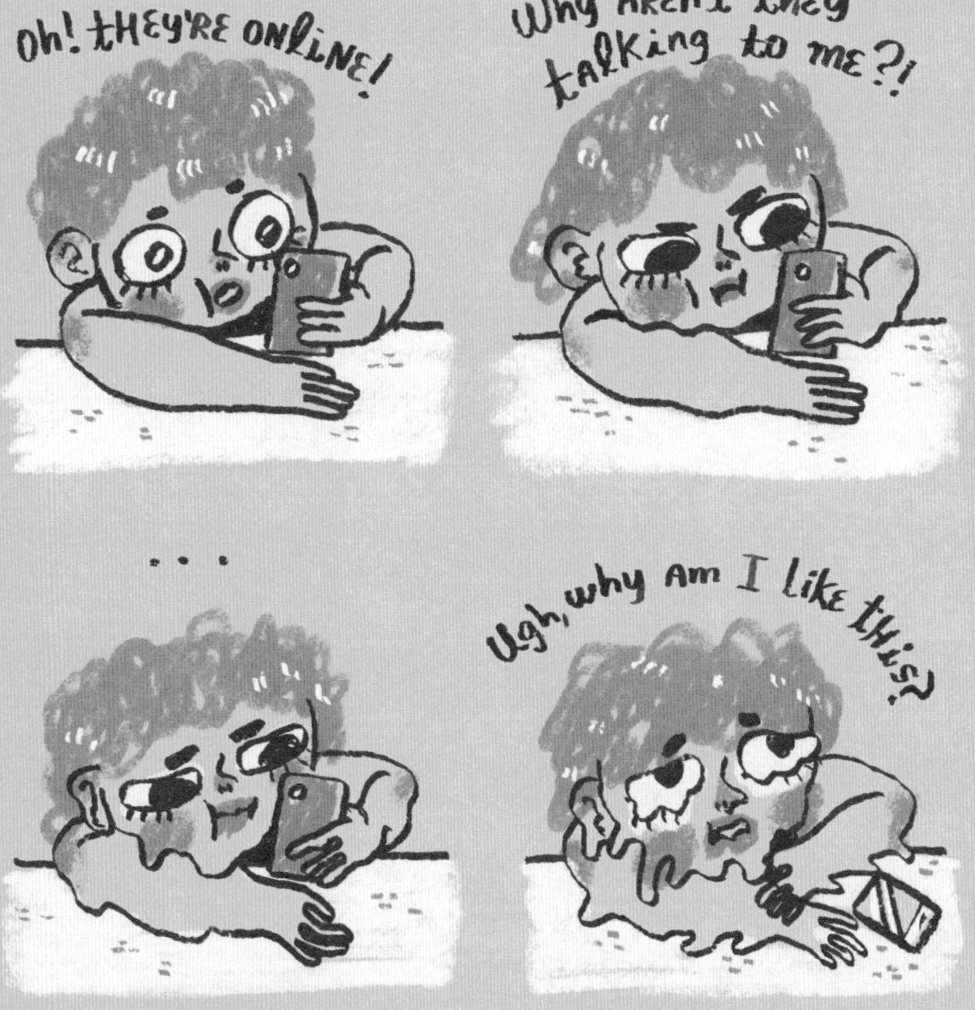
Oh! THEY'RE ONLINE!
Why AREN'T they talking to me?!
...
Ugh, why Am I like THIS?

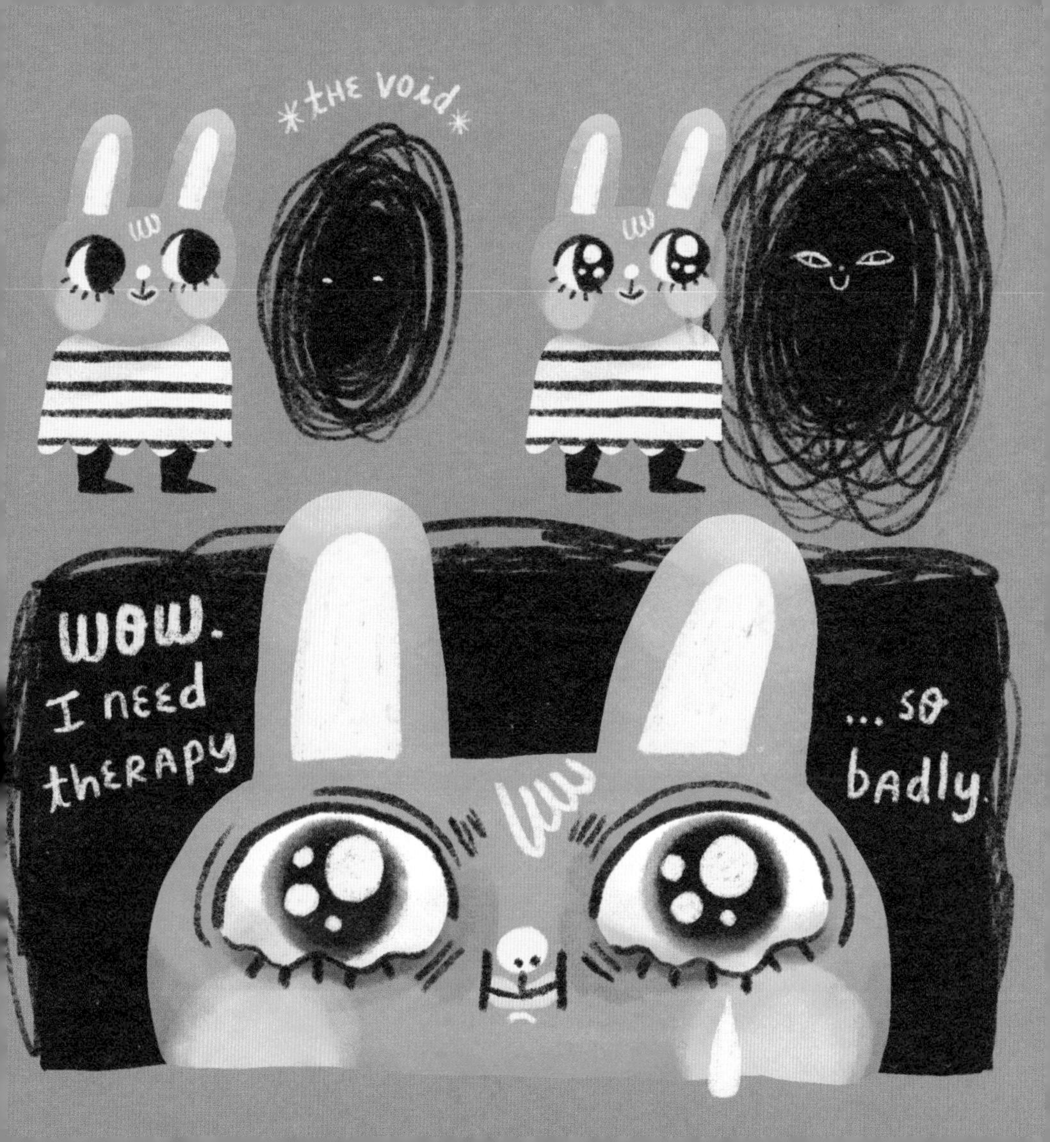
the void
WOW.
I need
therapy
...so
badly.

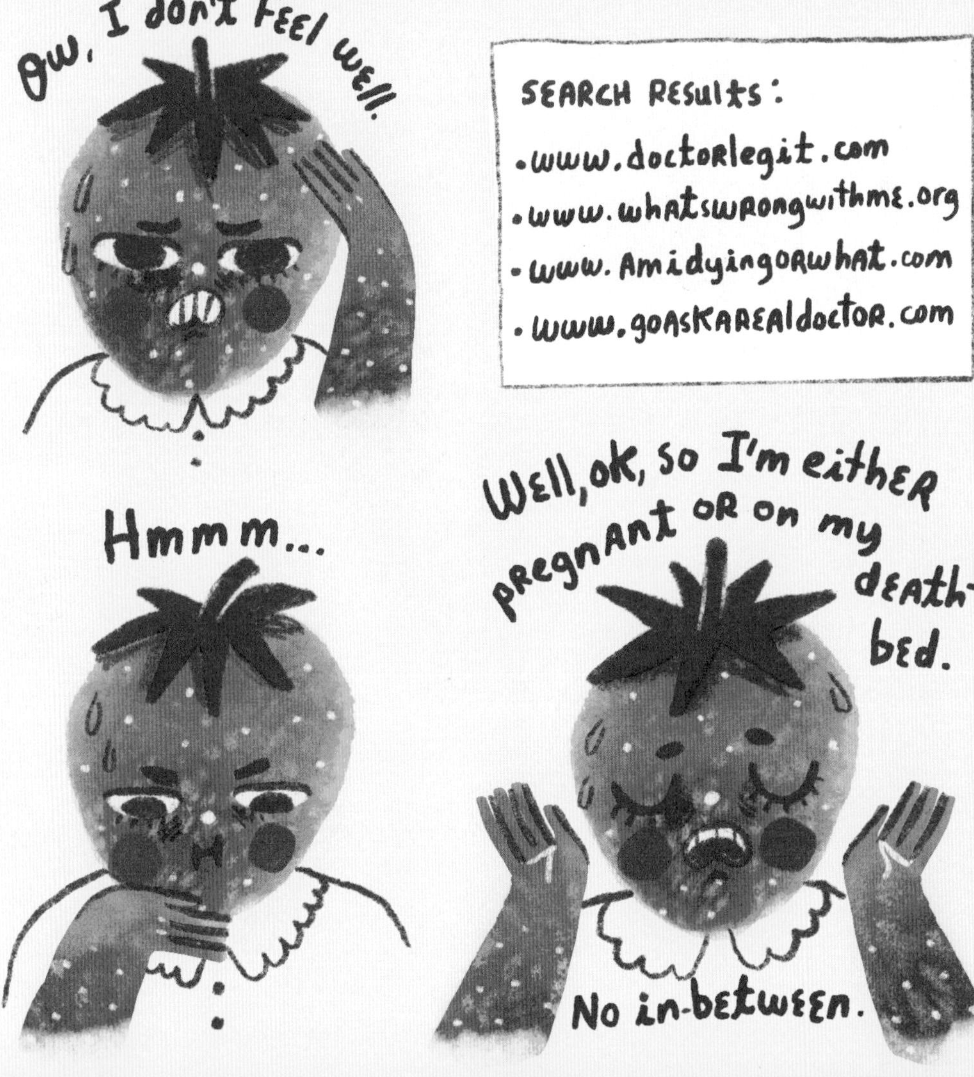
Ow, I don't feel well.
SEARCH RESULTS:
•www.doctorlegit.com
•www.whatswrongwithme.org
•www.Amidyingorwhat.com
•www.goaskarealdoctor.com
Hmmm...
Well, ok, so I'm either pregnant or on my death-bed.
No in-between.

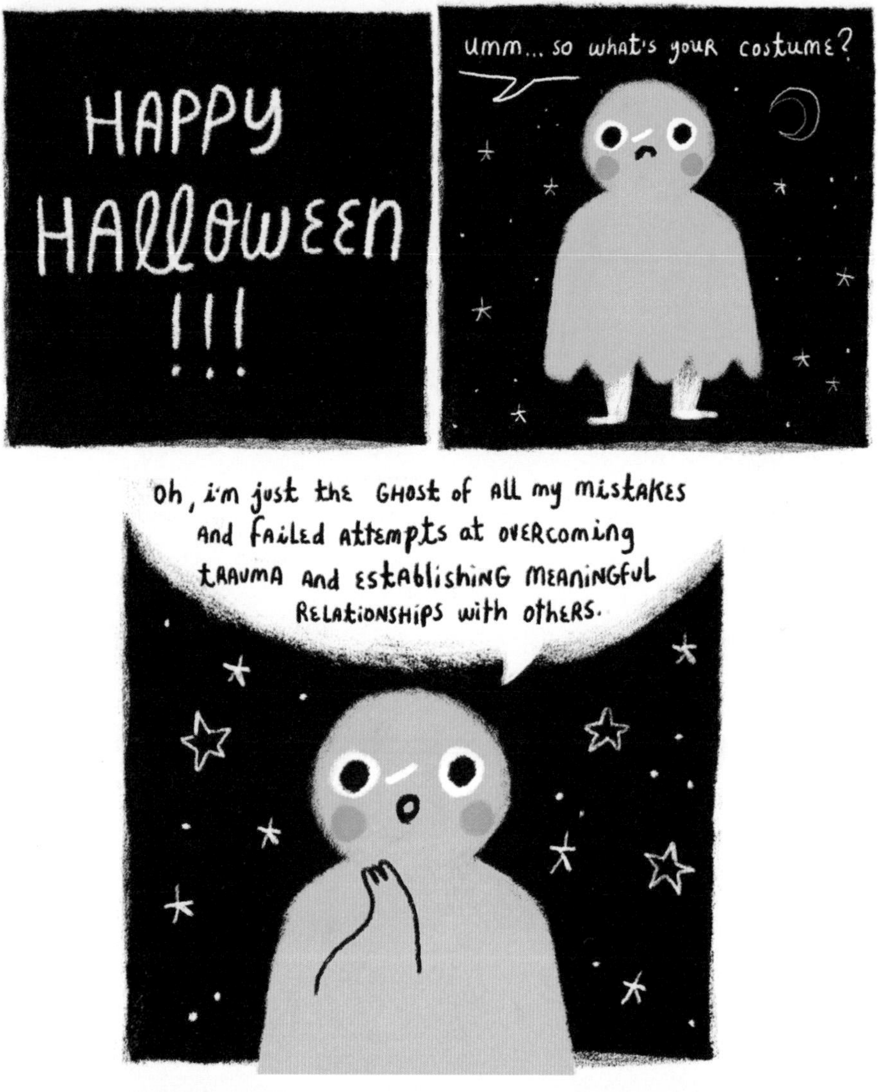
HAPPY HALLOWEEN !!!
umm... so what's your costume?
Oh, i'm just the GHOST of ALL my mistakes and failed attempts at overcoming trauma and establishing meaningful relationships with others.

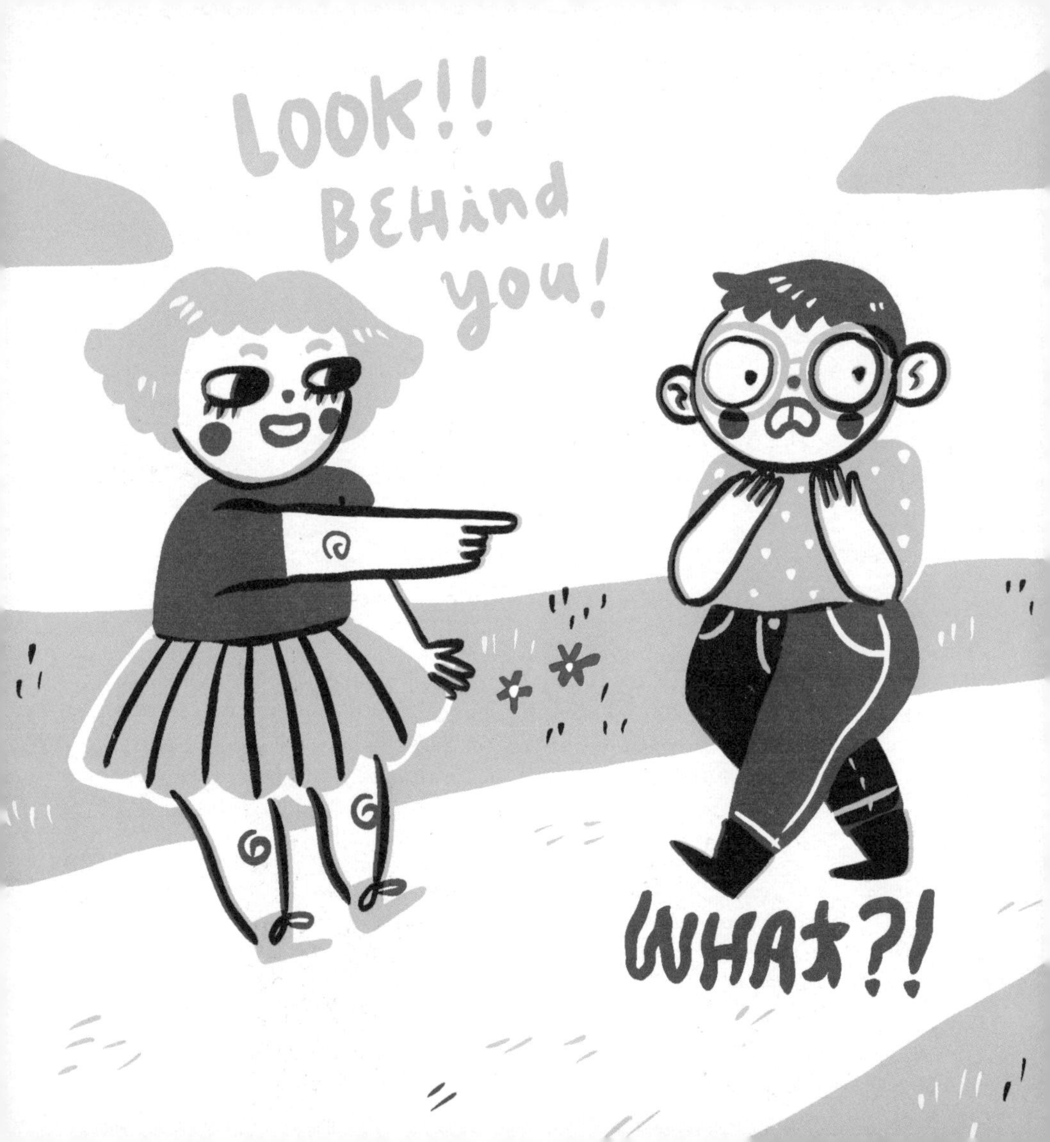
LOOK!! BEHind you!
WHAT?!

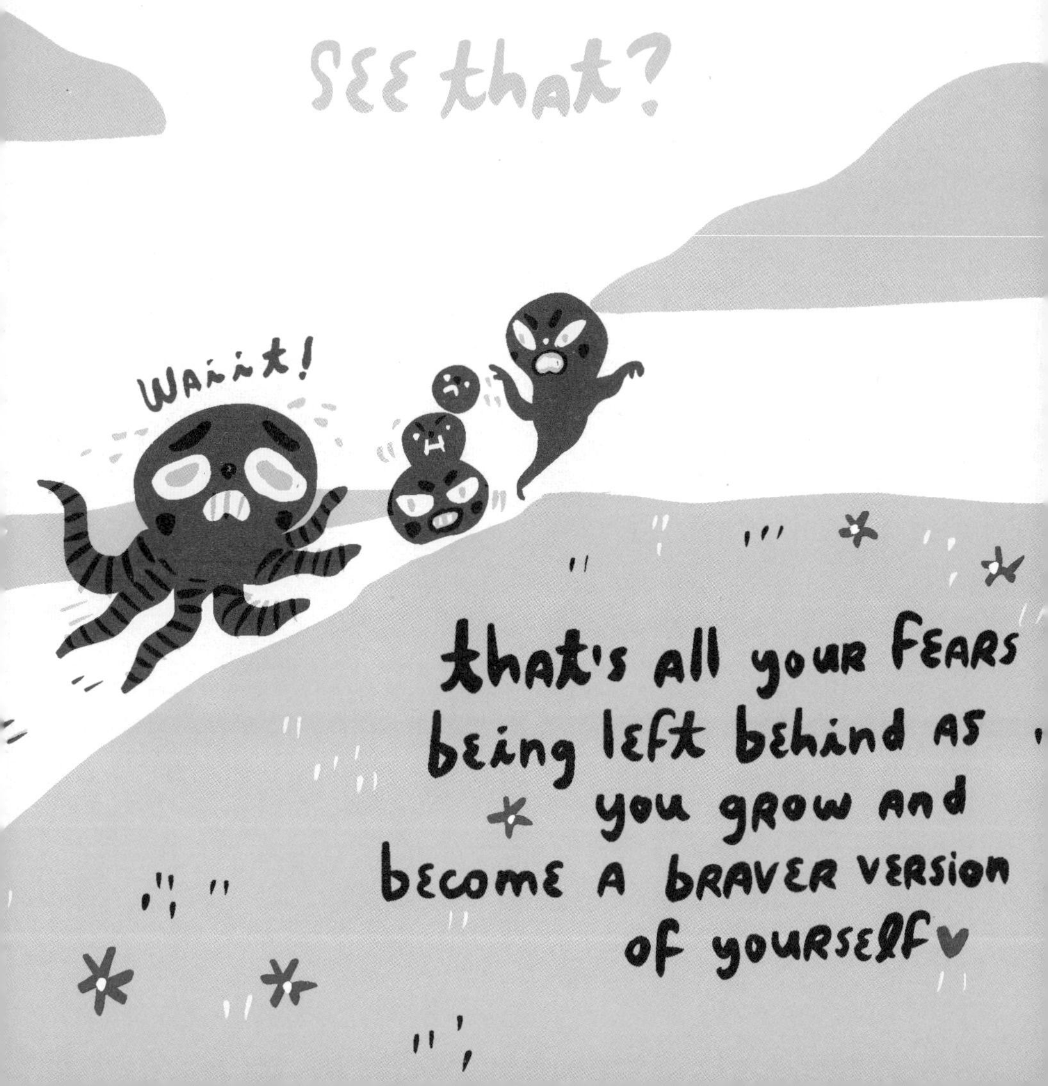
SEE that?
Waiiit!
that's all your FEARS being left behind as you grow and become a braver version of yourself

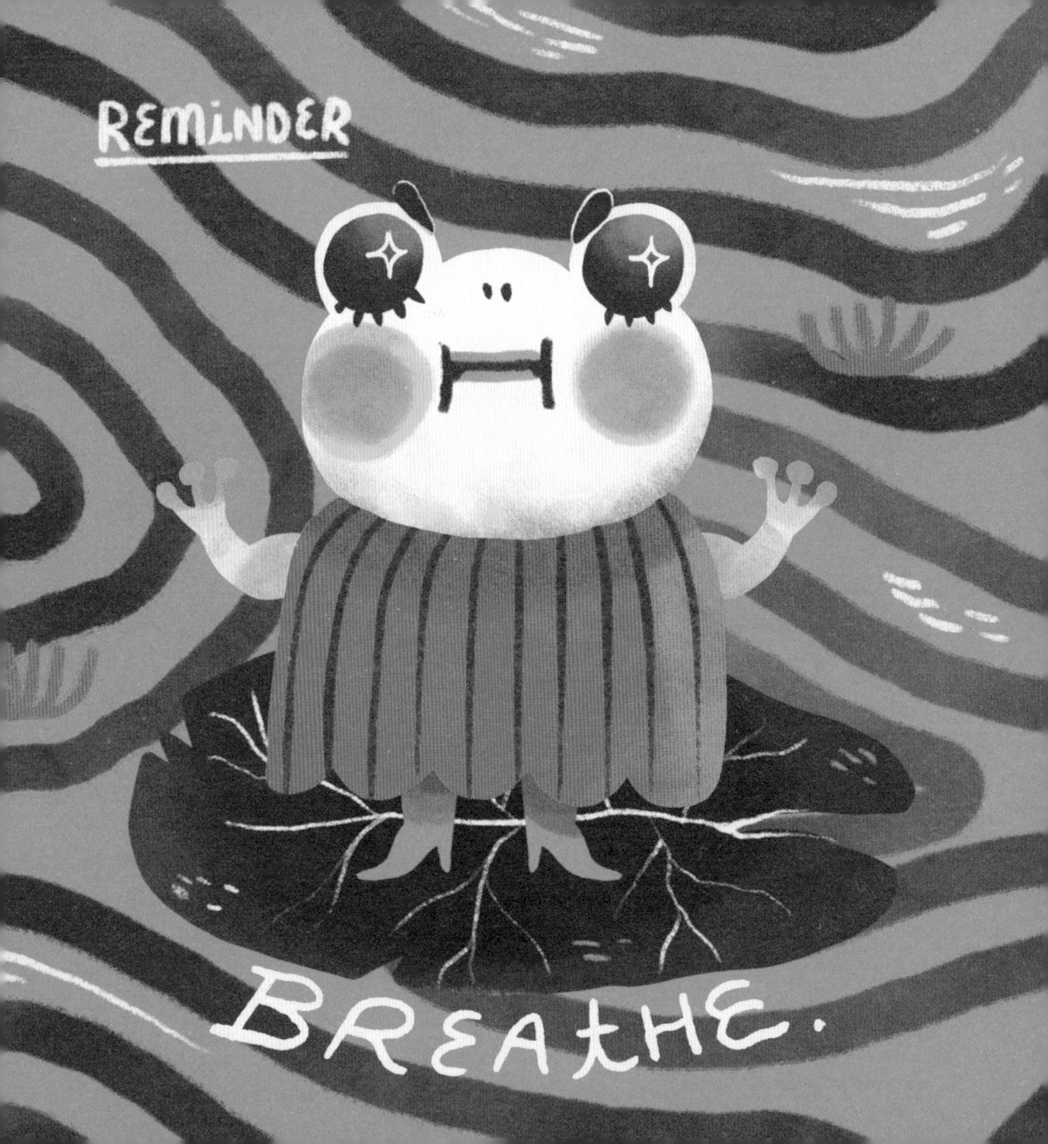
REMINDER
BREAtHE.

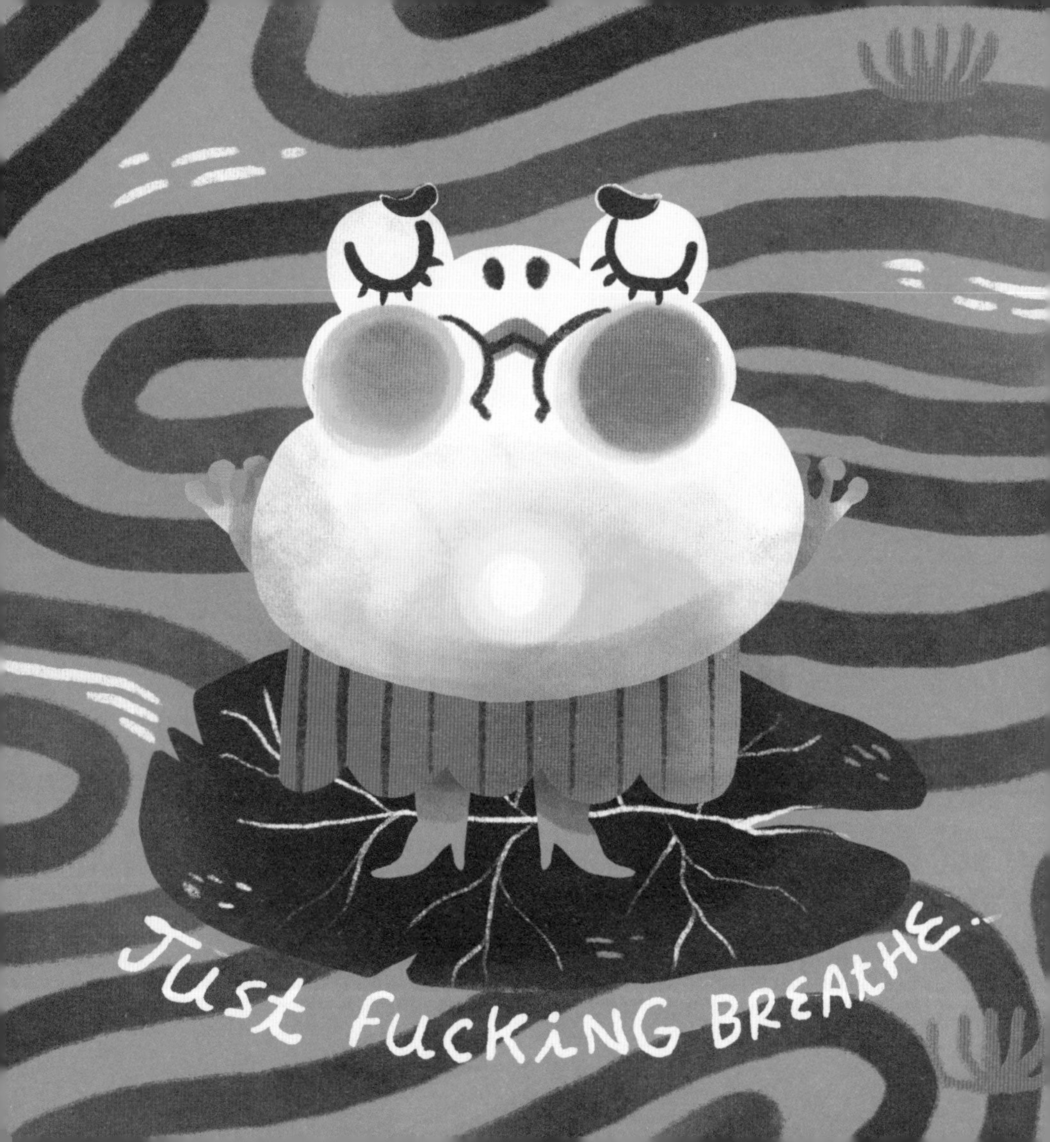
JUST FUCKING BREATHE.

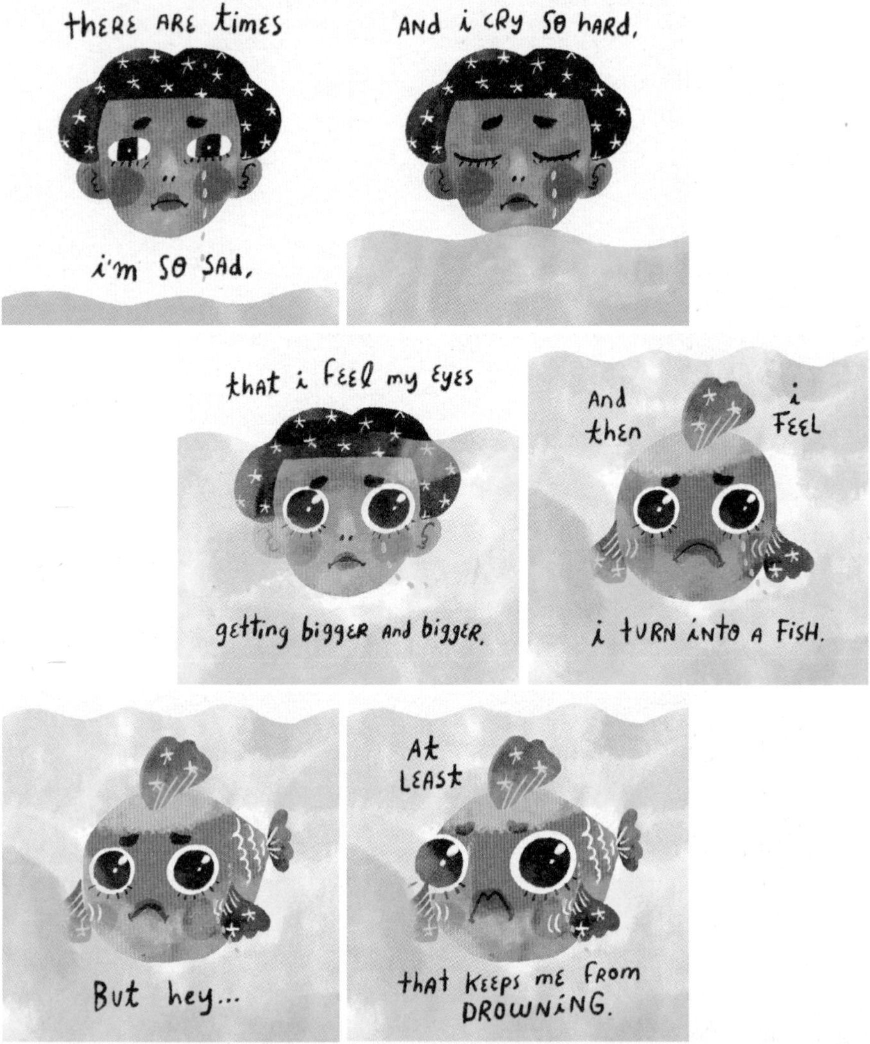
THERE ARE TIMES
i'M SO SAD,
AND i CRY SO HARD,
THAT i FEEL MY EYES
GETTING BIGGER AND BIGGER.
AND THEN i FEEL
i TURN INTO A FISH.
BUT HEY...
AT LEAST
THAT KEEPS ME FROM DROWNING.

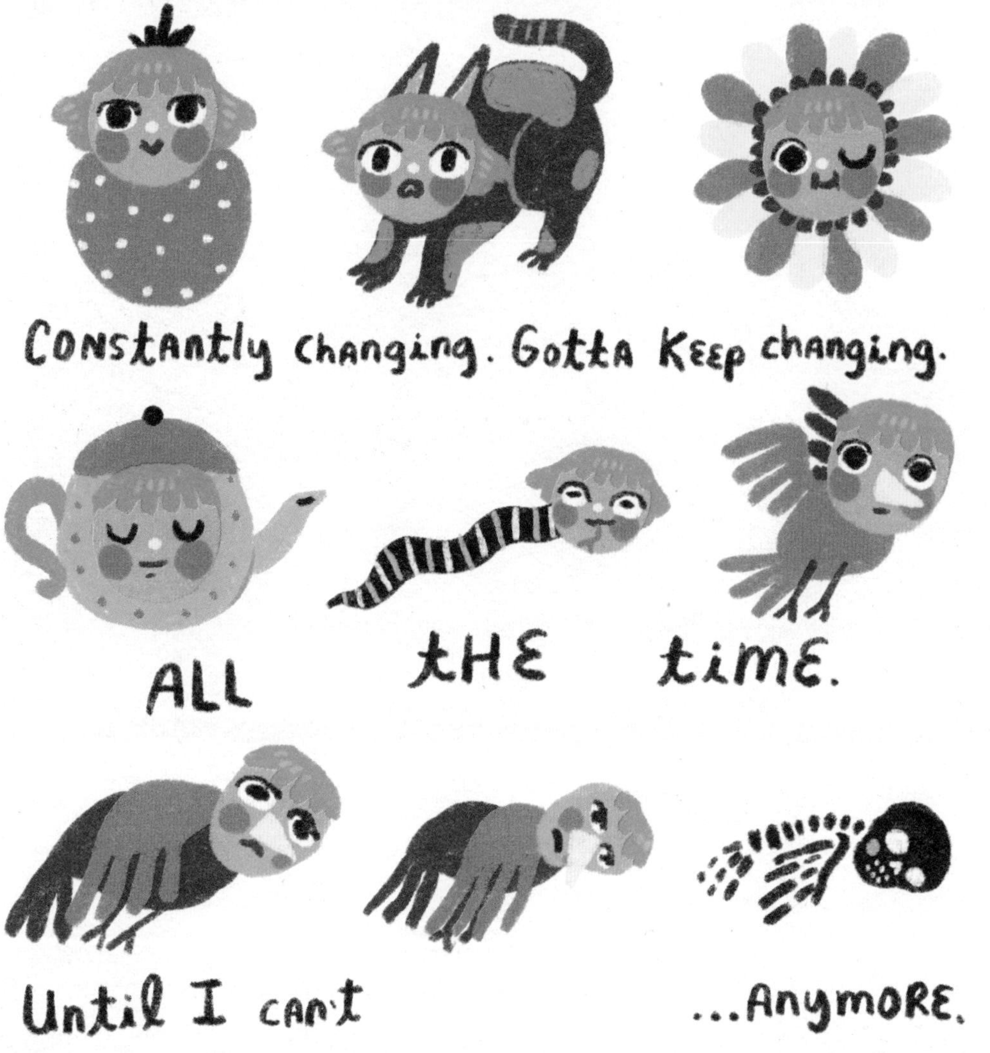
Constantly changing. Gotta Keep changing.
ALL
tHE
timE.
Until I can't
...Anymore.

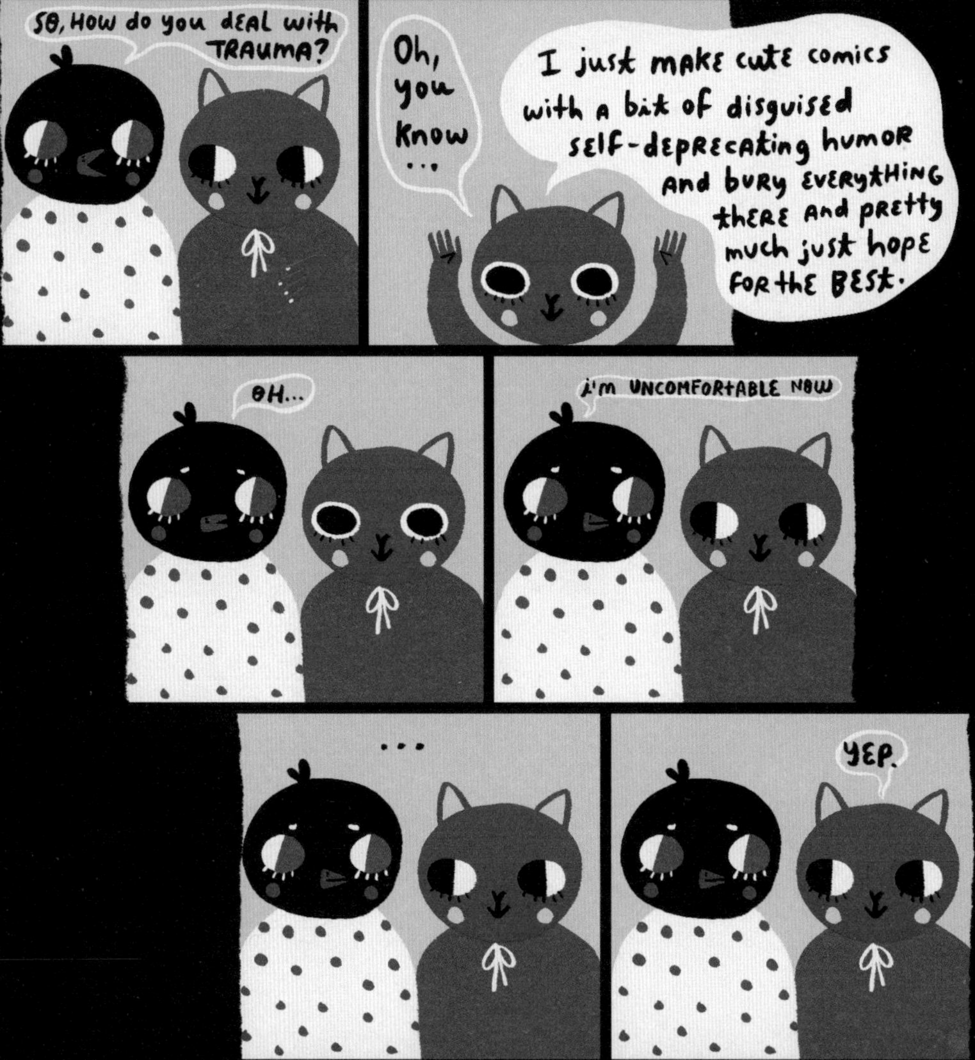
SO, HOW do you dEAL with TRAUMA?
Oh, you Know ...
I just MAKE cutE comics with A bit of disguisEd sElf-dEpREcAting humoR And bury EVERythiNG thERE And pREtty much just hopE FoR thE BESt.
OH...
i'm UNCOMFORtABLE NOW
...
YEP.

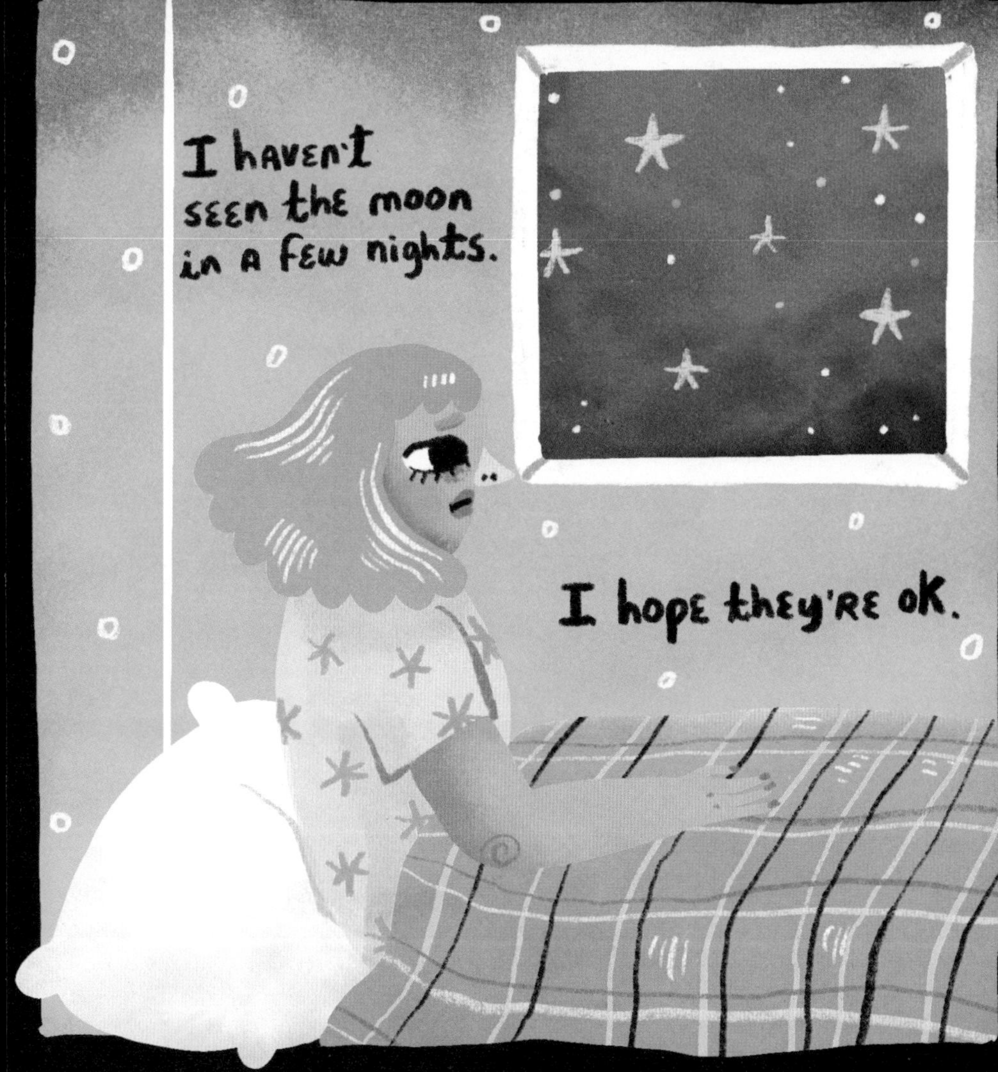
I haven't seen the moon in a few nights.
I hope they're ok.

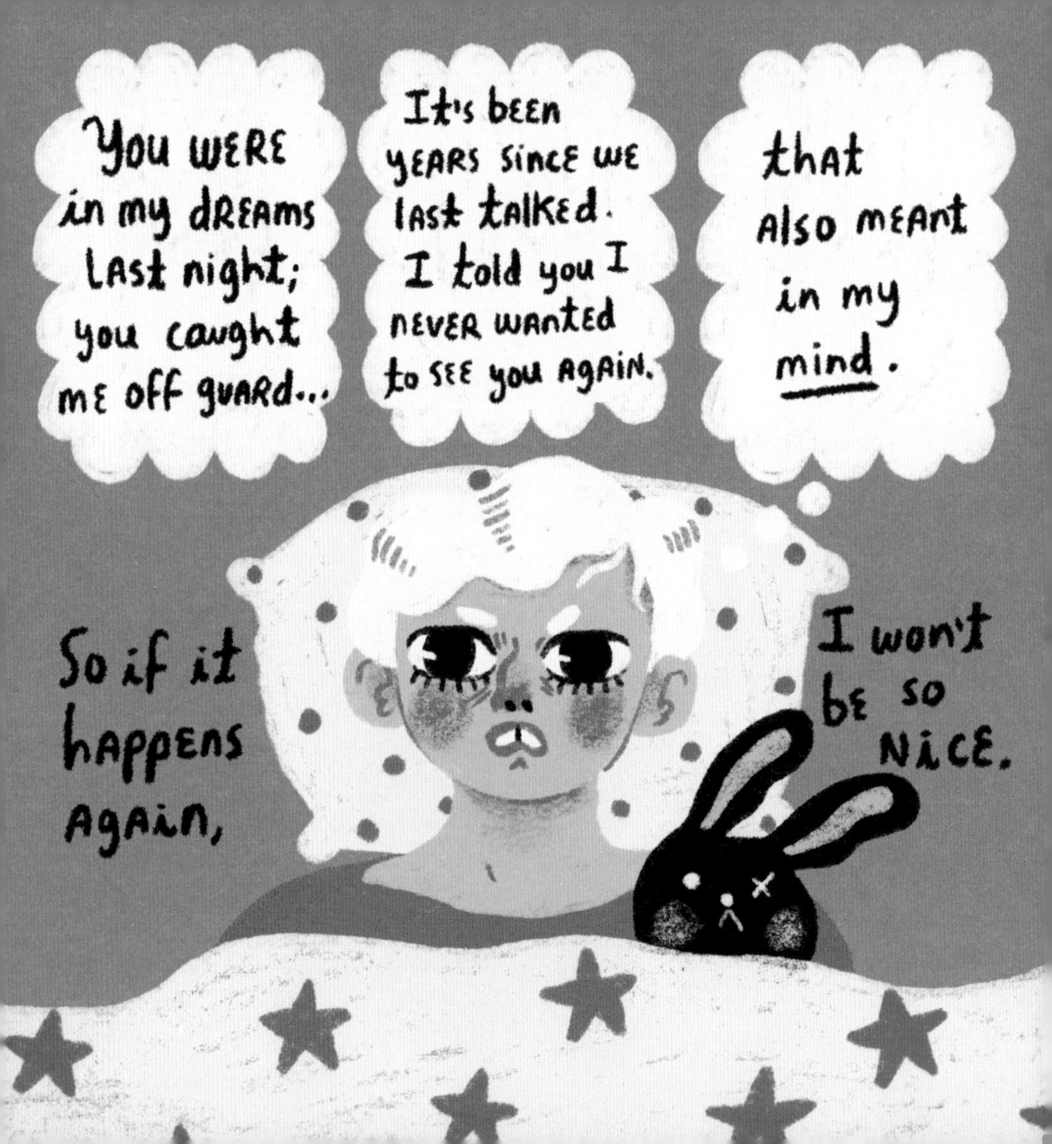
You WERE in my dREAMS LAst night; you caught me off guARd...
It's bEEn yEARS SincE wE lASt tAlKEd. I told you I nEVER wAntEd to SEE you AgAIN.
that Also mEAnt in my mind.
So if it happEns AgAin,
I won't bE so NicE.

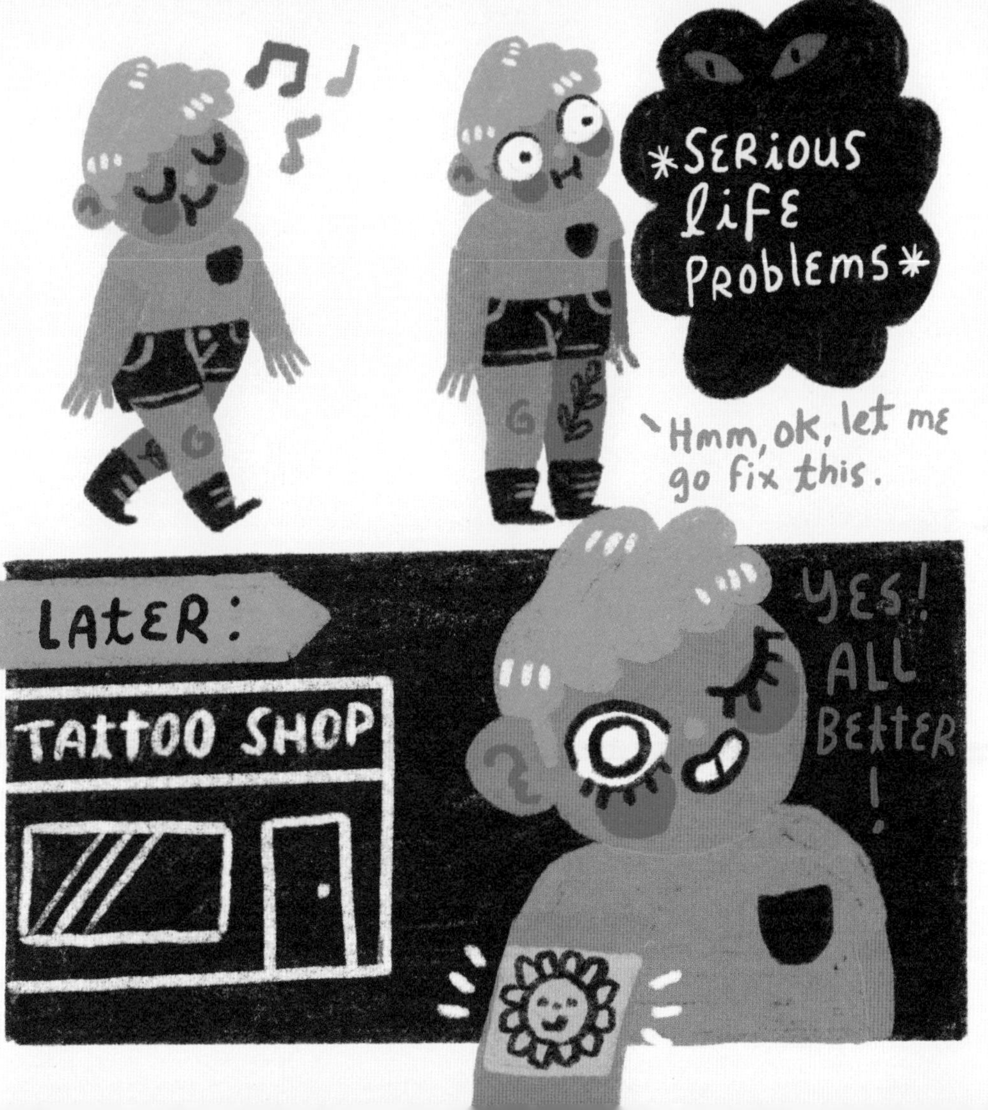
SERIOUS LIFE PROBLEMS
Hmm, ok, let me go fix this.
LATER:
TATTOO SHOP
YES! ALL BETTER!

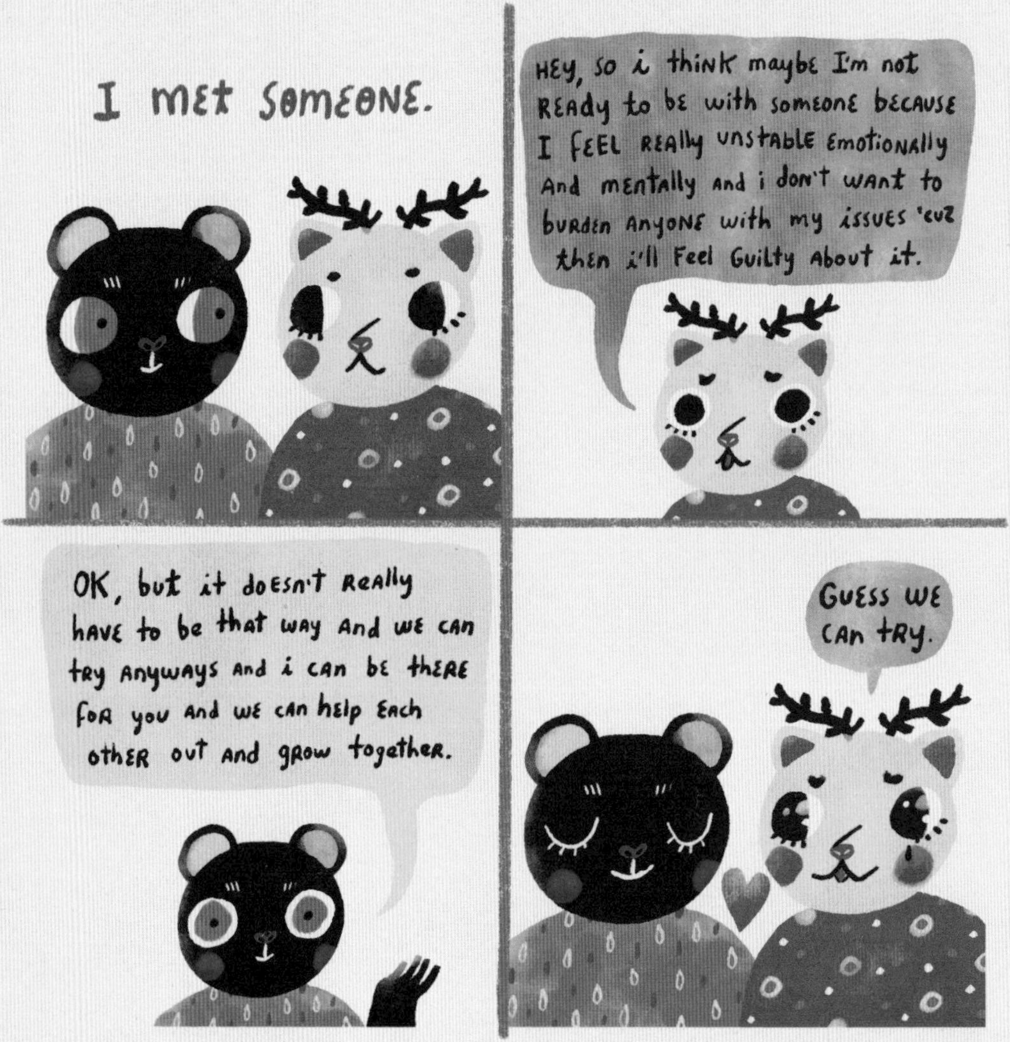
I MET SOMEONE.
HEY, SO i think maybe I'm not READy to be with someone because I FEEL REAlly unstable emotionally And mentally and i don't want to burden anyone with my issues 'cuz then i'll Feel Guilty About it.
OK, but it doesn't Really have to be that way and we can try anyways and i can be there for you and we can help each other out and grow together.
GUESS WE CAN try.

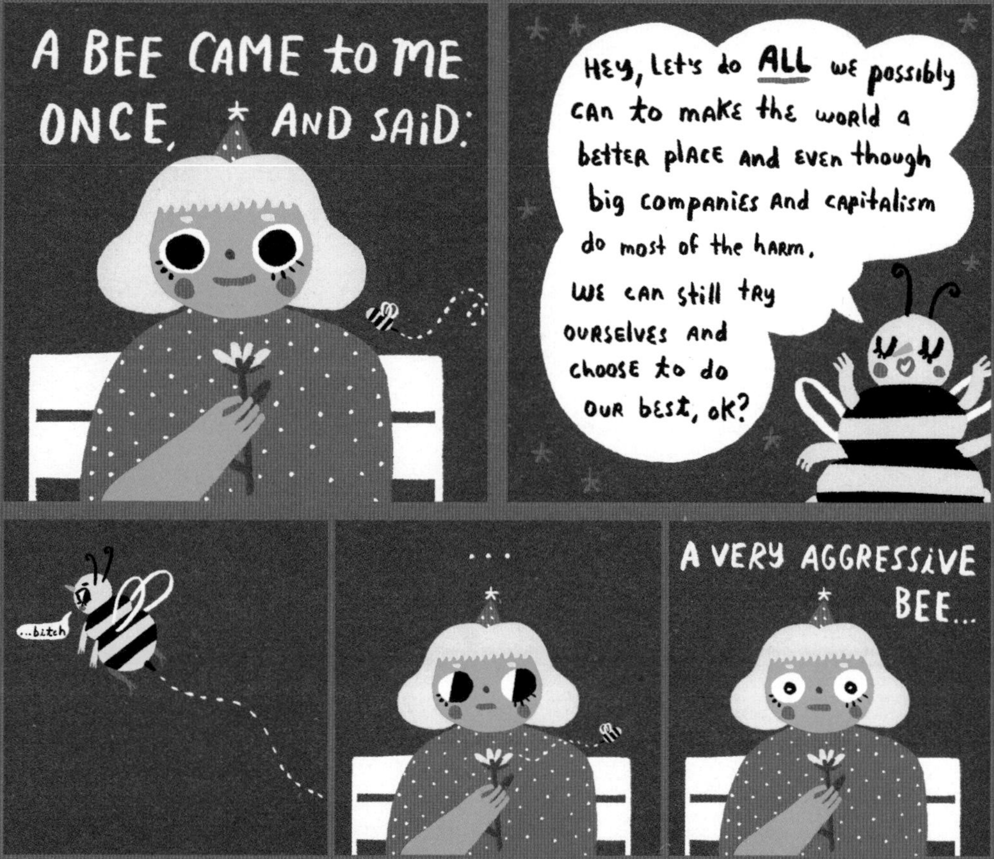
A BEE CAME to ME ONCE, AND SAID:
HEY, LEt's do ALL WE possibly CAN to MAKE the WORld a bEttER plACE And EVEN though big companiES And capitalism do most of the harm. WE CAN still tRY OURSElVES And choosE to do OUR bESt, ok?
...bitch
...
A VERY AGGRESSIVE BEE...

AND SUDDENLY...

LOCK-
DOWN

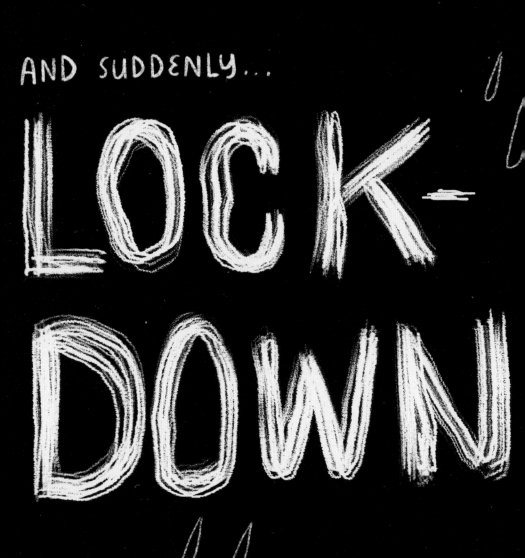

WHAT is HAPPENiNG?

I'm SO SCARED

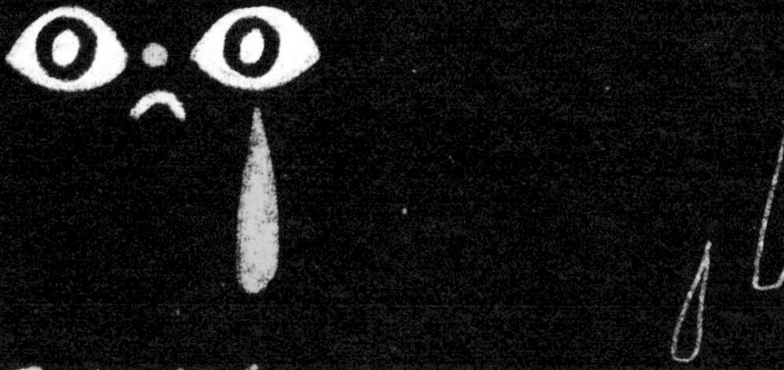

I miss my FRiENDS

LiKE i NEEd MORE time ALONE
with my thoughts...

REMINDER

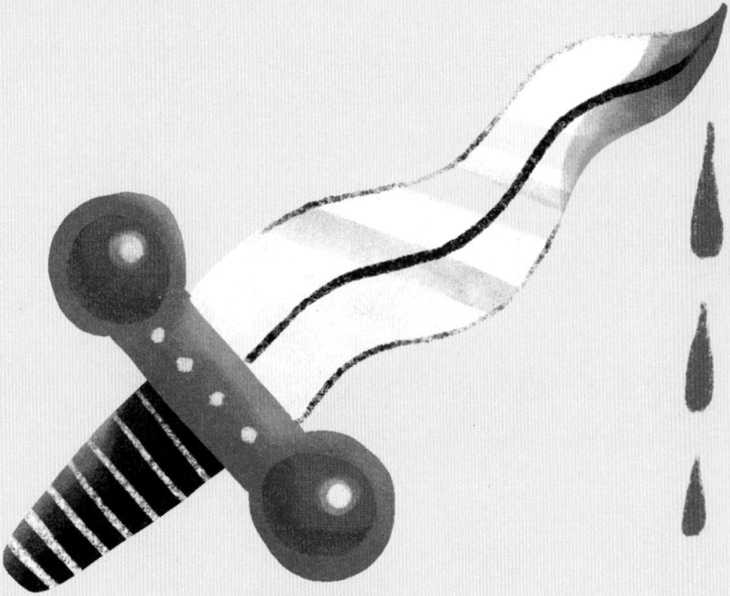

YOU CHOOSE tO HURt.

that's it, that's the REMINDER.

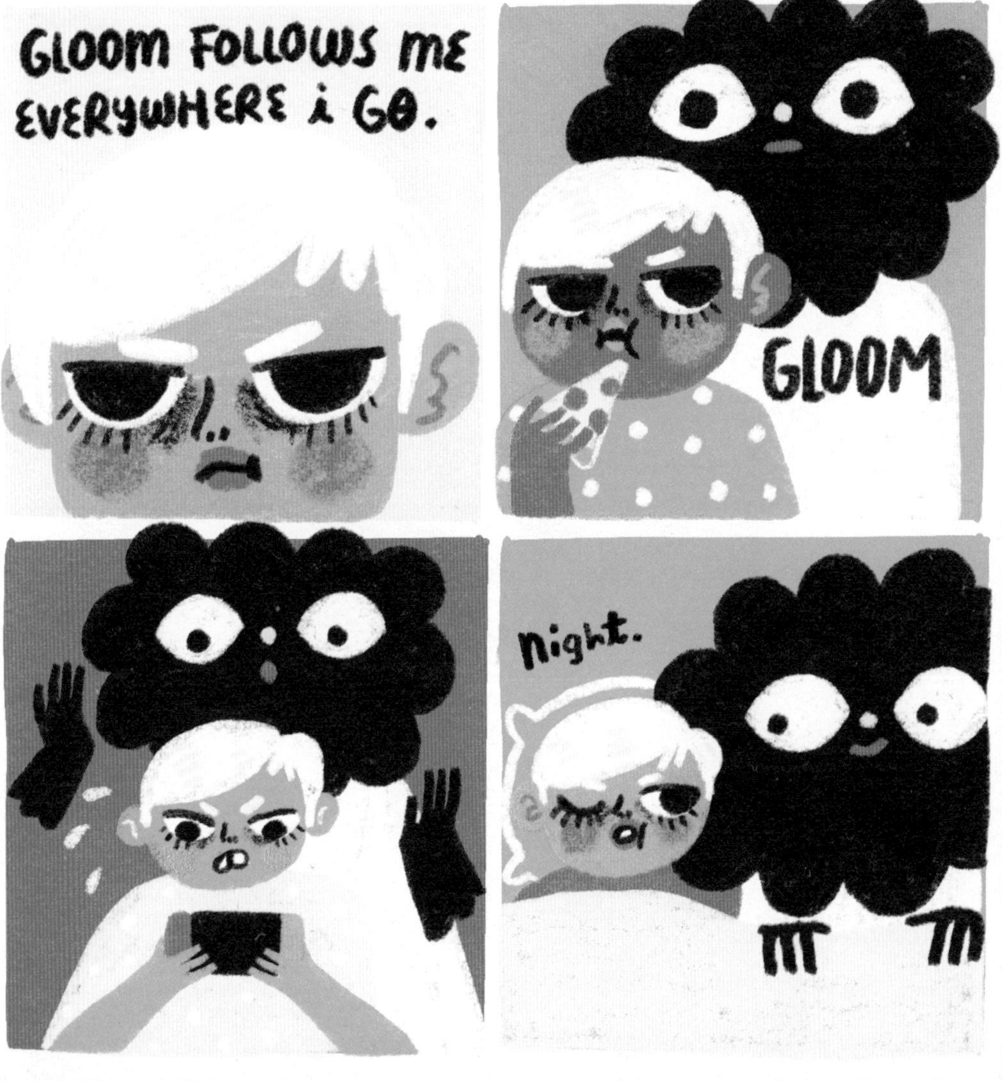
GLOOM FOLLOWS ME
EVERYWHERE i GO.
GLOOM
night.

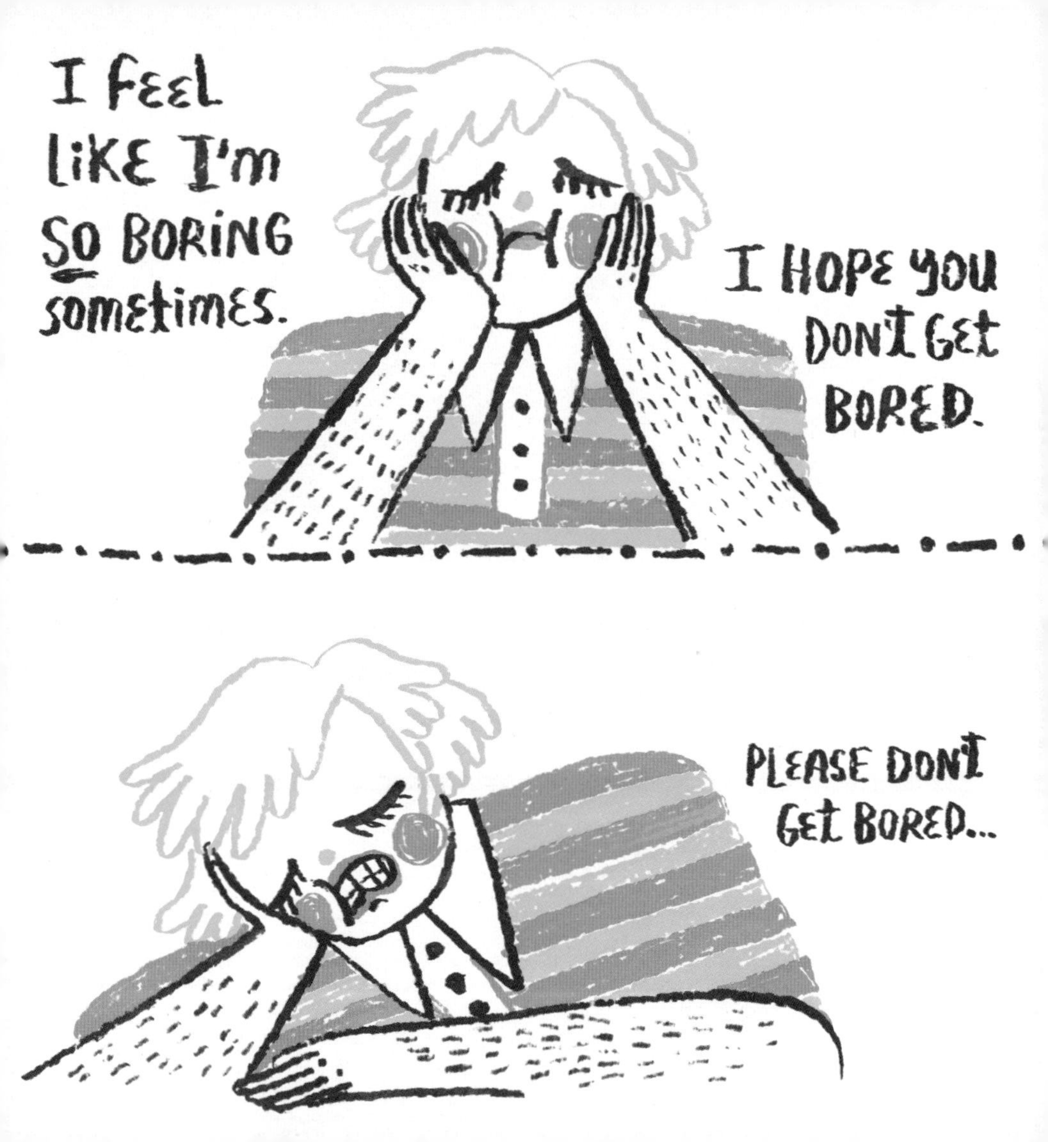
I FEEL LIKE I'm SO BORING sometimes.
I HOPE YOU DON'T GET BORED.
PLEASE DON'T GET BORED...

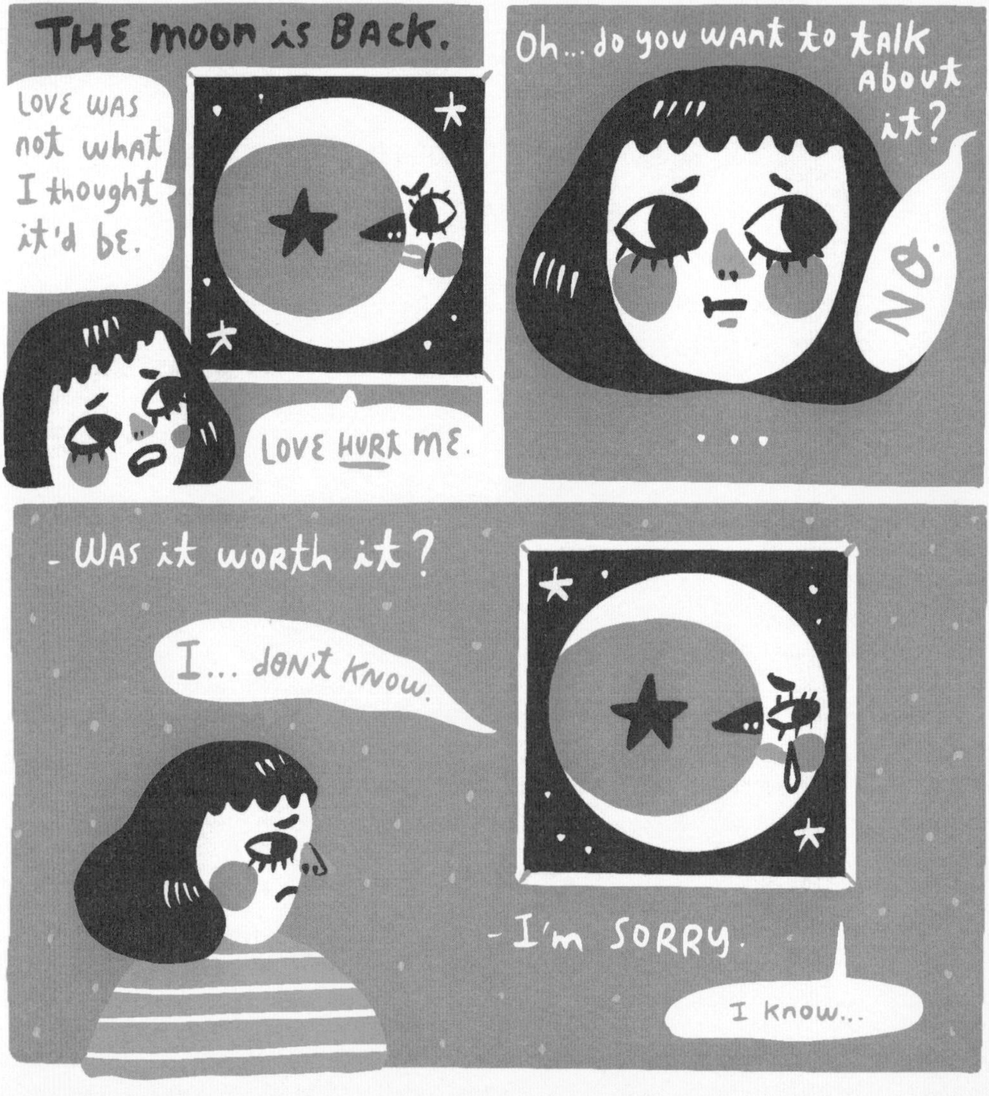
THE moon is BACK.
LOVE WAS not what I thought it'd be.
LOVE HURT ME.
Oh... do you want to talk about it?
NO.
. . .
- Was it worth it?
I... don't know.
- I'm SORRY.
I know...

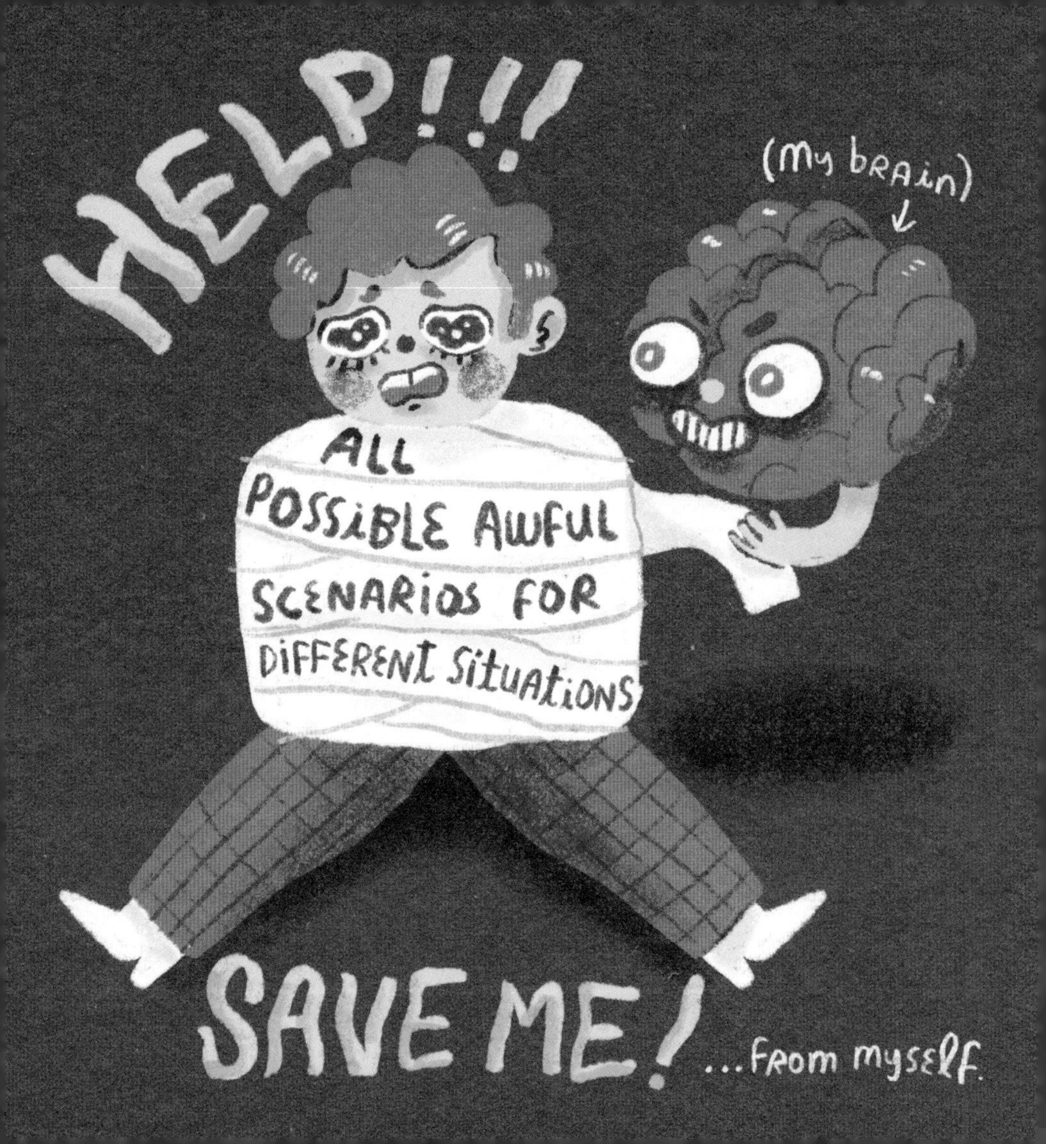
HELP!!!
(My brain)
ALL POSSIBLE AWFUL SCENARIOS FOR DIFFERENT SITUATIONS
SAVE ME!
...from myself.

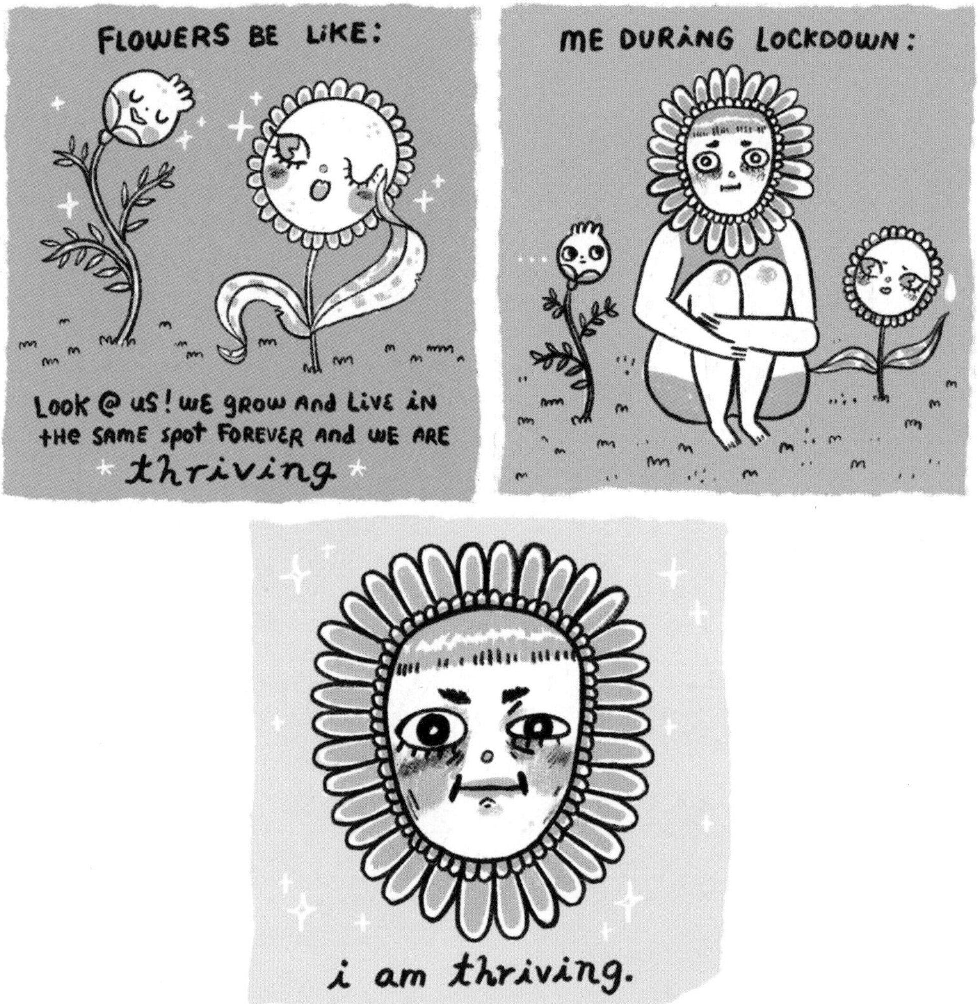
FLOWERS BE LIKE:
LOOK @ US! WE GROW AND LIVE IN THE SAME SPOT FOREVER AND WE ARE
* thriving *
ME DURING LOCKDOWN:
i am thriving.

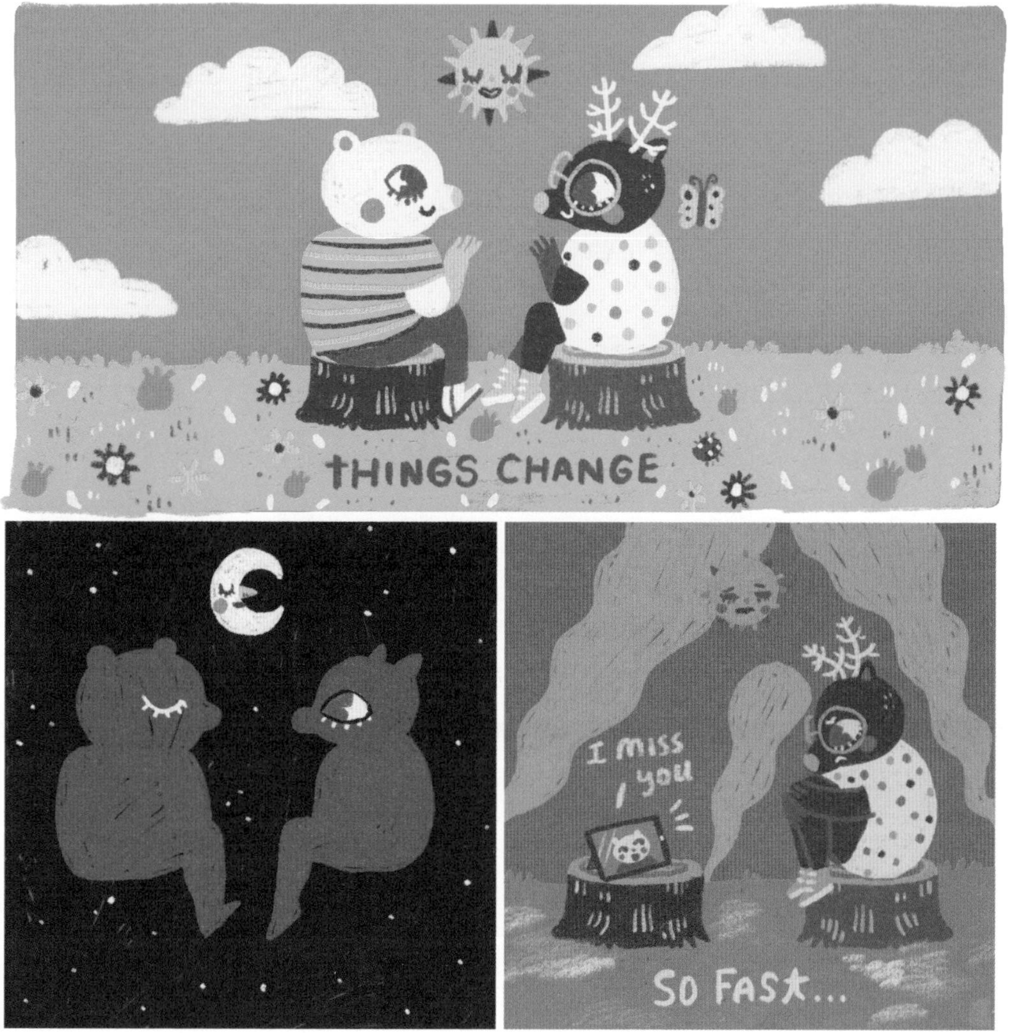
THINGS CHANGE
I miss you
SO FAST...

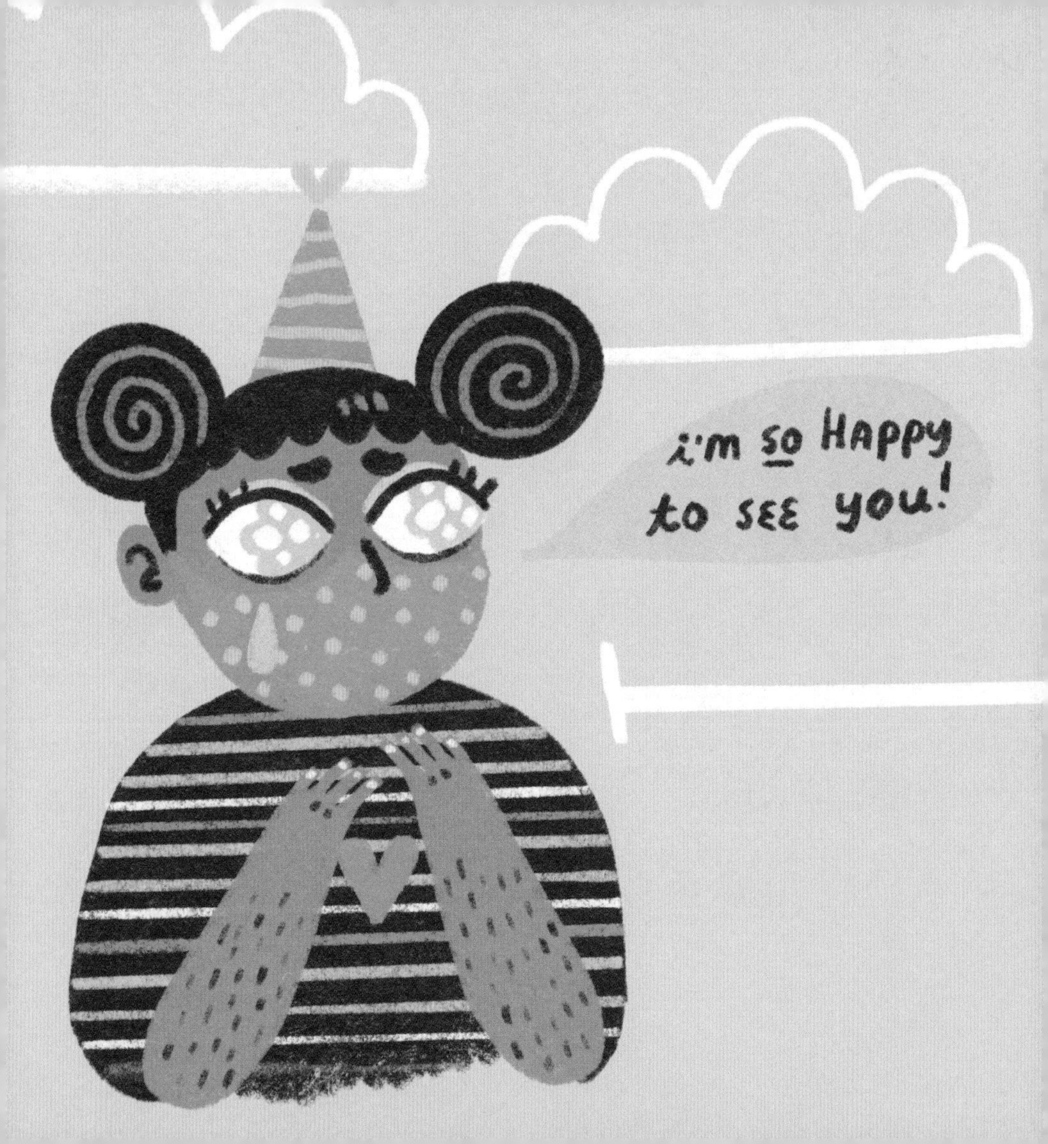
i'm so HAPPY to SEE you!

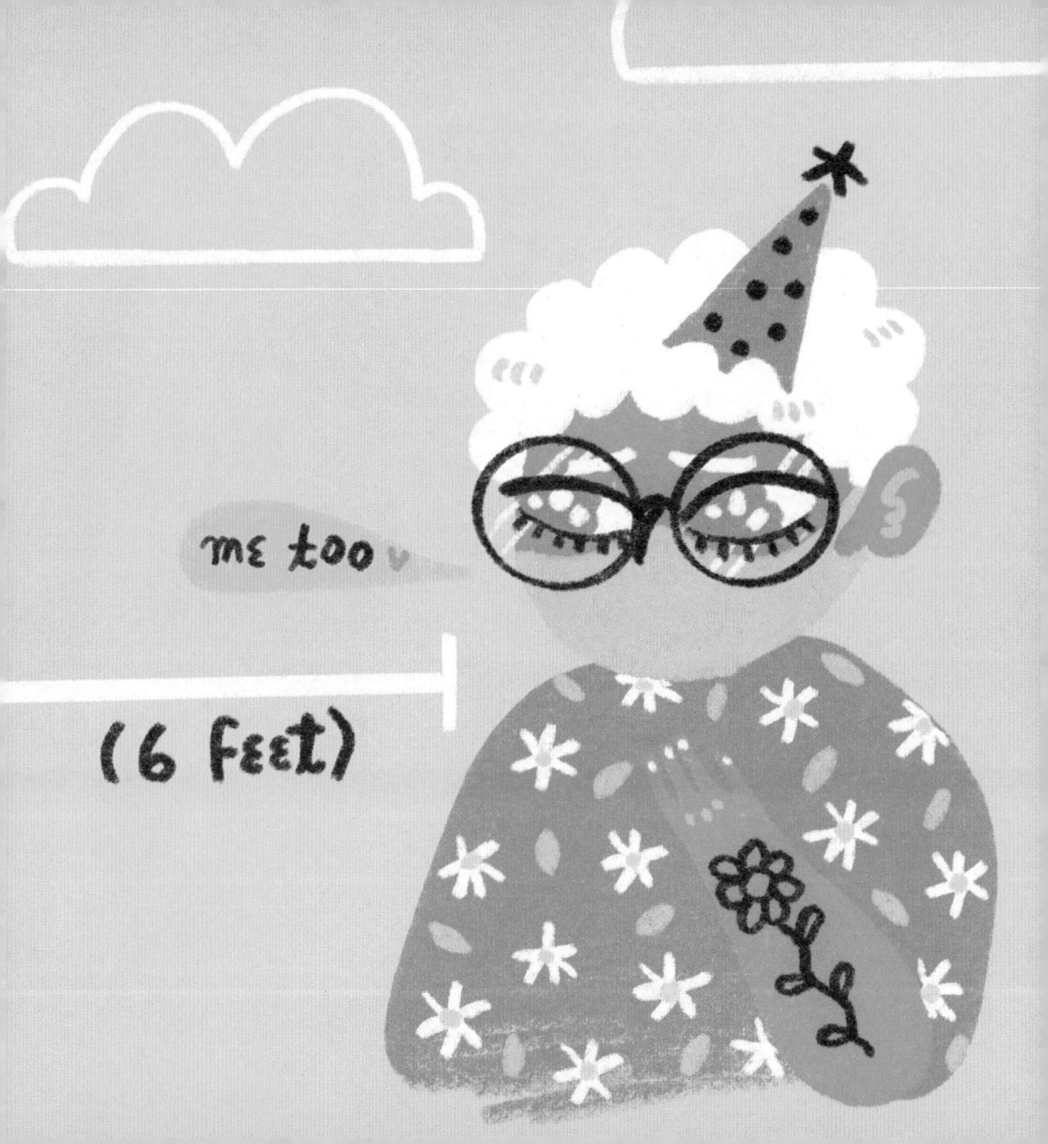
me too
(6 feet)

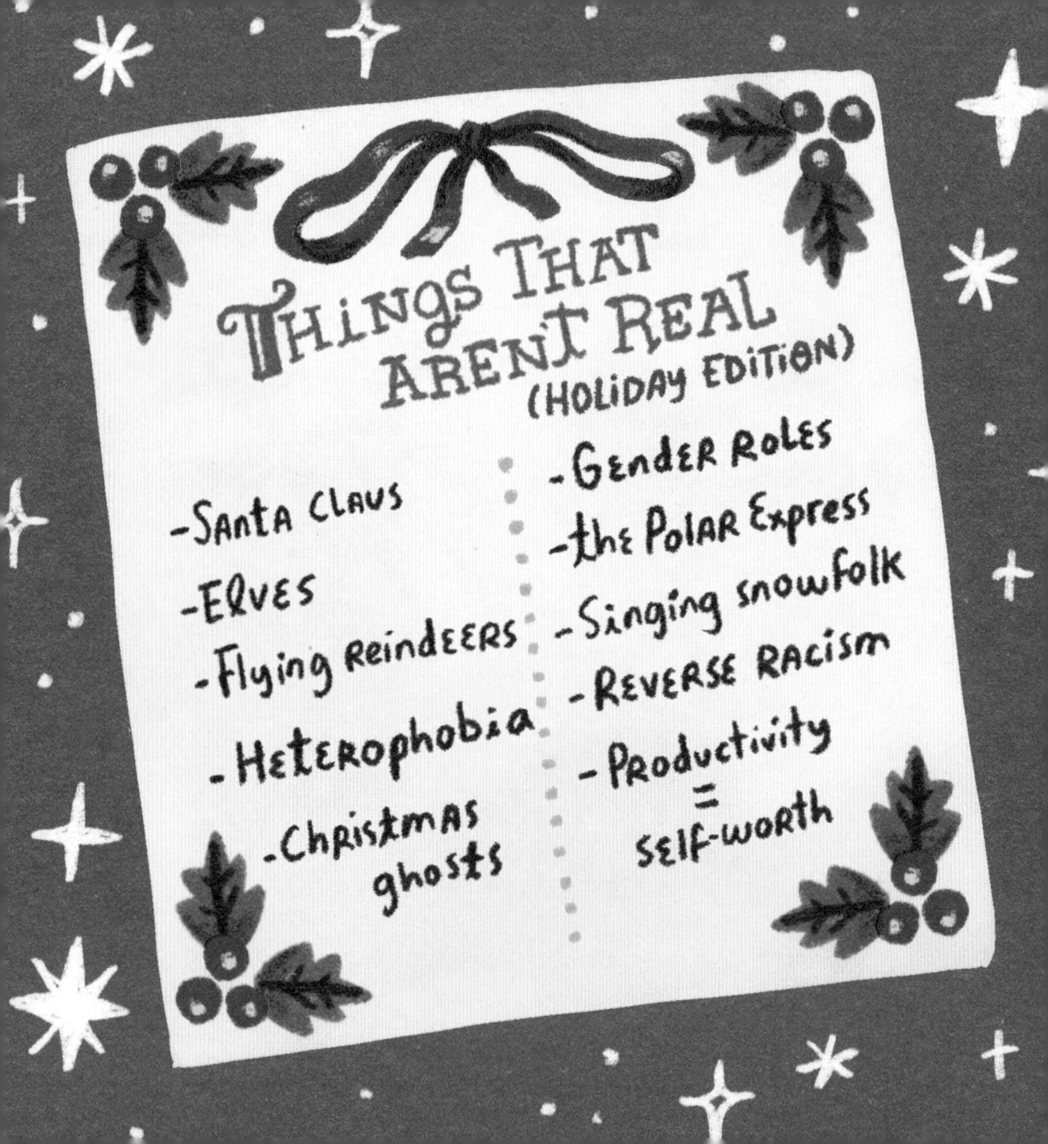
THINGS THAT AREN'T REAL
(HOLIDAY EDITION)
-Santa Claus
-Elves
-Flying reindeers
-Heterophobia
-Christmas ghosts
-Gender roles
-the Polar Express
-Singing snowfolk
-Reverse racism
-Productivity = self-worth

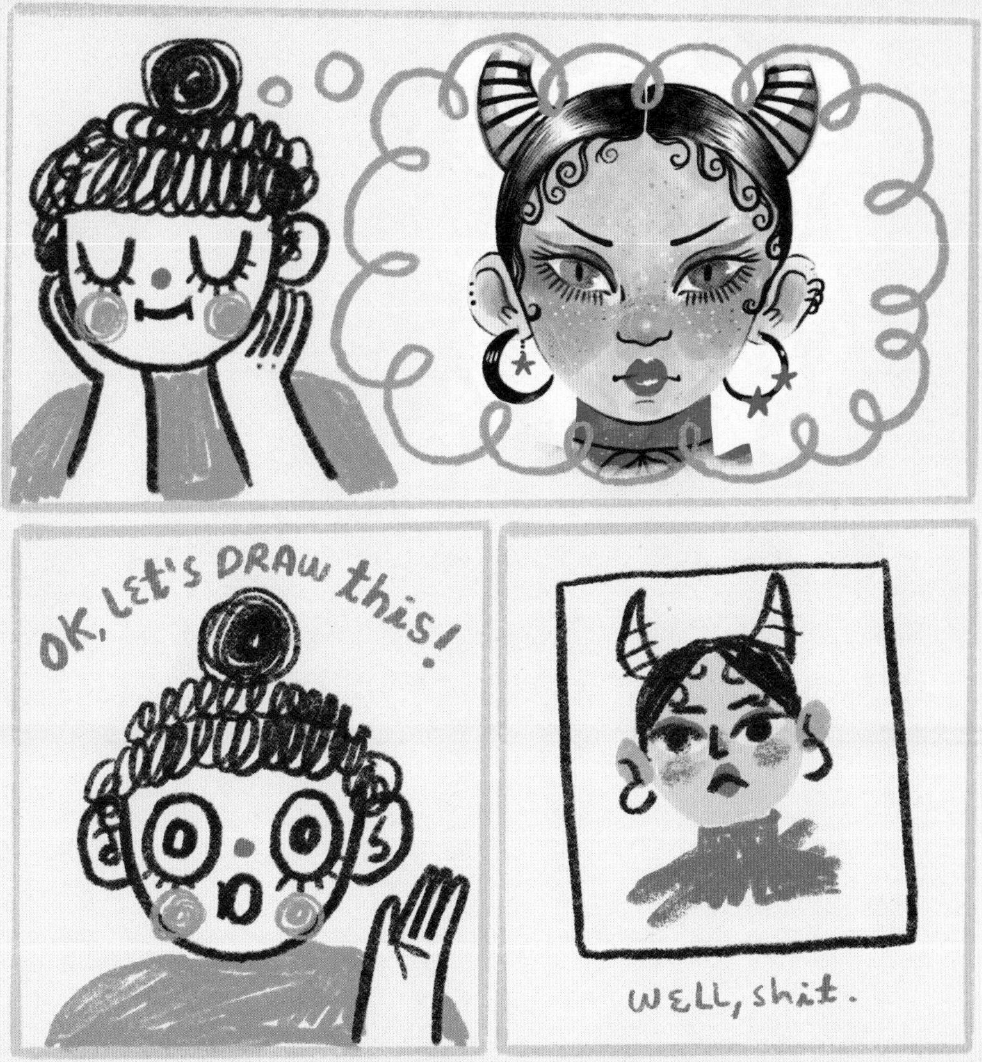
OK, LET'S DRAW this!
WELL, shit.

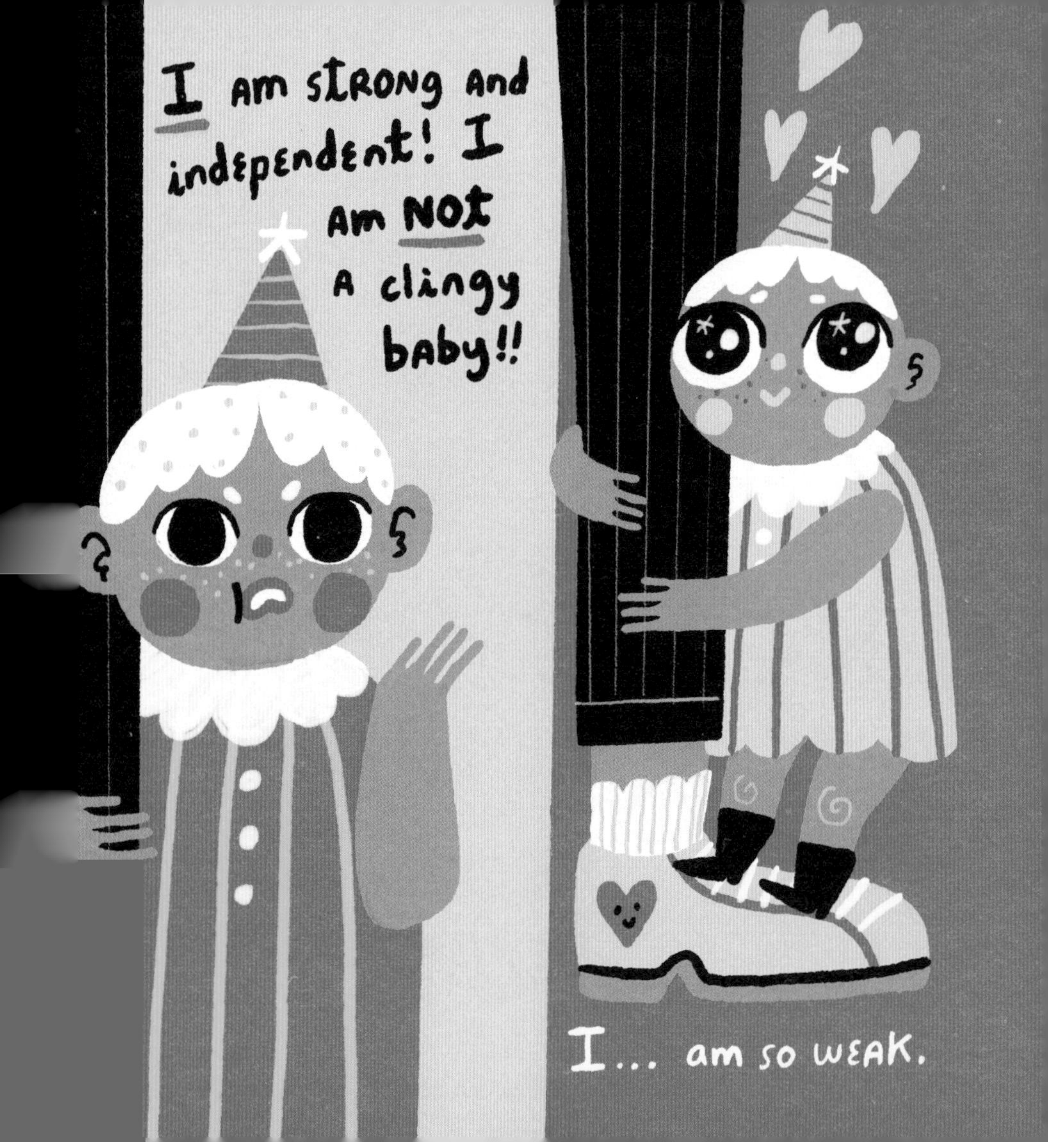
I am STRONG and independent! I am NOT a clingy baby!!
I... am so WEAK.

You can't play
with FIRE
And not expect
to get burned.

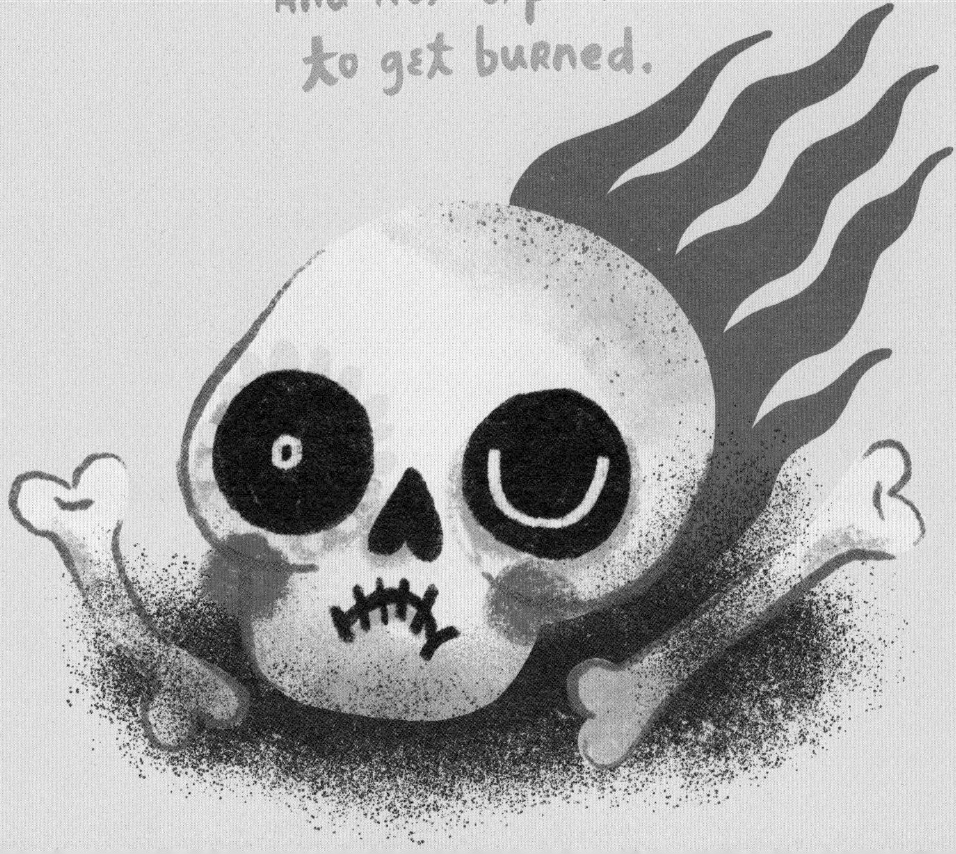

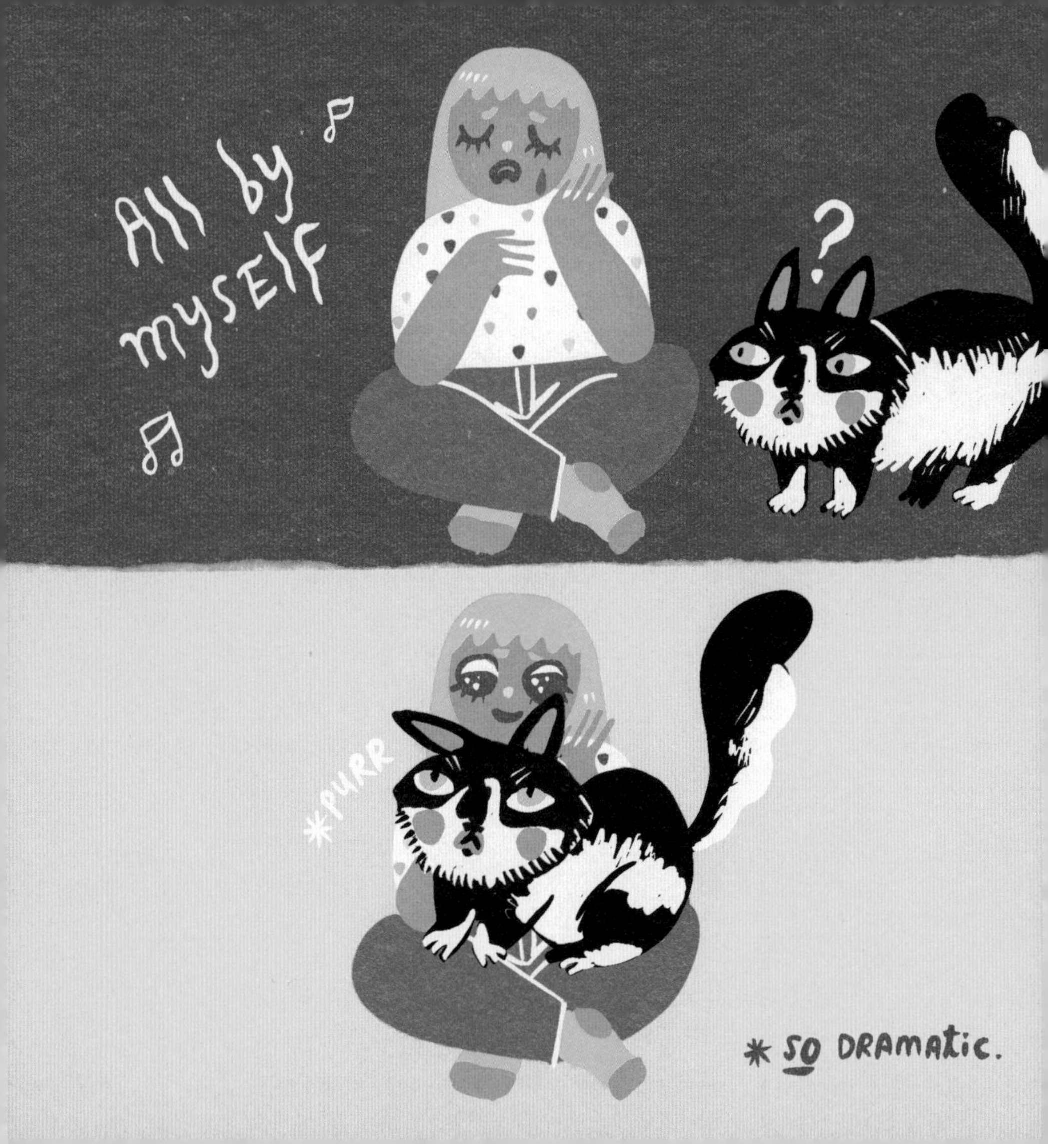
All by myself
?
*PURR
* SO DRAMAtic.

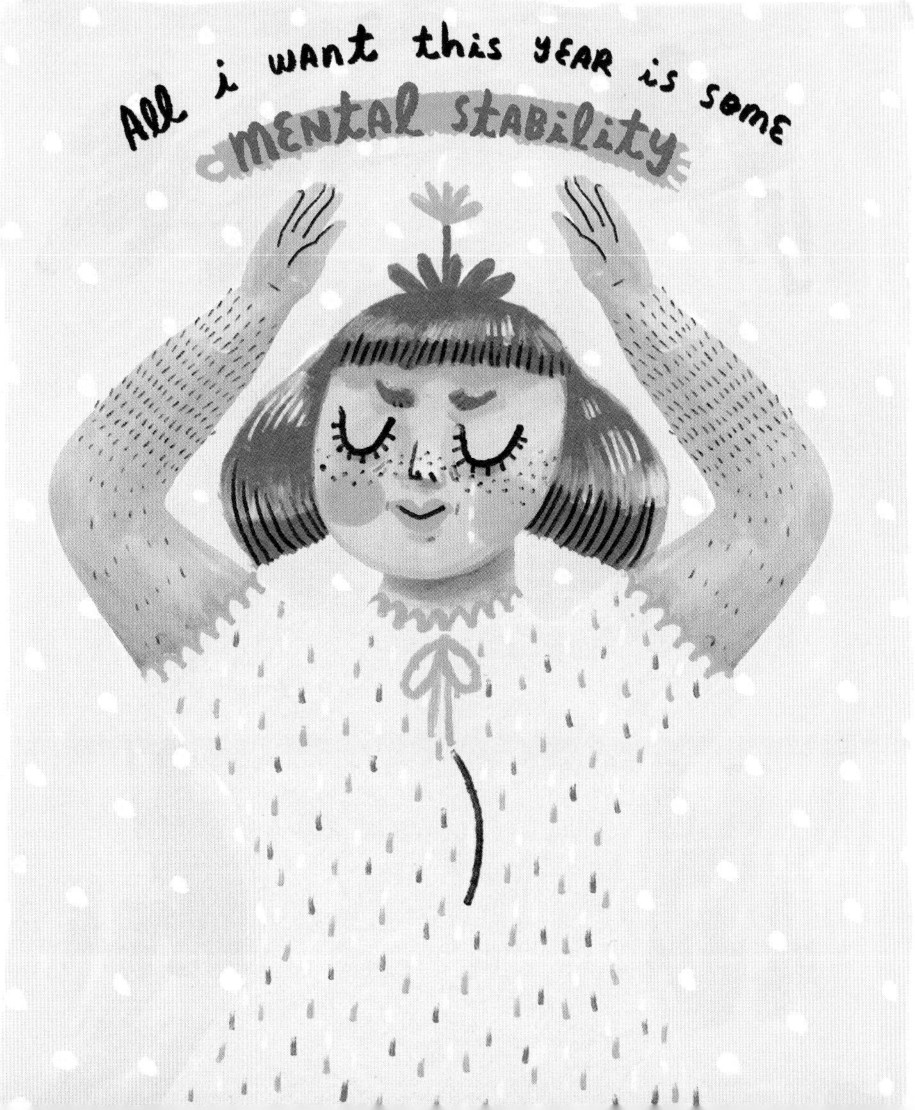
All i want this year is some
mental stability

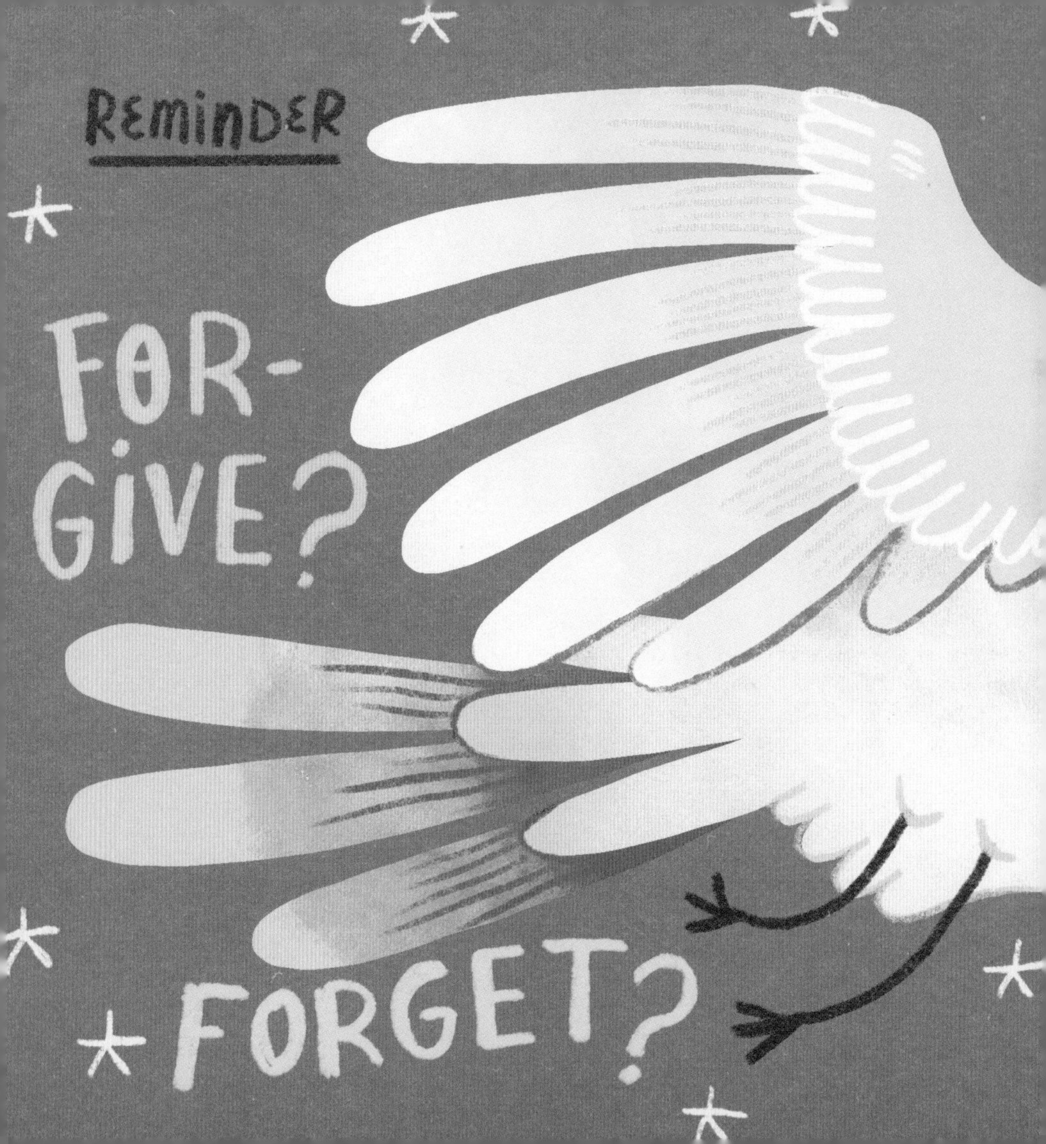
REMINDER
FOR-
GIVE?
FORGET?

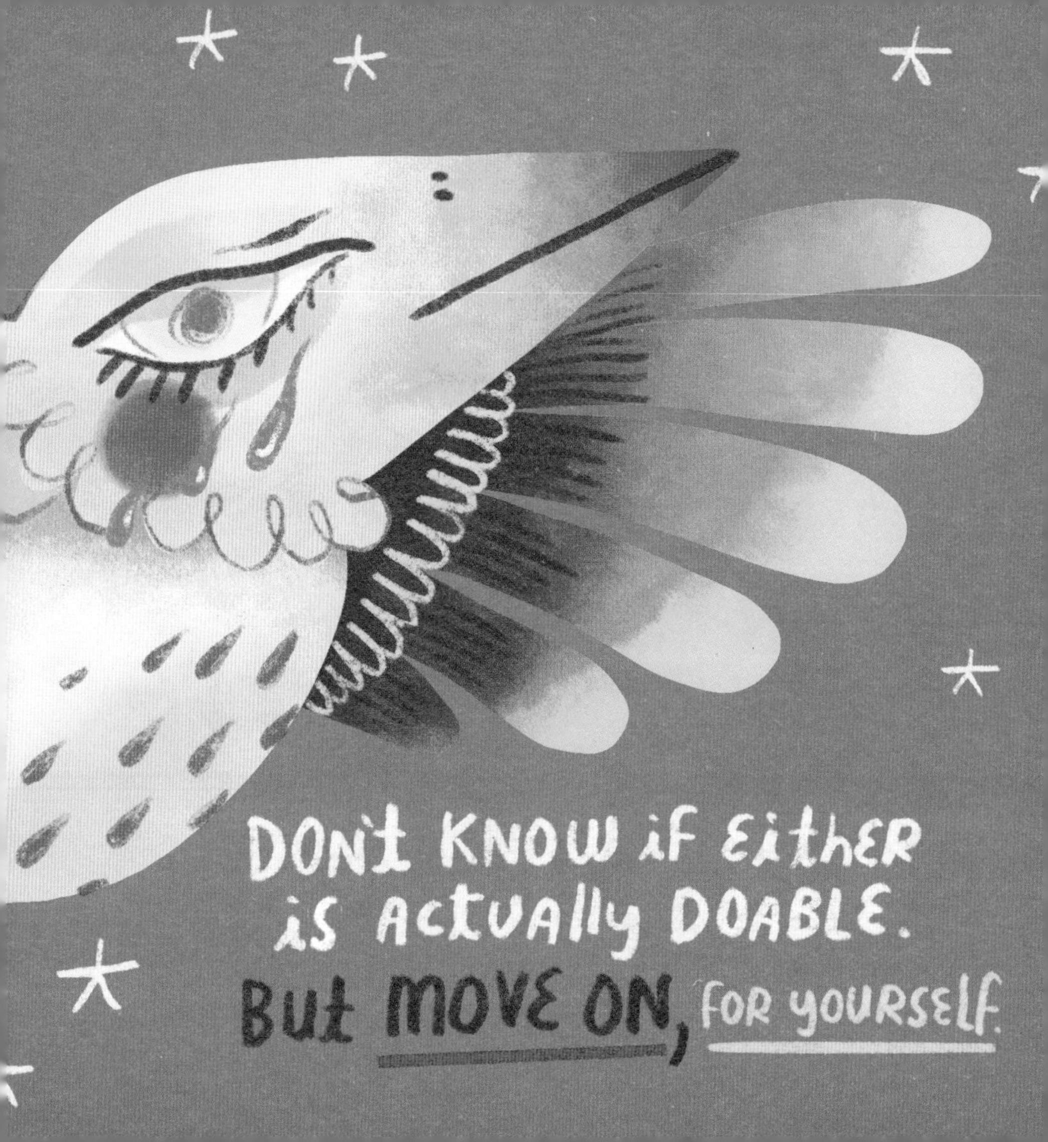
DON'T KNOW IF EITHER
IS ACTUALLY DOABLE.
BUT MOVE ON, FOR YOURSELF.

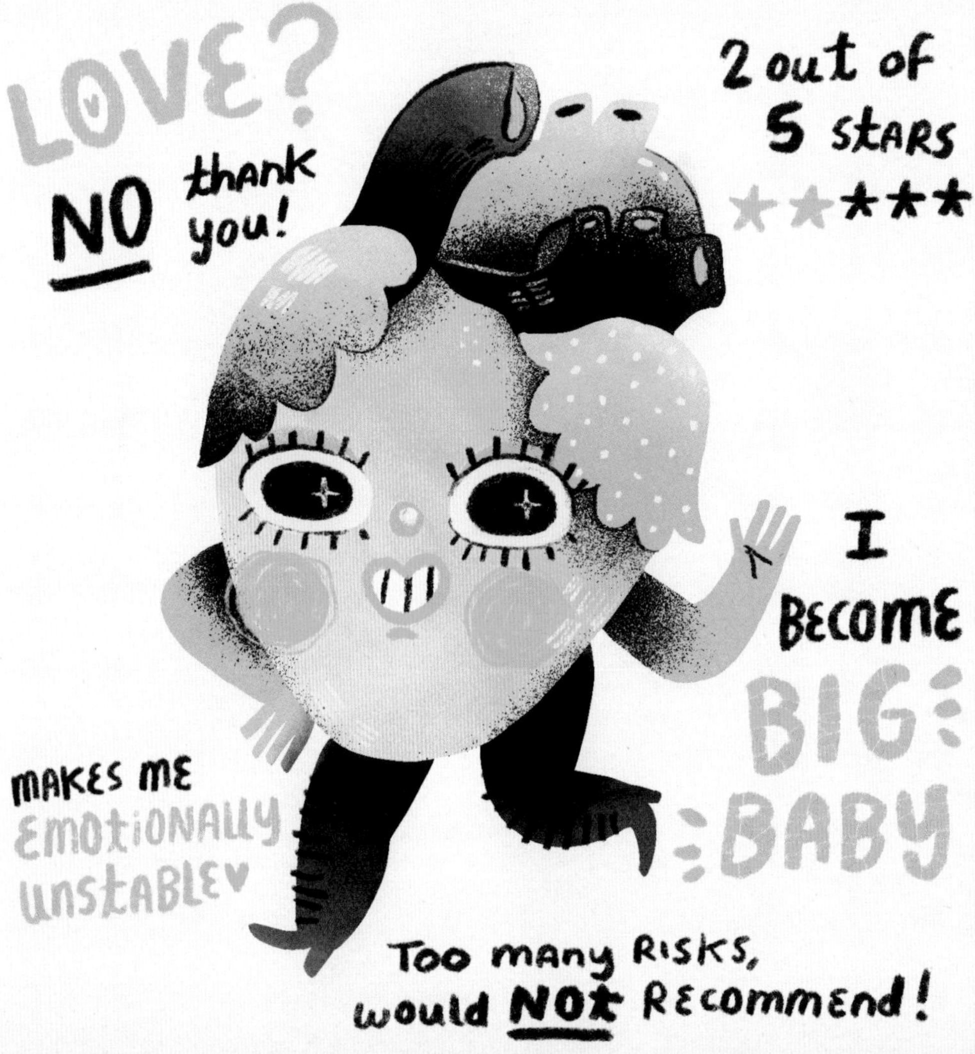
LOVE?
NO thank you!
2 out of 5 stars
I BECOME BIG BABY
MAKES ME EMOTIONALLY UNSTABLE
Too many RISKS, would NOT RECOMMEND!

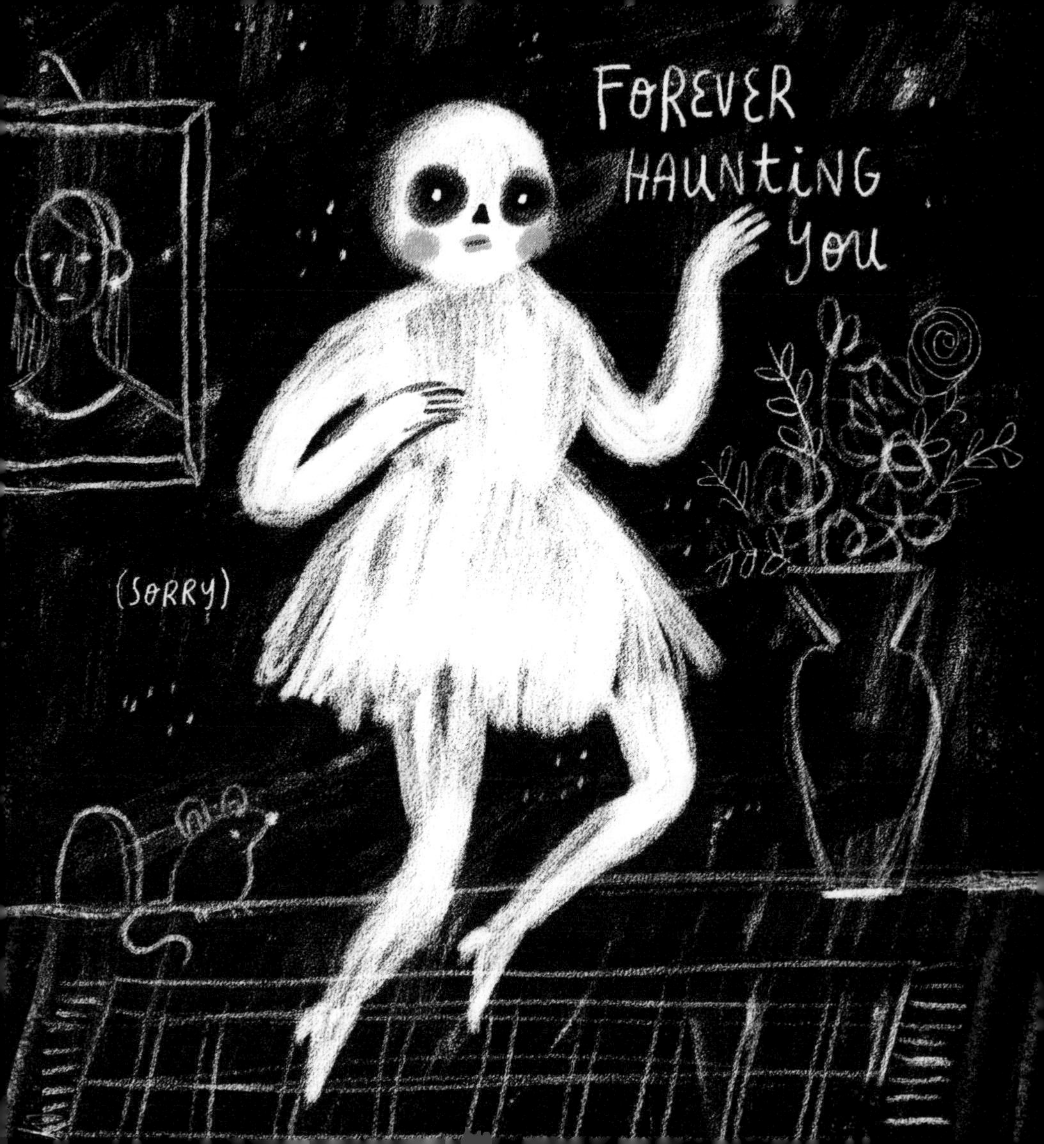
FOREVER HAUNTING YOU
(SORRY)

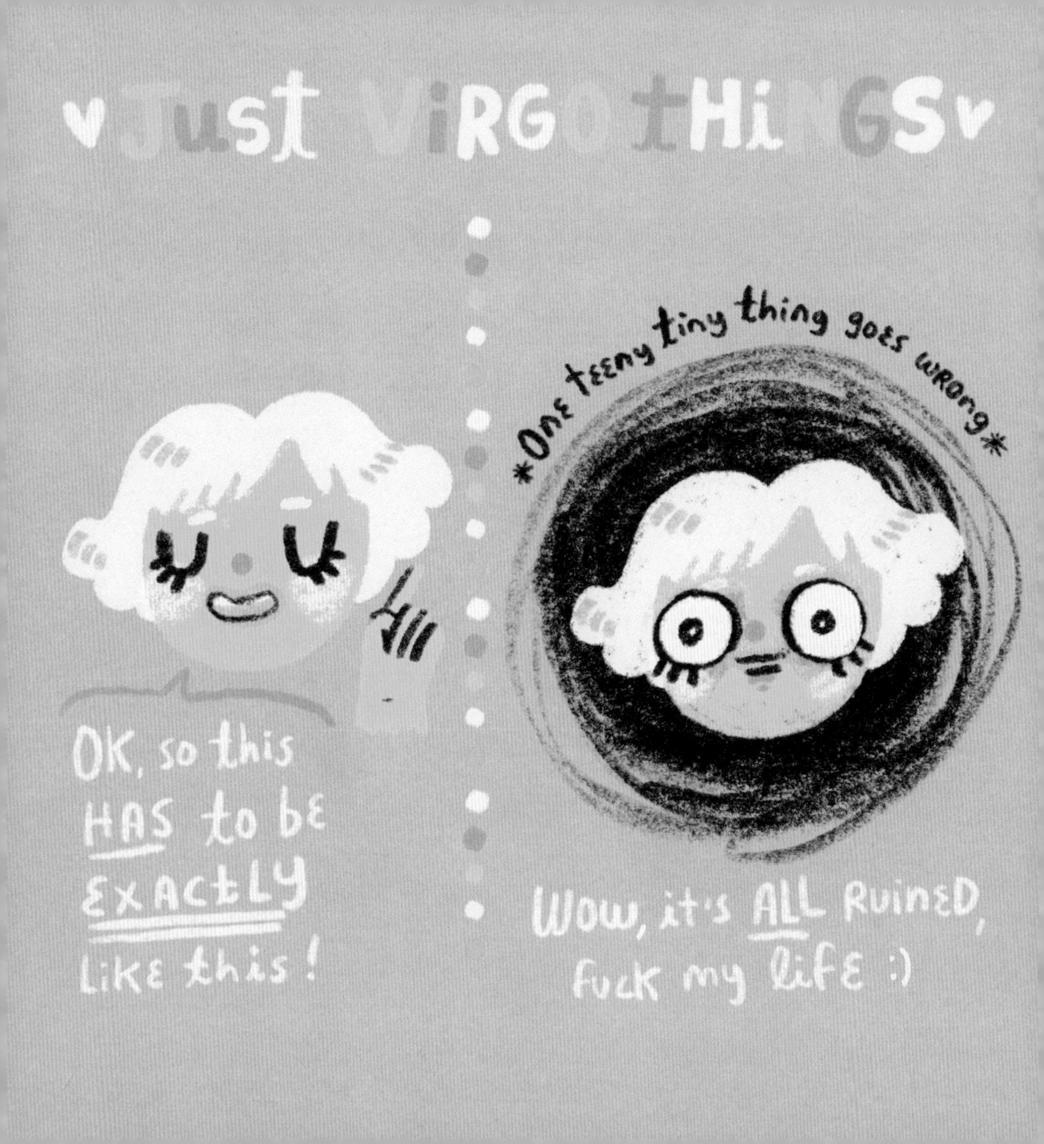

♥ JUST VIRGO THINGS ♥
OK, so this HAS to be EXACTLY like this!
One teeny tiny thing goes wrong
Wow, it's ALL ruined, fuck my life :)

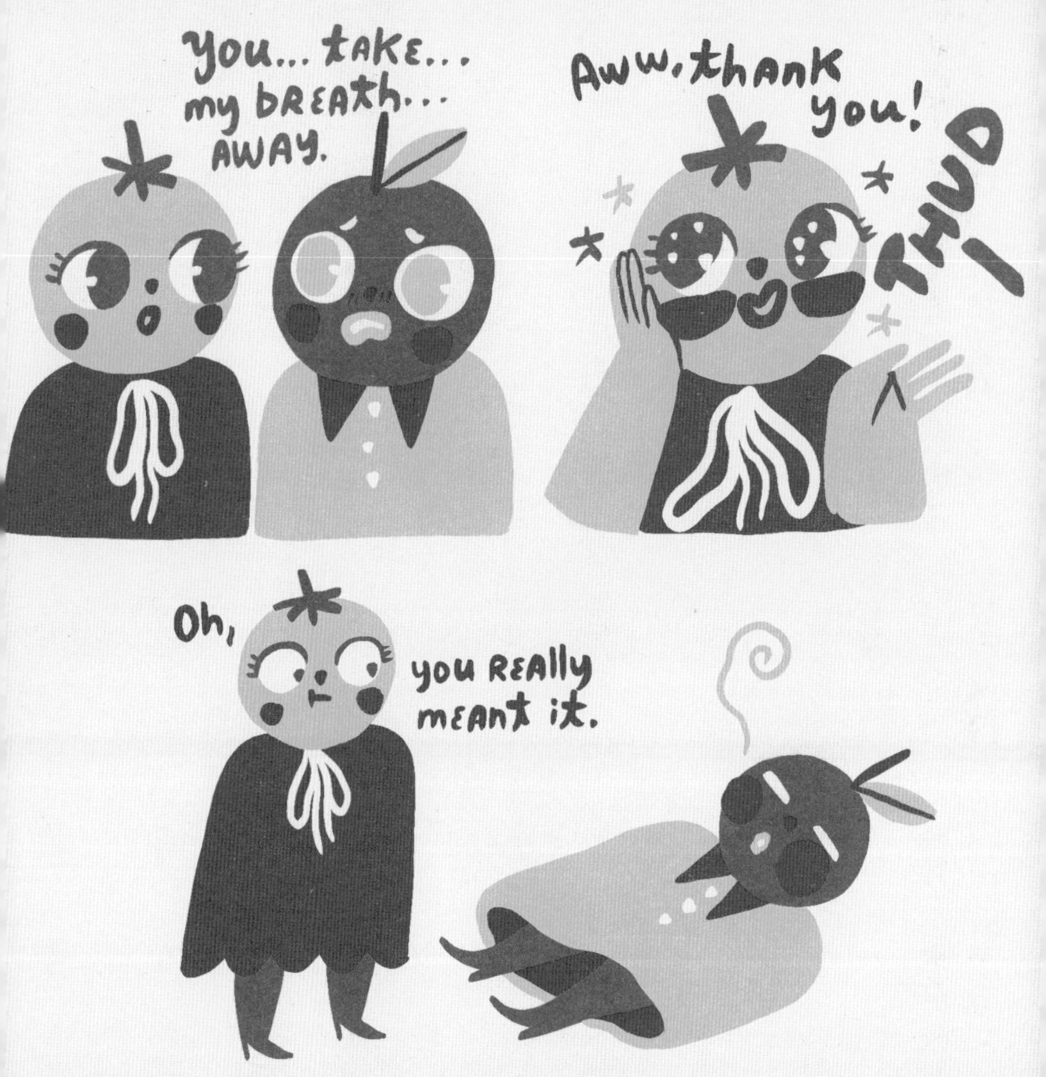
you... take...
my breath...
AWAY.
Aww, thank
you!
THUD
Oh,
you really
meant it.

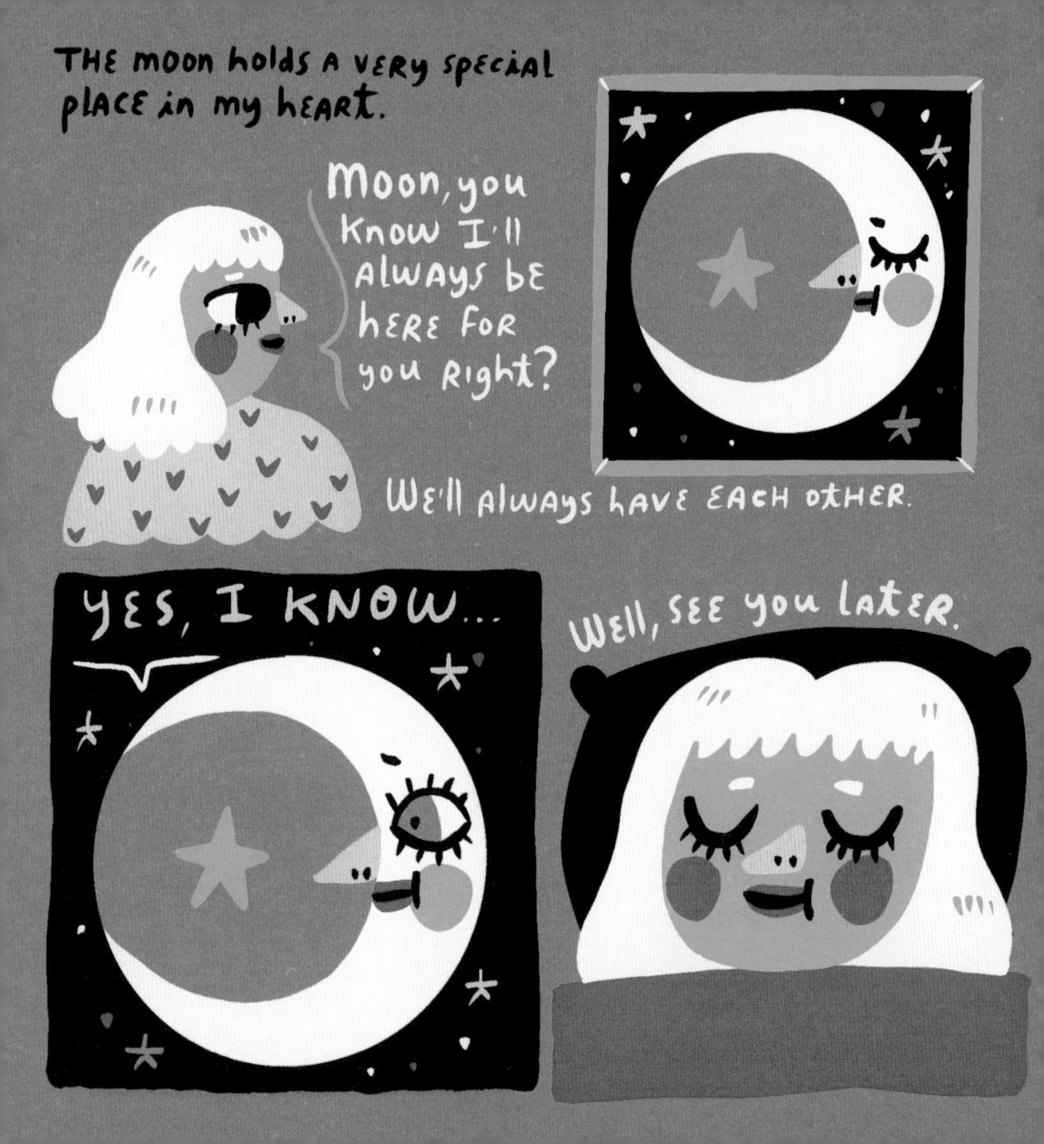
THE moon holds A VERY special place in my heART.
Moon, you Know I'll Always bE hERE FoR you Right?
We'll Always have EACH other.
YES, I KNOW...
Well, SEE you later.

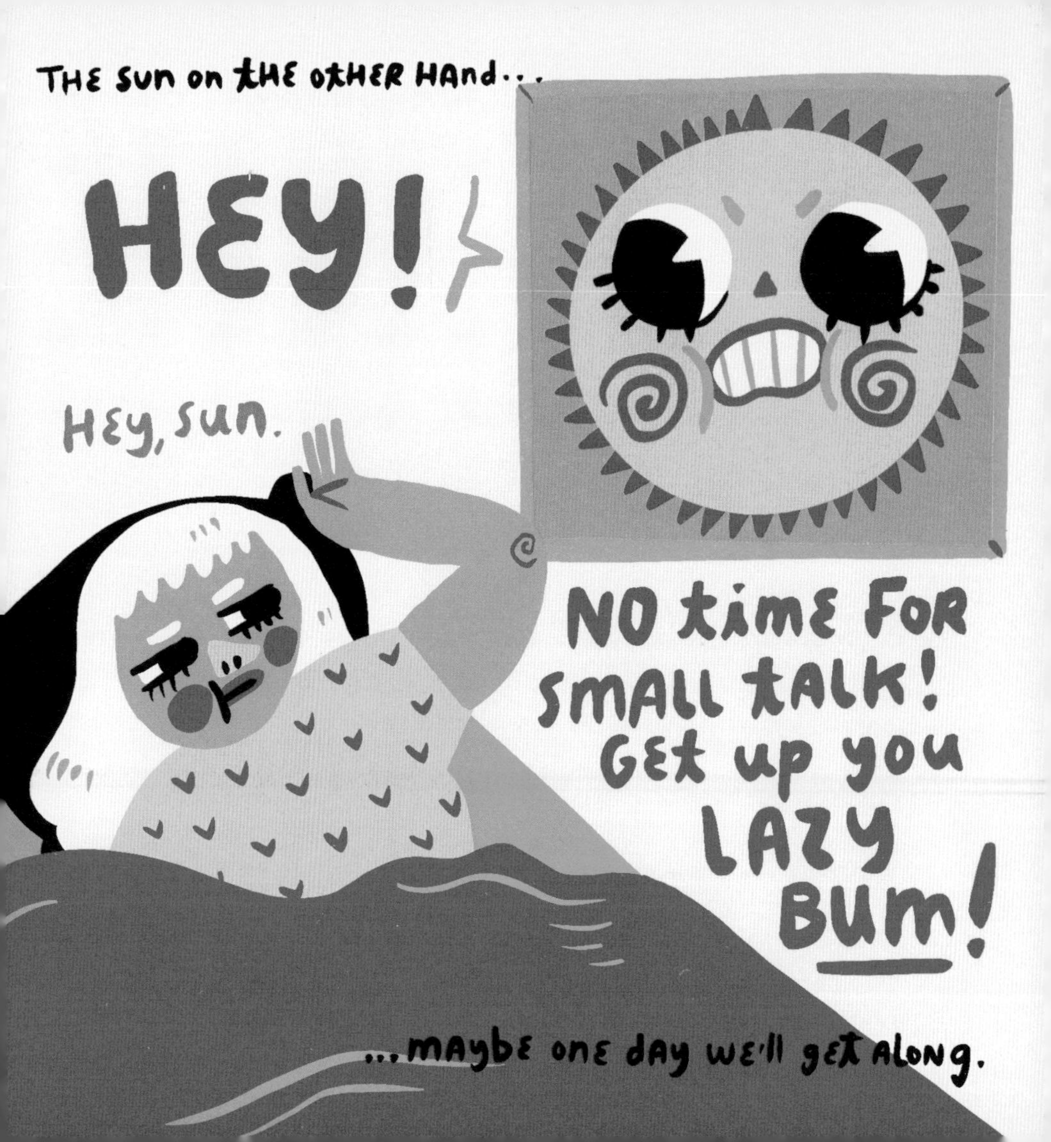
THE SUN ON THE OTHER HAND...
HEY!
HEY, SUN.
NO TIME FOR SMALL TALK! GET UP YOU LAZY BUM!
...MAYBE ONE DAY WE'LL GET ALONG.

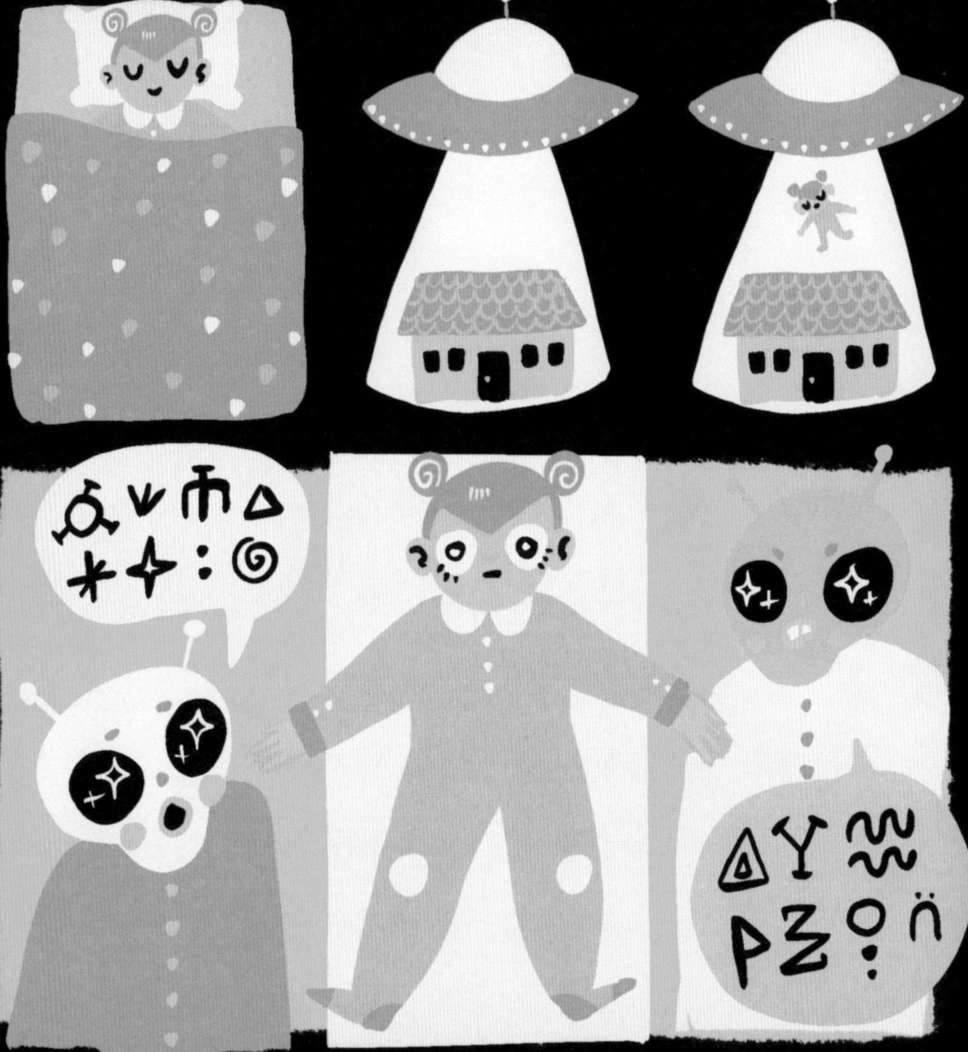

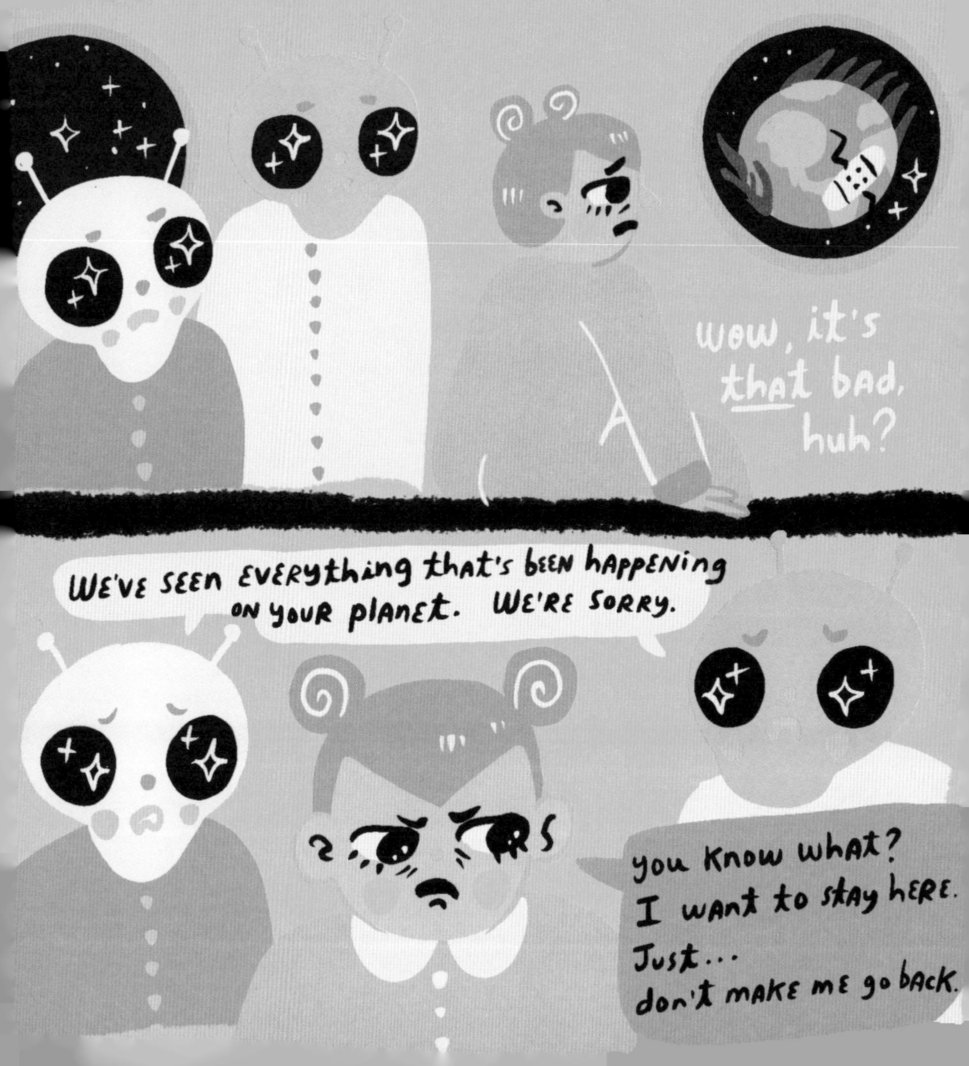
wow, it's that bad, huh?
WE'VE SEEN EVERYthing that's been happening on your planet. WE'RE SORRY.
you know what? I want to stay here. Just... don't make me go back.

SO I'M WITH SOMEONE.
IT PROBABLY WON'T LAST FOREVER.
IT'LL PROBABLY MAKE ME SAD.
BUT FOR NOW, IT FEELS GOOD.

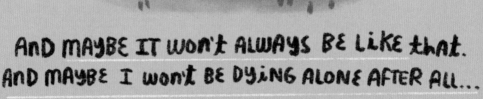

AND MAYBE IT WON'T ALWAYS BE LIKE that.
AND MAYBE I WON'T BE DYING ALONE AFTER ALL...
MAYBE...
WE'LL JUST WAIT AND SEE, I GUESS.

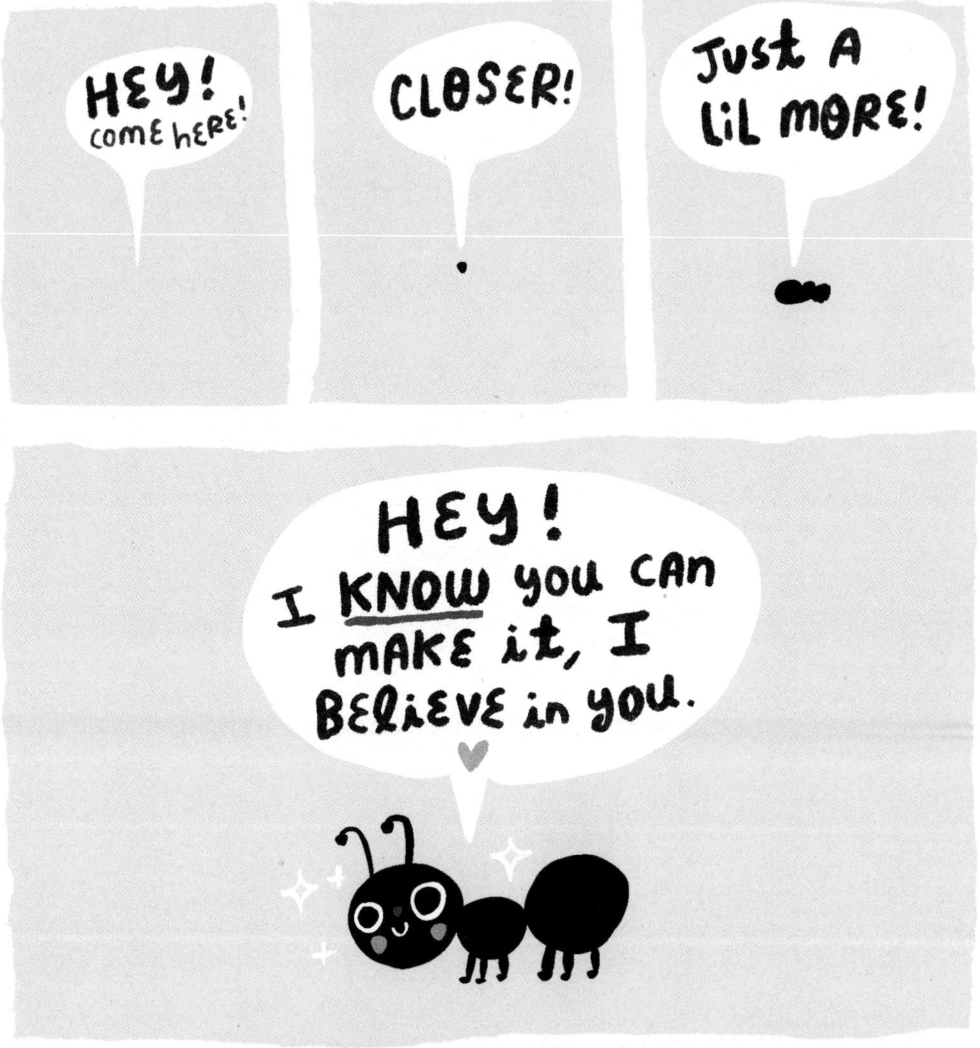
HEY! COME HERE!
CLOSER!
JUST A LIL MORE!
HEY! I KNOW YOU CAN MAKE IT, I BELIEVE IN YOU.

Final Reminder

OK, so I guess it's way too early to say if life will get easier one day. But even when I'm feeling down, I HAVE to REMEMBER:

* there will Always be beauty around.
* There will always be LOVE (of all kinds).
* there will be laughter.
* there will be PASSION (in many forms).
* there will Always be Amazing people around me.

And I'll always have me, trying my best.

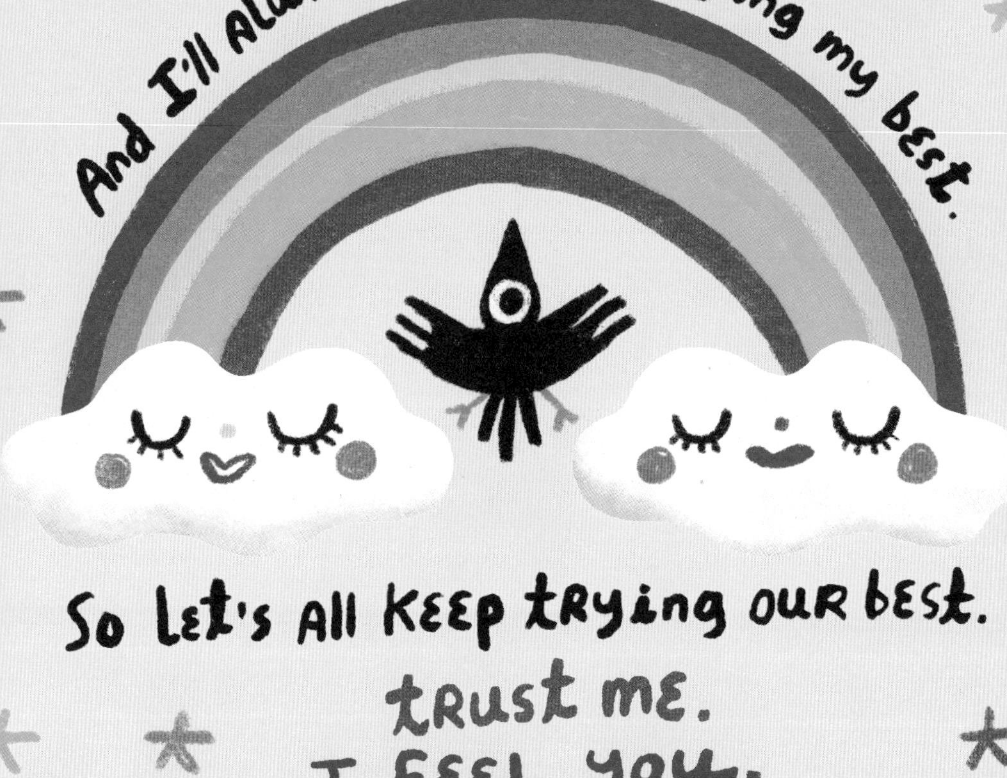

So let's all keep trying our best.

trust me.

I feel you.

you got this.

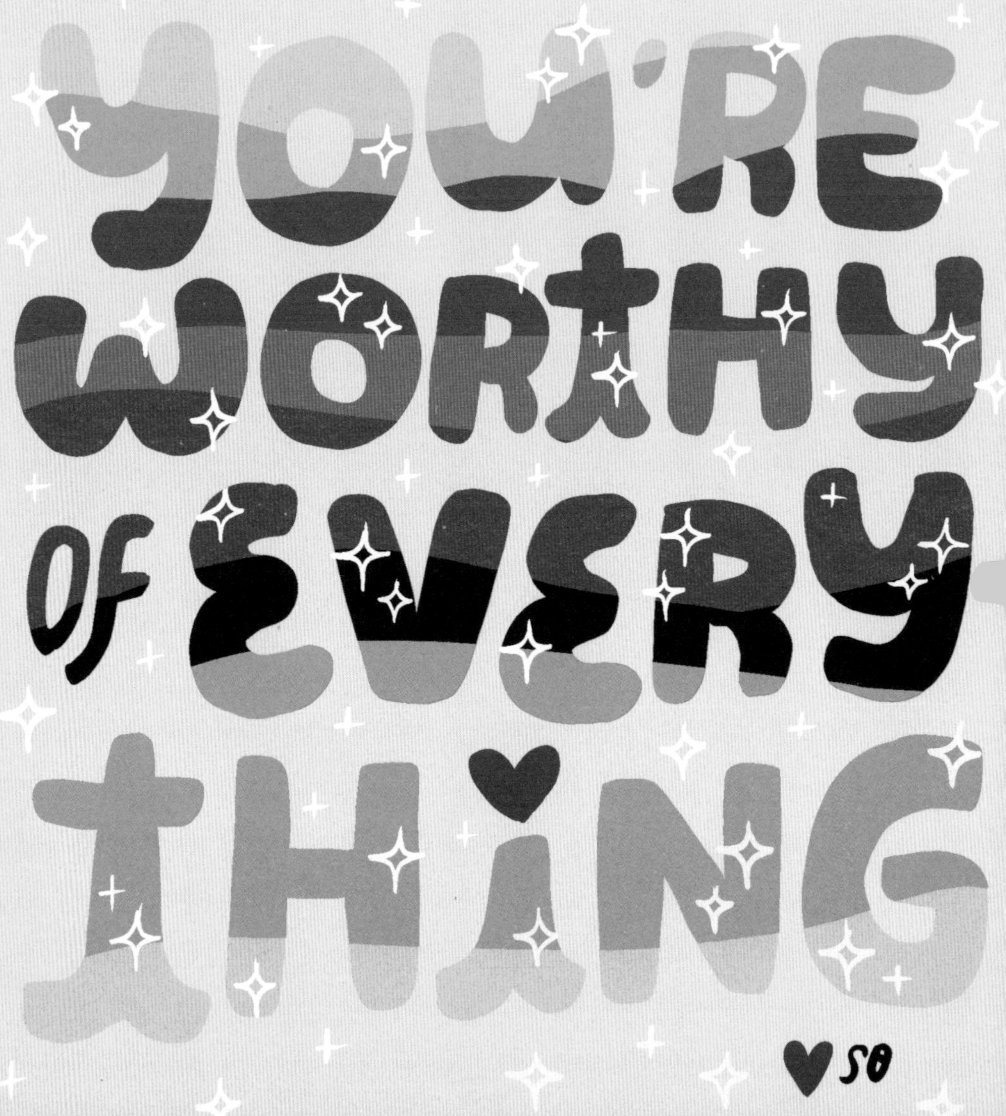
YOU'RE WORTHY OF EVERY THING
♥ SO

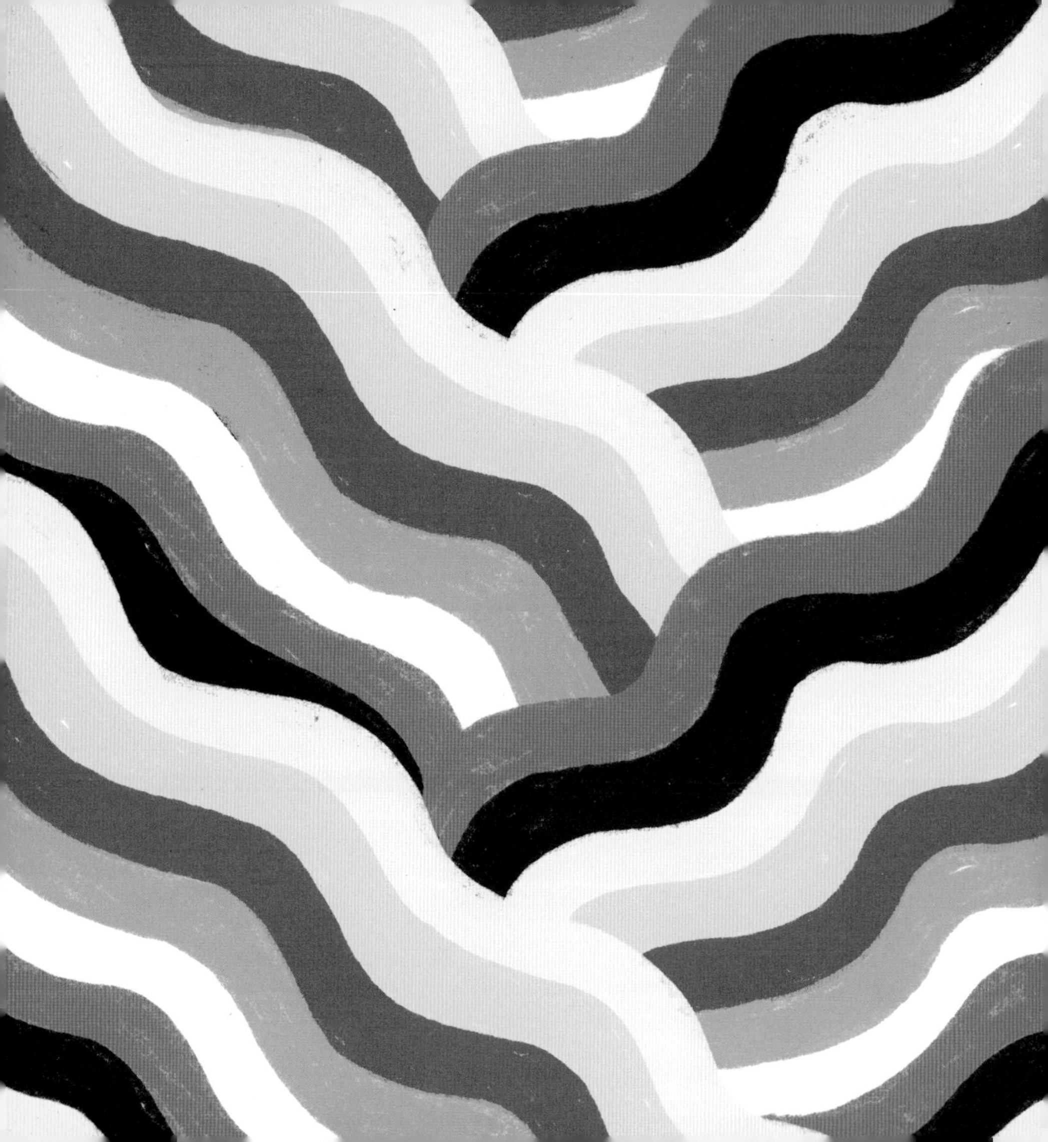

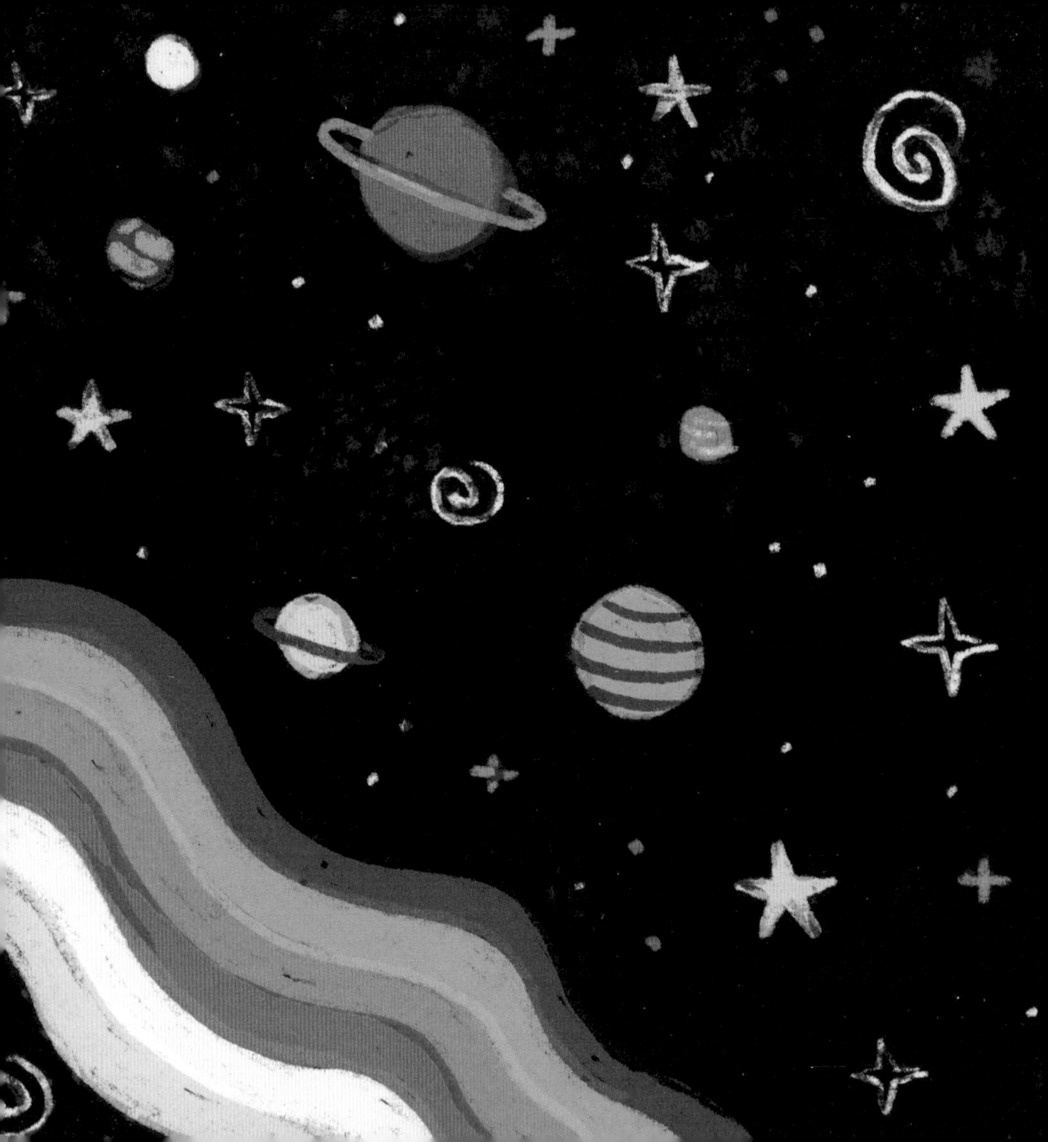